THE COMMON ROOTS OF EUROPE

THE COMMON ROOTS OF EUROPE

BRONISŁAW GEREMEK

Translated by
Jan Aleksandrowicz, J. K. Fedorowicz, Rosemary Hunt,
Agnieszka Kołakowska and Shayne Mitchell

Polity Press

English translation copyright © Polity Press 1996.
First published in Italy as *Le radici comuni dell'Europa* copyright © Arnoldo Mondadori
Editore, S.p.A., 1991.
Please see Acknowledgements on page vi for individual chapters.

First published in 1996 by Polity Press in association with Blackwell Publishers Ltd.

2 4 6 8 9 10 7 5 3 1

Editorial office:
Polity Press
65 Bridge Street
Cambridge CB2 1UR, UK

Marketing and production:
Blackwell Publishers Ltd
108 Cowley Road
Oxford OX4 1JF, UK

Published in the USA by
Blackwell Publishers Inc.
238 Main Street
Cambridge, MA 02142, USA

ISBN 0-7456-1121-4

A CIP catalogue record for this book is available from the British Library and the Library
of Congress.

Typeset in 11 on 13pt Sabon by Wearset, Boldon, Tyne and Wear.
Printed in Great Britain by Hartnolls Ltd, Bodmin, Cornwall.

This book is printed on acid-free paper.

Contents

Acknowledgements

The publishers gratefully acknowledge permission to reproduce or translate from previously published material in this book.

Chapter 1: reprinted from 'Western Europe in the Middle Ages', *Acta Polonae Historica*, XXXII, pp. 35–57.

Chapter 2: 'L'exemplum et la circulation de la culture au Moyen Age', *Mélanges de l'Ecole Française de Rome*, 92, 1980, pp. 153–79.

Chapter 3: 'Wiez i poczucie wspolnoty w sredniowiecznej Europie', in *Dziesiec wiekow Europy*, Warsaw, 1983, pp. 19–81.

Chapter 4: reprinted from 'Poland and the cultural geography of medieval Europe', in *A Republic of Nobles: studies in Polish history to 1864*, ed. and trans. J. K. Fedorowicz, co-ed. M. Bogucka and H. Samsonowicz, Cambridge, 1982, pp. 10–27, © Cambridge University Press.

Chapter 5: 'Geografia i Apokalipsa: pojecie Europy u Jakuba Paradyża, *I viaggi di Erodoto*, 2, 1984, pp. 108–16.

Chapter 6: 'Panstwo-narod w Europie XX wieku', in *Fermentum massae mundi*, ed. Agora, Warsaw, 1990.

The Introduction was translated by Shayne Mitchell
Chapter 1 was translated by Jan Aleksandrowicz
Chapters 2 and 6 were translated by Agnieszka Kołakowska
Chapters 3 and 5 were translated by Rosemary Hunt
Chapter 4 was translated by J. K. Fedorowicz

Introduction

In Search of Lost Europe

Francesco M. Cataluccio

Europa, Europa[1] is the title of the harrowing autobiography of Sally Perel, a German Jew who as a child in 1935 fled to Poland in order to escape Nazi persecution. The outbreak of war in 1939 forced him further east still, to the Soviet Union, where he became a young pioneer under Stalin. In 1941 he was captured by the Germans but claimed to be a Lithuanian German, and as 'Josef Pejrell' spent four years in the Hitler Youth. Perel knew only too well what Hitler stood for and what the Nazis were doing to the Jews. He may, as he writes, have been ignorant of what was meant by the 'final solution', but he was aware of washing himself in the communal shower at the Brunswick college for Hitler Youth with soap called 'Rip' (*Reinjudenpaste*), pure Jewish fat.

Perel's extraordinary story, with its accounts of atrocities, subterfuge and degradation, can seem to mark what many have regarded as the final destiny of the idea of a continent and of a civilization. 'Europa, Europa': a cry unheard? A scornful jibe? The search for an implausible lifebelt? Or all three? What cannot be denied is that at this time the lamp of European civilization burned low, even if there were a few who succeeded in keeping a glimmer of light alive in the encroaching darkness. Barbarity skulked behind a façade of civilization and progress: soldiers from the nation which had given humanity most philosophers, musicians and artists wore emblazoned on their gun belts 'God is with us' as they went on their massacring way. After this it became necessary to reconsider what Europe stood for, in the full knowledge that nothing could ever be the same again; Europeans could no longer claim a unique civilization which merited export to the rest of the world. Indeed, some even began to assert that 'the most implacable foes of the human race had come from Europe'. As Geremek wrote,

> Historical reflection on the concept of Europe has been intensive throughout the twentieth century, and particularly since 1945, following the experience of a total war which began in Europe and of totalitarian ideologies and political movements whose origins were also European. A shadow of uncertainty has fallen over the sense of identity of a common civilization. As a result of this attitude the common fates of European culture, and the consciousness of belonging to a common culture such as has been ascribed to the nations and peoples of Europe in the distant past, have been overestimated.[2]

And yet for the last fifty years this ideal of Europe, shattered by the Second World War, has given hope to the inhabitants of the eastern half of Europe, swallowed up in the Soviet bloc; it has enabled them to find the courage to resist totalitarianism. For the dissidents of Eastern Europe – as indeed for the majority of people there – Europe meant freedom, democracy and well-being. Their idea of Europe was similar to that which prevailed in 1848; Europe stood for the reaffirmation of national sovereignty, of political and cultural independence. The contradiction which flared up then, leading directly to the two world wars, menaces again today: the creeping cancer of nationalism and intolerance lurks in the idea of a triumphant Europe and her civilization. As the historian Lewis Namier, who was Galician by origin, perceptively remarked:

> The year 1848 marked, for better or for worse, the beginning of the age of linguistic nationalism which gave shape to mass movements and led to inevitable conflict between them; a nation which defines its oneness in terms of language will not readily accept that groups of its co-nationals should live side by side with those of its neighbour.[3]

The 'illusions of 1848' seem to be the same as those of today. While the Western part of Europe strives to reattach itself to the

Eastern, the East explodes in ethnic conflicts which seem almost medieval. The prospect of a united Europe (from the Atlantic to the Urals, as has been forecast) recedes just as it seemed at its closest.

What has Europe meant for the citizens of Eastern Europe in the second half of the twentieth century? And what image of it have academics and intellectuals created? In his book *Penser l'Europe*, Edgar Morin observed that 'Contrary to appearances, European culture is by no means on the decline in the East; it is there regenerating itself ... It is necessary to be cut off from Europe, wrenched from it, to be as deeply aware of belonging to Europe as those Czechoslovak writers, émigrés in New York after 1968, who, as they went on holiday, to France or to Italy, would say "we're going home".'[4]

In the years after the war Europe was reborn as an ideal precisely in that part where in reality she had ceased to exist. It is the same phenomenon as in the nineteenth century, when national feeling was all the stronger among peoples who had ceased to exist as a nation (the most obvious example is Poland, which vanished from the map for almost a century and a half). The idea of Europe was reborn, but as an aspiration, in the Soviet bloc. The poet Czesław Miłosz was acutely aware of this feeling. His *Rodzinna Europa* ['Native Europe'],[5] written in 1959 when the author was already in exile, is one of the most profound and heartfelt paeans to Europe ever written. Miłosz, of Lithuanian origin and Polish mother-tongue, is a classic example of the attachment that smaller nations, buffeted by the storm of history, have for a conception of civilization which both elevates their own culture and binds them to the rest of the continent, preventing them from disappearing. What is striking about Miłosz's story is that for him the most important of the features that make Europe one is *smell*: in Switzerland he notices smells which remind him of Lithuania and Poland. The same is true of the writer Witold Gombrowicz: after years of exile in Argentina he sniffs the air in the Tiergarten in Berlin and realizes that he is 'back home'.[6] For us in Western Europe, Europe is no longer, if it ever was, defined by smell! Naturally Miłosz also describes the common tradition which links Lithuania and Poland to Europe: Latin culture and the Catholic religion. The city of Vilna (Wilno, Vilnius), with its baroque architecture, Jesuit tradition and a cultural life which made it 'the outpost of Europe against the East', symbolizes this common heritage. It was a city both Catholic and Jewish (Jews called it the 'Jerusalem of the North'), in which the most disparate ethnic groups and cultures, from Karaites to Muslims, lived together in an atmosphere of tolerance.

This world was swept away by the Second World War. In the early 1950s, unable to live under Stalinism, Miłosz fled to the West. He left behind ruins and ashes; he found himself in countries like France where everything was done to make him feel an outsider: people either sought to exploit him for political ends or felt irked by him, an 'exile from a better world'. And yet,

> Europe herself gathered me in her warm embrace, and her stones, chiselled by the hands of past generations, the swarm of her faces emerging from carved wood, from paintings, from the gilt of embroidered fabrics, soothed me, and my voice was added to her old challenges and oaths in spite of my refusal to accept her split and her sickliness. Europe, after all, was home to me.[7]

Miłosz is one of the first émigrés to create the potent image of one half of Europe, immersed in suffering and wretchedness, which is destined to be the spiritual saviour of the other, Western, half, the half of 'calm and orderly countries' which are susceptible to 'the melancholy of things that are simply here, yet are opaque'.[8] United by its deep-rooted shared past and culture – even by intangibles such as smell – Europe is divided by historical events. Its Eastern half will reunite with the rest, and save itself by saving the West.

In the gallery of visions of Europe created by the intelligentsia of Eastern Europe over the past fifty years, the idea of a 'third Europe' has a special place. Credit for opening the debate on Central Europe as a 'third Europe' goes to the Czech writer Milan Kundera. In his essay 'The sequestrated West, or the tragedy of Central Europe',[9] which draws together political ideas already articulated in his novels and journalism, Kundera argues that Europe as a geographical entity (from the Atlantic to the Urals) has always been divided into two separate parts which developed differently: one linked to ancient Rome and to the Catholic Church (characterized by the Latin alphabet), and another linked to Byzantium and to the Orthodox Church (characterized by the Cyrillic alphabet). The Second World War created a third Europe: 'that part of Europe which is geographically in the centre, culturally in the West and politically in the East'. For Kundera Central Europe is, in a certain sense, 'the quintessence of Europe and of its rich variety, a Europe in miniature'. The two enemies of Central Europe are Russia and neglect by Western Europe, which does not see European unity as important and fails to understand that its own spiritual salvation lies there.

> For this reason revolts in this region are partly conservative, almost backward-looking; they strive desperately to bring back a past age of civilization, of the modern age, for only in that age is it possible to defend one's own identity.

But the central point of Kundera's argument is that Russia is not part of Europe. Their histories and civilizations are too different. According to Kundera, Europe can be defined by what she is not; she is the opposite of everything Russian. From a historical and geographical point of view, therefore, Europe ends with Lithuania and the Baltic states, that is, where the advance of Catholicism came to a halt in the East. From a cultural point of view, Kundera picks up the argument of the Polish writer Kazimierz Brandys in his published diary:

> Russia's fate is not a part of our consciousness. It is alien to us; we feel no kinship with it or responsibility for it. It weighs on us, but it is not our heritage. I have always felt that way about Russian literature. I was afraid of it. To this day I am still afraid of some of Gogol's stories and of all of Saltykov-Shchedrin. I would prefer not to know their world, not to know it exists. One has to be a Frenchman to feel safe with that literature. Reading Dostoevsky, I have to remind myself that I will emerge in one piece from this illness, that I will somehow escape it, for to allow oneself to be gripped by it and to succumb to it means a spiritual death sentence, and I am not sufficiently submissive to accept that.[10]

But this view of Europe as a culture and civilization quite different from Russia has had many critics. One is Timothy Garton Ash, who in an essay on fact and fiction in Central Europe[11] attacks Kundera:

> If we want the expression 'Central Europe' to acquire real meaning, the debate must move on from rhetoric, sentiment and

illusion to a dispassionate and rigorous examination of what history has bequeathed to Central Europe – as much division as unity – and of the actual situation in East-Central Europe today, characterized as much by differences as by similarities ... All attempts to distil some common 'essence' from the history of Central Europe are absurdly reductionist, or pointlessly vague.

The Czech sociologist Milan Šimecka and the Hungarian philosopher Mihály Vajda have also entered the fray, Šimecka opposing Kundera's argument, Vajda supporting it.[12] Moreover, Georges Nivat, the scholar of Russian literature, has voiced the unease felt by many Russian intellectuals:[13]

Russian civilization, so in its infancy compared with the other European civilizations, is varied enough to have given us, from Pushkin to Mandelshtam, some of the most thoughtful and passionate Europeans. In politics as in literature Pushkin was an admirer of Benjamin Constant ... True, Saltykov-Shchedrin can be unsettling, but let us not forget that his great genius for satire had but one cause: the struggle against Asiatic Russia. Dostoevsky and others were scornful of Europe, which Ivan Karamazov saw as one great graveyard ... But consider how many Russian poets and painters have translated European poetry or went to study in Rome or Munich. It is also true that from the creation of the new Russia up to today we have witnessed a fervently pro-European Russia: the Russia of Pasternak, Mandelshtam and Akhmatova ...

The poet Joseph Brodsky shared this view. In a debate on this theme organized by *Zeszyty Literackie*, a Polish review published in Paris, he commented:

There is nothing surprising about the fact that Kundera, who has spent so much of his life in Eastern Europe (on occasion also called Western Asia), should want to be more European than the Europeans. Apart from anything else, this stance must attract him because he endows his past with logical links to the present, a privilege seldom possible for an émigré. It also places him in a splendid position from which to reproach the West for having betrayed its own values (those which used to be defined as European civilization) and for having abandoned to their fate a number of countries which wanted to remain at the heart of that civilization ... The only problem is that the definition of European civilization which Kundera uses must be quite narrow, even one-sided, if it omits Dostoevsky, and goes so far as to number him among the dangers which threaten this civilization.[14]

In 'Our Europe'[15] Czesław Miłosz argues that the debate about Central Europe is a debate about a credo, a programme, a utopia. He goes on to draw attention to the fact that the situation does not justify a clean distinction between West and East.

> The old religious border between Catholicism and the Orthodox Church cannot be regarded as a precise factor. Nor did the countries between Germany and Russia have much in common with Western Europe. Ideas which penetrated from outside were tempered and refashioned until they took on a new character. Local customs were evidently deep-rooted, and institutions took on a different form from that in the western part of Europe, which, discomfited, could only persecute Hussitism in the late Middle Ages or the 'paradise of heretics' (*paradisum hereticorum*) in Poland and Transylvania . . . Apart from this, and setting aside a sense of superiority in admiring things Western, we who come from these predominantly rural marches have had more than one reason to regard ourselves as different from the societies devoted to trade and industry. The complex present relationship with the capitalist West has nothing new about it in the least.

This debate on Europe between 1984 and 1987, which inspired the birth of several reviews of which the most important is the Polish *Europa*,[16] as well as publications of varying legality, foreshadowed and in some ways fostered the so-called 1989 revolution which changed the face of the central and eastern part of the continent and ended the division between the two Germanies. Yet the debate aroused little interest among most Western academics until the Soviet leader Mikhail Gorbachev launched his proposal for a 'common European home'. This was a vague, ill-defined catch-phrase which, however, had the result of promoting a new debate in Western Europe about Europe, her borders, and her relationship with Russia. For its part, the Soviet Union established an institute for the study of Europe, part of the Academy of Sciences.[17] Ralf Dahrendorf, in his essay *Reflections on the Revolution in Europe: in a letter intended to have been sent to a gentleman in Warsaw, 1990* is frank:

> The more difficult question is that of the place of the Soviet Union and it also deserves an unambiguous answer. I have already shown my cards and said that so far as I am concerned, Europe ends at the Soviet border, wherever that may be. If Lithuania, Latvia and Estonia manage to establish their claim that they do

not belong to the Soviet Union, then they are a part of Europe (though Azerbaijan would not be even if it attained independence) . . .[18]

In Dahrendorf's view, there are three reasons to reject Russia's claim to belong to Europe: 1) there is 'something suspicious in yesterday's hegemonic power wishing to set up house with those whom it occupied and held under its tutelage for so long'; 2) 'the Soviet Union, with all its European history, is a vast developing country which has a much longer way to go than others in its European orbit before it becomes a full part of the modern world'; and, most importantly, 3) 'Europe is not just a geographical or even a cultural concept, but one of acute political significance.'

> This arises at least in part from the fact that small and medium-sized countries try to determine their destiny together. A super-power has no place in their midst, even if it is not an economic and perhaps no longer a political giant . . . If there is a common European house or home to aim for, it is therefore not Gorbachev's but one to the West of his and his successors' crumbling empire.

Moreover, simultaneously with the opening up of the Soviet Union to Western Europe, nationalism is exploding in the republics; and this, with the exception of the Baltic states and Ukraine, is driving the country far from the 'common home'. In addition, Slavophile sentiment is re-emerging in the Russian republic, as well as the kind of antagonism to the West which was articulated so clearly by the phonetics scholar Nikolai Trubetskoi in 1921. His *The Apogee and Nadir of Russian Culture*, in particular, expresses a deep-seated contempt for the West in which traditional respect for the origins of European civilization is turned on its head:

> As long as the edifice of Russian culture was crowned by its byzantine cupola there was stability. But since it has begun to be replaced by Germanic Romanesque architecture from the top floor, all stability and proportion in the different parts of the structure have been lost, the top has cracked more and more, and has finally collapsed. And we, the Russian intelligentsia, who wasted so much time and energy trying to support the Germanic Romanesque roof which was falling away from the Russian walls

on which it sat uneasily, we now gaze in astonishment at these vast ruins and wonder how to build a new roof, still in the same Germanic Romanesque style. Such a project must be firmly rejected.[19]

According to Trubetskoi Western Christian culture has only very slightly penetrated the Russian people; it has left untouched the depths of the soul of the people. 'Everything which came from Byzantium', on the other hand, 'was thoroughly assimilated and served as a model for a creation which adapted all these elements to the requirements of the national psyche.'

Today, when politics has brought the idea of Europe back to centre stage, and when debate of its nature and its borders is no longer restricted to intellectual argument between dissidents, the question of how to define its roots becomes crucial. As has often been the case during the last half-century, history becomes an instrument of politics, and the more open-minded historian must bear in mind Witold Kula's warning:

Historians have to be translators who can translate the values of other cultures into our own language. They must always be conscious of the individual values which they are translating, and of the possibility, in spite of everything, of achieving such a translation. Historians make societies aware of their uniqueness, and at the same time make this uniqueness comprehensible to others.[20]

Among the historical works on Europe which appeared in Eastern Europe after the 1939–45 war, those of the Hungarian historians István Bibó and Jenő Szűcs are particularly important. Bibó, who also served in Imre Nagy's revolutionary government in 1956,[21] was the first to give a reading – in the spirit of Witold Kula's injunction to struggle against myth-making – of the history of Central Europe which departed from both 'official' history-writing and that of the 'opposition'.

As can be seen from the volume *Misère des petits États de l'Europe de l'Est*,[22] a collection of French translations of some of his more important writings, Bibó regarded the failure of the liberation movements of 1848–9 in East-Central Europe as the cause of a 'progressive degeneration of healthy relations between communities'. In his eyes, nineteenth-century nationalism should be seen as the death of Europe and the prelude to the two world wars (Lewis Namier, as we have seen, had also argued this, and indeed Geremek refers to Namier in his essay 'The Nation-State in Twentieth-Century Europe', Chapter 6 in this volume).

Jenő Szűcs takes up Bibó's argument in his book *Les Trois Europes*.[23] Trained, like that other great Hungarian historian Sándor Kopácsi – and Geremek – in the Annales school, Szűcs writes a 'longue durée' history of Europe, from Charlemagne to the end of the Second World War. He demonstrates how, starting from one common race and a shared idea of Europe (Europe as cradle of Christianity and heir to Latin culture), Europe had within a few centuries shifted to the formation of three Europes: Western Europe, East-Central Europe (in Hungarian *keleti-közép Európa*) and Eastern Europe. Russia and Western Europe were to develop autonomous 'world economies' while the central nations would lose their political and economic independence. Western Europe was unique in having created, in the mid-thirteenth century, 'civic society' and 'political society'. Because of this, Szűcs argues, Western Europe is a product not of the classical world but of feudalism; this is as true of the concept of the dignity of man as it is of the constituent elements of political relationships. These are processes which exclude East-Central Europe because of the constant pressure from neighbouring powers. In the case of Hungary, the greatest danger came from the Ottoman empire which, after the battle of Mohács in 1526, occupied the country for a hundred and fifty years.

The Polish historian and philosopher Krzysztof Pomian, who continues Szűcs's argument in his book *L'Europe et ses nations*,[24] is therefore correct in declaring that

> The history of Europe is that of her borders. And that is the history of what was inside those borders, imposed on her by words and deeds. It is therefore a history of the forces which, consciously or not, have acted to produce the unification of a space which was initially fragmented; it is also a history of those forces which have pulled in the opposite direction and undone everything which the first had produced. It is thus a history of conflicts, between Europe and that which contained her, even crushed her, and of the internal conflict at the heart of Europe herself, between the forces which impelled her towards unity and uniformity and those which sought to divide and diversify.[25]

Pomian succeeds in giving a comprehensive view of the current situation in, and problems of, Europe as a whole, where no change is regarded as inevitable and irreversible. In his conclusion he merely gives this thought:

> For Europe the lesson is clear: her worst enemy, which has infiltrated her genetic inheritance like a virus, and which like a virus is capable of the most extraordinary transformations, is separatism, be it ethnic, national or ideological: the choice of autarchy or the aspiration to a hegemonic role, whatever the justifications may be.[26]

In the Middle Ages, as Geremek notes in his essay 'Geography and Apocalypse: The Concept of Europe According to Jakub of Paradyż' (Chapter 5 in this volume), the word 'Europe' was used to indicate a geographical place. Only towards the end of this period did it acquire a historical and cultural meaning, and was used increasingly in historical and philosophical works, replacing the word *christianitas*. 'Europe' was no longer synonymous with 'Christendom' but was becoming something more specific.

At the beginning of the 1980s Geremek abandoned twenty years of research on the marginalized in society[27] to devote himself to a series of studies on the 'uniqueness' of Europe, on the relations between Poland and Europe, and on the idea of Europe. This was a crucial period in the history of modern Poland. At the end of the 1970s opposition to the communist government had created independent institutions (trades unions, underground universities, publishers) which had shaken up Polish political and cultural life. This phenomenon, entirely new in a Warsaw Pact country, meant that the blue-collar strikers of August 1980 soon became a revolutionary movement which convulsed the entire country. No sooner had the workers, led by Lech Wałęsa, occupied the Gdańsk dockyards than Geremek, along with Catholic Mazowiecki, went there to demonstrate their solidarity. Geremek was to become a councillor of the Independent Union of Solidarność. Thus began the political career of a historian who had been dramatically saved as a child from the Warsaw ghetto. Geremek had subsequently become first a communist, then a dissident, returning his party card in 1968 in protest at the Soviet invasion of Czechoslovakia. From that time his work as a historian had to coexist – and often conflict – with his involvement in politics: Geremek was one of the main architects of the turning-point of 1989 with the 'Round Table',[28] and he became one of the most respected politicians in the new Poland, a result of his intelligence and his negotiating skills, but also of the determination with which he defended his 'lay' view of politics and of his conviction that Poland can live only in a Europe of democratic and tolerant states.

As a result, the focus of Geremek's research since the early 1980s does not seem coincidental. This is also true from a political perspective: during the 16 months of Solidarity (August 1980 to December 1981) it was often remarked that Poland was returning to Europe.

During this period the Vatican, which has played so great a part in recent Polish affairs, organized an international colloquium at the Augustinianum Patristic Institute in Rome on the theme of 'The Common Christian Roots of the European Nations'. Responding to Pope John Paul II's appeal on 3 June 1979 in Gniezno, during his visit to Poland, two hundred scholars (of whom two-thirds were Slav, for the most part Polish) assembled in the Vatican City between 3 and 7 November 1981.[29] The written message sent by Alexander Solzhenitsyn gives a sense of how some understood the theme of the conference:

> The further we venture into the dark maw of the twentieth century, while in the distance the gashes of decades disappear, all the more clearly do we perceive that the entire change of course which the world has embarked on in the last three centuries is part of a single terrible process, that of the loss of God by humanity. If we do not allow ourselves to be distracted by the immediate political minutiae of today and of individual countries, we will find ourselves on the brink of an abyss into whose depths all Christian civilization could plunge for ever. We who are conscious of this have one last chance, to strive for the unification of our forces in order to proclaim the danger and to urge its avoidance.[30]

Geremek also took part in the colloquium, giving a paper called 'La notion d'Europe et la prise de conscience européenne au bas Moyen Age'.[31]

> The modern conception of Europe was born in the Middle Ages. And yet the central institutions of that age seem to contradict the

ideals of political, economic and cultural unity which Europe might seem to stand for. Studies of the history of the idea of Europe generally regard the Middle Ages as an inevitable stage in the creation of a European consciousness. The imprint of a Western-centric view which characterizes these studies, and the absence of a sociological perspective in the examination of social awareness, paradoxically combine to make this more likely. The success of the idea of Europe was associated not only with the gradual secularization of the mind but also with the disintegration of *christianitas*, a community identified with Western Europe; on these two levels the idea of Europe appears to be the opposite of medieval universalist ideas. In the Middle Ages social links and the awareness of being part of society were extremely limited; equally, the sense of solidarity and of wider social bonds was extremely weak and was usually found only in narrow elite groups. The history of the idea of Europe, or of the European ideal, is not therefore identical with that of the growing awareness of the European community ... Compared to traditional *christianitas*, which had developed over earlier centuries, the common bonds of Europe seem much less coherent but, in compensation, from a geographical point of view distinctly wider. The geographical frontiers of Christendom derived, obviously, from the spread of conversion and submission to the Roman Church. However, the regions on the edge of this community seem to be little integrated into Western Latin civilization. Equally, the cohesion of the central area of Europe should not be overestimated.

Geremek's interpretation of the idea of Europe goes beyond any idealization of, and nostalgia for, the Middle Ages; it also goes beyond a simple equation of Europe-Christianity-civilization.

The month after the Rome conference, following the military coup of 13 December 1981 in Poland, Geremek was interned. Historians did not stop working in prison. Karol Modzelewski writing his book on the organization of the Polish state from the tenth to the thirteenth century thanks to the help of Aleksander Gieysztor, who brought his books and notes when he visited, is well known.[32] Geremek worked on Jacobus de Paradiso (Jacobus Carthusiensis, Jakob z Paradyża) and on his 'certainty' of an imminent apocalypse which would come from the East to assail the West. Reading these pages, one is aware of the amusement of the historian who can maintain a dialogue with the past and can 'see in perspective' his own immediate situation. In the following years, Geremek's research has been a preparation for a comprehensive appraisal of the idea and nature of Europe which will hopefully one day be published as a monograph.

In 1990 Geremek wrote an article on Europe entitled 'An open border'. In this he states:

> I believe that in Western Europe the sense of belonging to European civilization is felt less strongly than in the countries of Central Europe. For us it has always been an aspiration, while in Western Europe the process of unification has advanced with difficulty and has been associated with squabbles over agricultural policy. It seemed that the European Community would never be able to resolve the issue of the production and sale of eggs. In Central Europe, on the other hand, the issue of Europe is seen as a challenge, a political, economic and cultural challenge. I believe that it is in everyone's interest to understand Europe in a wide sense . . . Europe is not a geographical concept but a political concept, a cultural one . . . To identify Europe with Western Europe is good neither for Europe nor the world. I am convinced that the phrase once used by De Gaulle is still valid: according to him Europe is an ensemble of nations, and the wealth of national traditions and character does not in any way conflict with the concept of the European community.[33]

The concept of Central Europe and of our common Christian roots as a still central part of European civilization and as a pivot of unification with the Catholic and Orthodox communities of Russia seems to recur in Geremek's most recent writings: 'The heritage of Europe is a particular way of living in societies, nations and cultures. It is rooted in what Europe has built: in the Christian tradition.' And yet, faced with an increasingly multi-racial Europe, the Europe–Christianity equation is of doubtful validity. The Czech Antonin Liehm, editor of the journal *Lettera internazionale*, is correct in identifying as the characteristic feature of modern Europe the 'citizen'.

> To be European is in fact to be a citizen. Europe stands for civic society. Europe's shared past lies in the culture of civic society, in urban culture, not rural, not in peasant superstition . . . Europe does not mean a return to the Middle Ages, but the civic society which developed in the nineteenth century when America was still akin to Europe. From this point of view Russia is a European civilization, but not a European society, precisely because she still has to complete the long march towards civic society.[34]

Notes

1 S. Perel, *Europa, Europa*, Paris, Editions Ramsay, 1990. A film based on the book and with the same title, by the Polish director Agnieszka Holland, was released in 1990.
2 Cf. Chapter 5 in this volume.
3 Lewis Namier, *La rivoluzione degli intellectuali ed altri saggi sull'800 europeo*, Turin, Einaudi, 1957, p. 193.
4 E. Morin, *Penser l'Europe*, Paris, Gallimard, 1987, pp. 191, 199–200.
5 C. Miłosz, *Rodzinna Europa*, Paris, Instytut Literacki, 1959 (Eng. trans. by Catherine S. Leach as *Native Realm: a search for self-definition*, London, Sidgwick & Jackson, 1981 [first published New York, Doubleday, 1968]).
6 W. Gombrowicz, *Dziennik 1961–1966*, Paris, Instytut Literacki, 1971 (Eng. trans. by Lillian Vallee as *Diary: Volume 3 (1961–1966)*, Evanston, IL, Northwestern Press, 1993, p. 103).
7 Miłosz, *Native Realm*, p. 293.
8 Ibid., pp. 299, 300.
9 M. Kundera, 'L'Occidente sequestrato, ovvero la tragedia dell'Europa Centrale', *Nuovi Argomenti*, 9, Jan.–March 1984.
10 K. Brandys, *Miesiące 1978–1981*, Paris, Instytut Literacki, 1982 (Eng. trans. by Richard Lourie as *A Warsaw Diary 1978–1981*, London, Chatto & Windus, 1984, p. 47).
11 T. G. Ash, 'Mito e realtà dell'Europa Centrale', *Lettera Internazionale*, 9–10, summer–autumn 1986. On this theme, see Ash, *Pomimo i wbrew: eseje o Europie Środkowej*, London, Polonia, 1990, an anthology of articles originally published in the *New York Review of Books, Granta, New Republic* and the *Times Literary Supplement*.
12 M. Šimecka, 'Another civilization? An other civilization?', *East European Reporter*, I, 2, 1985; M. Vajda, 'Who excluded Russia from Europe?', ibid., I, 4, 1986; M. Šimecka, 'Which way back to Europe?', ibid., II, 3, 1987.
13 Cf. *Le Débat*, 3, 1984, and G. Nivat, *Vers la fin du mythe russe: essais sur la culture russe de Gogol à nos jours*, Lausanne, L'Age d'Homme, 1982.
14 J. Brodsky, 'Si può escludere Dostoevskij dall'Europa?' *Ottavogiorno*, 4, Oct.–Dec. 1987. Cf. Barbara Toruńczyk, 'Le voci, lo spirito, la coscienza', ibid.
15 C. Miłosz, 'O naszei Europie', *Kultura*, 4 (463), 1986 (It. trans. as 'La nostra Europa', *Ottavogiorno*, 4, Oct.–Dec. 1987).
16 Founded in Warsaw in 1987 as the journal of the Instytut Europy Wschodniej (Institute for Eastern Europe) and published clandestinely. Five issues appeared in 1989.
17 See A. Bonanni's interview with the institute director Vitalii Vladimirovich Zhurkin, 'Ecco l'Europa sognata da Mosca', *Corriere della sera*, 31 Oct. 1988.

18 *Reflections on the Revolution in Europe: in a letter intended to have been sent to a gentleman in Warsaw*, 1990, London, Chatto & Windus, 1990, p. 110.
19 N. Trubetskoi, *Verkhi i nizy russkoi kul'tury*, 1921 (It. trans. as *Il vertice e la base della cultura russa*, in N. Trubeckoi, *L'Europa e l'umanità*, Turin, Einaudi, 1982, pp. 101, 109.
20 W. Kula, 'Moja edukacja sentymentalna', *Trwórczość*, 9, 1976 (It. trans. as 'La mia educazione sentimentale', *Rivista storica italiana*, XCIX, 3, 1987).
21 On Bibó, see Agnes Heller, 'Un democratico senza democrazia', *Micro-Mega*, 3, 1986, and Gabriele Nissim, 'Olocausto, responsabilità, identità', *Ottavogiorno*, 2–3, April–Sept. 1987.
22 I. Bibó, *Misère des petits États de l'Europe de l'Est*, Paris, Harmattan, 1986.
23 J. Szűcs, *Les Trois Europes*, Paris, Harmattan, 1985; it includes an enthusiastic introduction by Fernand Braudel.
24 K. Pomian, *L'Europe et ses nations*, Paris, Gallimard, 1990.
25 Pomian, *L'Europe et ses nations*, pp. 7–8.
26 Ibid., pp. 232–3.
27 For an intellectual biography of Geremek, see F. M. Cataluccio, 'I vagabondi e i poveri nell'opera di Bronisław Geremek', introduction to Geremek, *La stirpe di Caino*, Milan, il Saggiatore, 1988.
28 For Geremek's role in Poland's transition to democracy, see J. Żakowski's interview with him in *Rok 1989: Bronisław Geremek opowiada, Jacek Żakowski pyta* [The year 1989: Bronisław Geremek replies to Jacek Zakowski's questions], Warsaw, Plejada, 1990.
29 *The Common Christian Roots of the European Nations*, 2 vols, Florence, Le Monnier, 1982.
30 Ibid., vol. 1, pp. 45–6.
31 Ibid., vol. 2, pp. 1247–69.
32 K. Modzelewski wrote, in Italian, a paper for the Settimana di Studi del Centro italiano di studi sull'alto Medio Evo (Spoleto, Italy, 15–21 April 1982): *L'organizzazione dello stato polacco nei secoli X–XIII: la soicetà e le strutture del potere*. It was read on Modzelewski's behalf by Girolamo Arnaldi (cf. G. Arnaldi, 'Due amici polacchi', *Il Giornale*, 21 Sept. 1982).
33 B. Geremek, 'Un confine aperto', *Ulisse 2000*, 81, Dec. 1990, pp. 124–5.
34 A. Liehm, 'Praga, rovine dell'Europa', *L'Unità*, 24 Feb. 1988.

1

Western Europe in the Middle Ages

Research on the history of foreign countries[1] has a solid tradition in Polish medieval studies. It has always been motivated by the need to interpret the history of one's own country in connection with processes of civilization on the scale of universal history, by the need for a comparative framework for historical investigation and by a curiosity to investigate similarities and dissimilarities between processes and developments taking place in different geographical and political or ethnical formations. When one of the great founders of modern Polish historiography, Joachim Lelewel (1786–1861), undertook to present a systematic and modern approach to Poland's history, he presented it throughout against the background of the history of other peoples and countries and inscribed it in the framework of European history; it was from that procedure of bringing into relationship the Polish and the general history that grew his brilliant studies in the geography and numismatics of medieval Europe and the amazing parallel between the history of Poland and of Spain in the sixteenth to eighteenth centuries. In the subsequent decades of the nineteenth century and in the first decades of the twentieth, the positivistic programme of historiography assumed a distrustful attitude towards synthetical constructions and philosophical reflection on the past which tended naturally to widen the geographical horizons of historical research and to cultivate general history; at the same time, however, it took into account the needs of comparative studies and encouraged the practice of research into foreign history. Such research was to serve as a school of historical analysis utilizing different – and in most cases also very rich – source material and, at the same time, provide an opportunity of confronting methodological rigour with more trained historical centres; hence the particular preference shown in this research for the French and German Middle Ages. The universality of institutional and ideological structures of the medieval West also inclined scholars to investigate institutions and ideas where they developed in the fullest and most classical form – so as to understand better the mechanisms and results of reception in an area that was younger in respect of civilization. In this way, modern medieval studies in Poland have constantly retained the concept of research into general history.

Indeed, general history which, for institutional and administrative reasons, is treated as one of the specialized fields of historical science, is rather a general perspective of historical synthesis in which can be included equally research into the history of one's own country and that of foreign countries. In the present review, which merely outlines the main directions of studies and does not aspire to completeness, I shall discuss works concerned with the general history of the Middle Ages in this narrower sense, that is, excluding studies devoted to the history of medieval Poland and including works by Polish medievalists in the field of foreign history.

The geographical range of the main body of these works remains within the confines of the circle of civilization to which Poland also belonged; it comprised on the one hand the Slav world, on the other the Christian West. The intensity of that research is different with regard to the various countries and to the various centres of historical science in Poland. Thus research on medieval Russia (in Warsaw, Poznań, Toruń), Bohemia (Wrocław), Hungary (Cracow), France (Warsaw) and Germany (Poznań, Warsaw) has been particularly extensive; to a lesser extent and rather sporadically represented, on the other hand, are studies on the medieval history of Italy or England (Cracow, Warsaw).

The needs of university instruction and the interest of broad circles of the reading public brought about the appearance of several attempts at a synthetical exposition of European history of the Middle Ages. Tadeusz Manteuffel, who had published before the war a history of the early Middle Ages (in the Great General History series), is the author of a full general history of the Middle Ages. He did not go in this work beyond European history, considering that the very notion of general history had grown from the history of the succession states of the Roman empire, and the contacts between the various civilizations had been so faint in the Middle Ages that a joint presentation of the history of Europe and Asia would have been an artificial procedure.[2] Keeping within the confines of post-Roman succession, the author included the history of the Slav world and Byzantium in his uniform synthetical exposition.

Departing from similar assumptions, Benedykt Zientara attempted to include non-European history in his comprehensive (and very good) manual of general medieval history;[3] he introduced in an interesting manner the history of the Arab world, showing the close cultural and political ties between Europe and the Islamic world (the exposition of the medieval history of the Far East has rather the character of synoptic information).

The various sections of the medieval historical process, especially those which have a separate status in university studies, have also been the subject of presentation in compendium form; in some cases they went beyond the classical type of textbook formulations and were based on the author's original research; this is true in particular of outline histories of states and institutions and of histories of philosophy or aesthetics.[4] The economic and social history of the Middle Ages has also become the subject of works of encyclopedic and popularizing character.[5] The small book which Jan Baszkiewicz devoted to the political thought of the Middle Ages, largely containing the results of his own analytical research,[6] was intended as popular reading for the general public. Aleksander Gieysztor has presented the history of Latin paleography as part of an encyclopedic series devoted to the auxiliary sciences of history;[7] this excellently documented work is not only a modern manual of Latin paleography *sensu largo* but in a considerable part the result of the author's own research. Finally, in the various series presenting the national histories of individual countries, the Middle Ages have been the subject of synthetical exposition by distinguished Polish medievalists.[8]

Detailed research into general medieval history, conducted in

Poland in various centres and by various research groups, is characterized by considerable dispersion, both chronologically and thematically. The list of works is also quite long. Without aspiring to present a full register of Polish research in this field, I propose only to indicate certain groups of problems on which that research has been more concentrated than on others, and where important scientific conclusions have been reached.

A domain of wide interest on the part of Polish medievalists has been the formation of social, economic and political structures of early medieval Europe through a confrontation and blending of the heritage of Mediterranean antiquity with the social realities of the barbarian peoples. Polish medieval studies had excellent antecedents in the research conducted at Warsaw University in the interwar period. The seminars conducted by Professor Marceli Handelsman produced a considerable number of works on society and power in Merovingian and Carolingian Europe. In the postwar years, the dynamic research, conceived on a wide scale, on the origins of the Polish state also initiated analogical and comparative studies on the formation of early medieval states. However, these studies concerned only marginally the territories of the post-Roman succession. Gerard Labuda undertook the investigation of the character of state organization formed on the periphery of the Christian West, on Slav lands, in the seventh century.[9] In this work, a true masterpiece of medieval analysis, Labuda performed a subtle reconstruction of the process as a result of which the Frankish merchant Samo became the leader of a Slav state with Moravia as its central territory. While in this case we remain within Merovingian Europe – and the problems of contacts between Slavs and Franks as well as the figure of Charlemagne have attracted the attention of Polish historians[10] – Polish studies on the early medieval period have concentrated primarily on Slav countries. A unique place in this respect is held by the scientific output of the eminent medievalist from Poznań, Henryk Łowmiański. Before the war, when he was attached to the University of Vilnius, Łowmiański published a work on the society of medieval Lithuania[11] which, in a manner innovatory in Polish historiography, introduced sociological and economic problems into medieval studies; then, in 1953, he presented the first attempt at a comparative investigation of the economic bases for the formation of state structures in the Slav countries.[12] Pointing to the connection between the formation of states and the development of plough tillage, the author demonstrated the interrelation between the disintegration of kin community and the formation of feudal property. These theses became the object of vivid discussion; the author himself, in the course of further studies, connected in particular with his monumental work on Poland in the early Middle Ages, introduced considerable nuances into his statements; he also greatly expanded the scope of research on the migrations and stabilization of Slav tribes in the social, economic and political structures of the Slav world.

In Polish research concerned with the origins of states, Scandinavian problems are represented by separate works. Marian Małowist has dealt with economic structures of a broadly outlined area which he calls the Baltic zone; in this, he utilized largely the results of archeological research.[13] Stanisław Piekarczyk undertook an analysis of economic relations in Sweden in the early Middle Ages,[14] striving to determine the distinct features of feudalization processes in Scandinavian societies. Gerard Labuda presented an interesting sketch of peculiarities in the processes of the formation and evolution of German statehood in the tenth to the thirteenth centuries.[15]

In the course of research on the origins of the Polish state and society, the cooperation between historians and archeologists has proved particularly important and fertile. This has also been the case with the attempted synthetical presentations concerning the entire Slav world. I should cite here above all the syntheses and compendia of the history of Slavs in the early Middle Ages by Witold Hensel, who, in addition, engaged in comparative studies on the origins of Slav towns.[16] Important hypotheses and research proposals in this respect have also been advanced by Aleksander Gieysztor; in particular, he outlined the processes of development of a monetary economy and of urbanization against a comparative all-Slav background.[17] The combined research efforts of Polish historians and archeologists yield numerous works of major importance.[18] The *Dictionary of Slav Antiquities*, published in 1961, was a scientific project of great importance for research on the Slavs in the early Middle Ages; this encyclopedia (covering to the end of the twelfth century) has no precedent in Slav studies.[19] Among the latter I should cite many works and subjects discussed in connection with the problems of Poland's own history. I shall limit myself to pointing out Labuda's excellent studies on the history of Western Slavs,[20] their place in the Slav community, the contacts of Slavs with Huns and Goths, and their relations with Scandinavia.

In the postwar years, the methodological reorientation of Polish historiography has contributed to an important development of research into social and economic problems. This is reflected by the subject-matter of works devoted to general medieval history, although the overall proportions among the various fields of social and economic history have not always been fully maintained. While in regard to Polish history research on agrarian history has been decidedly predominant (and the number of analytical and monographic studies has led to important attempts at synthetical and model constructions), in the studies of general medieval history agrarian problems have engaged little attention. I might cite here Karol Modzelewski's thorough work on the *exploitation directe* system in the estates of a Venetian monastery, and a more general attempt to interpret the pattern of manorial economy on the basis of north Italian polyptychs from the ninth and tenth centuries.[21] In an analytical study on the interrelation between the grain trade and the agrarian structure of the Uckermark in the fourteenth century, Zientara tackled the problem of agrarian depression towards the end of the Middle Ages, and demonstrated that it was the transformations in the economic structure and not the natural calamities that were the basic cause of the phenomenon of abandoned fields and farms.[22]

Problems of urban history enjoyed much greater interest; in this respect, significant achievements can be noted in investigations of the forms of urban economic activity and the social structure of the medieval town. In connection with the initiated team research on the history of Polish crafts, Małowist took up the problems of European crafts in the late Middle Ages. The proper perspective for this research was provided by one of the crucial problems of European medieval discussions – that of structural transformations in the economics of the late Middle Ages. Seeing in these transformations the signs of the first crisis of the feudal system, Małowist in three comprehensive studies made an analysis of the organization of production and the social relations in the cloth industry of Flanders, England and Holland in the fourteenth and fifteenth centuries, pointing to the decline of traditional luxury production and the development of new manufacturing designed for a wider trade.[23] The author connected these phenomena with the process of expansion of a monetary economy in the countryside and new social groups entering urban economic activity and the market. Using contemporary cloth-making as an example, he made an interesting analysis of the primitive forms of capitalistic organization of production. The crafts in late medieval Paris became the object of a separate study.[24] Characterizing the forms of urban wage work in the Middle Ages, the author pointed to the limited scope of function of the labour market and to the peculiar place that an unskilled labour force held in that market. In the economic and psychosociological processes shaping the modern labour market, a particular role was played by migrant journeymen, and a comparative analysis of their migrations has also been made.[25] Tadeusz Rosłanowski presented the mining and metallurgy of Westphalia in the Middle Ages in connection with the problems of colonization of that region,[26] and the history of money became the subject of a monograph by Ryszard Kiersnowski, who examined the course and the economic background of monetary reform in Europe in the thirteenth and fourteenth centuries.[27]

The problems of European trade were studied in particular by Małowist, who had pursued that line of research since before the war. Shortly after the war he published a comprehensive work on transformations in Black Sea trade in the third quarter of the fifteenth century and on Kaffa's economic role after the seizure of the Black Sea region by the Turks. He also carried out extensive research on the history of Baltic trade in the late Middle Ages, pointing in particular to the role that trade had played in consolidating the division of Europe into economic zones.[28] Małowist's works found a continuation in the studies of Henryk Samsonowicz, who, from research on the economic activity of Gdańsk in the fifteenth century, reconstructed an overall economic picture of the Hanse on the Baltic; he argued that in the fourteenth and fifteenth centuries the Baltic region constituted an economic entity as a result of both the functioning of the international division of labour and the specific natural conditions.[29] The problems of shipping on the Baltic Sea also attracted the interest of historians: Edmund Cieślak and Stanisław Matysik undertook to investigate the question of the winter pause in Baltic navigation in the light of legal rules, as well as several other detailed problems related to maritime law.[30]

In the studies on the social structure of the medieval town, the attention of Polish historians was attracted by the problem of the patrician order on the one hand and the urban populace on the other. Samsonowicz's preliminary and discussible supposition that up to the fourteenth century the notion of an urban patriciate had been connected with definite forms of economic activity and in a later period it had been identified with the power elite[31] has not become the object of detailed verification. Rosłanowski undertook to investigate the problems of the urban patriciate, taking as an example three cities on the Rhine – Bonn, Andernach and Koblenz – in the twelfth and thirteenth centuries (utilizing, especially for Andernach, several previously unpublished documents).[32] The author made a thorough study of three successive stages in the evolution of the urban elite: first the group of ministerials, then the *meliores*, evolving towards the status of rentiers of feudal type, and finally, at the turn of the fourteenth century, the group of *maiores oppidani*, drawing their strength from economic activity but, like the former, evolving towards rentiership. The opposite extreme of the medieval urban community has been discussed in a work on marginal groups in Paris in the fourteenth and fifteenth centuries.[33] This study, based primarily on court records, tried to determine the place of beggars, vagrants, prostitutes and outcasts in the topography and social structure of the late medieval town; the author stressed the common features in the way of life of these diverse groups and the basic absence of a sense of community or class consciousness. The passive and instrumental role played by these groups in social movements bears witness, in the author's opinion, to the low degree of their internal cohesion.[34]

Urban history has also been represented in Polish medievalist literature by minor works. In the field of historical demography, attempts have been made to determine the population of Hanseatic cities and the trends of its evolution, as well as the proportions of the population of Paris in the fourteenth century (arguments were set forth to prove that Paris had more than 200,000 inhabitants).[35] The monograph on a small Provençal town, Salon-de-Provence, in the fourteenth century showed the functioning of a small-town market and its connections with its 'hinterland' (the work provided interesting information on the forms of urban credit).[36] Urban life was also the subject of a small book of popular character,[37] in which, apart from economic structures and forms of urban activities, the peculiarities of urban culture and its sociopsychological aspects are dealt with.

Finally, I should note in this field an original attempt at comparative synthesis: in an extensive confrontation of social and economic structures of Europe's east and west in the late Middle Ages, Małowist[38] summed up his studies on the difference of developmental trends in the various zones; the author introduced into scholarly circulation interesting material concerning South-Eastern Europe, little utilized thus far in comparative research, and demonstrated how the East supplied raw materials and the West gave in return industrial and luxury goods.

In the vast field of research on the history of law, Polish historiography has some considerable achievements, especially with regard to the Middle Ages. Studies have been directed to the comparative history of Slav laws,[39] where discussions and investigations have concerned the possibilities of reconstructing ancient Slav custom-law, the legal systems and monuments of the neighbouring territories,[40] and the problems of laws and institutions of the West. Michał Patkaniowski's research on the origin of the legal system of Italian communes, started before the war, has been continued in several directions. Irena Malinowska-Kwiatkowska has studied the institutions of the commune of Bologna and certain detailed problems of Italian law, as well as private law in the Sicilian legislation of the twelfth to thirteenth centuries (the latter work containing an interesting analysis of agrarian contracts and property relations);[41] Michał Staszków has presented the theoretical and practical origins of the evolution of legal views on the commune, studying in particular the inquiries of Italian glossators.[42] Wojciech M. Bartel has considered the evolution of state institutions in Anglo-Saxon Britain and the problems of protection of personal liberty up to the time of the Norman conquest.[43] The legal problems of the feudal system, outlined before the war by Marceli Handelsman and Tadeusz Manteuffel, were dealt with in the postwar years above all by the latter's works[44] of both popular and research character.

An important place in this field is held by Michał Sczaniecki's work with its penetrating analysis of a peculiar type of feudal contract, namely enfeoffment.[45] I should also mention here several minor studies, for example, on the character of vassalage in Anglo-Saxon Britain or on the role of feudal institutions in the formation of Slav states.[46] Finally I should note the works by the distinguished historian of medieval law Adam Vetulani, whose studies on *Decretum Gratiani* and the decretists have already become classics in the literature of the subject.[47]

Interesting research has been undertaken on the history of the formation of the institutions of state representation in Central Europe. Karol Górski has presented an attempt at comparative examination of state privileges and institutions,[48] and Stanisław Russocki has investigated the birth and typology of state assemblies.[49] Russocki is also the author of important studies devoted to *ius resistendi* in Slav countries and the influence of provincial synods on political assemblies in the tenth to thirteenth centuries.[50]

History of law has also inspired one of the most interesting Polish works on general medieval history, namely Jan Baszkiewicz's book on state sovereignty in the political doctrine of the Middle Ages.[51] Baszkiewicz concentrated his attention on the external aspect of state sovereignty, developing in the course of confrontation of national monarchies the universalism of empire and the papacy. The author linked the doctrine of state sovereignty with the elimination of feudal fragmentation and with the restoration of royal power in the thirteenth and fourteenth centuries, rejecting the thesis that the theory of the modern sovereign state was elaborated by twelfth-century canonic lawyers and in papal circles.

The history of the papacy and of the Church is the subject of numerous research projects in Polish historiography; predominant among them are monographs and analytical studies. Taking up the study of the ideological origin of the Crusades, Gieysztor[52] pointed out that there were no grounds for supposing any antecedents of the Crusades in the plans of Sergius IV (1009–1012) and demonstrated that the encyclical ascribed to that pope was a forgery produced in the milieu of Cluny on the eve of the First Crusade. Manteuffel investigated the history of monastic orders in the medieval Church[53] and devoted a detailed monograph to the place of the Cistercians in papal policy.[54] The original results of this study include both the internal evolution of the order (and, in particular, of its economic policy) and the special missionary role the Cistercians were to play in the policy of the papacy in Slav and Baltic countries.

In Polish research into religious life and consciousness, a particular role has been played by the problem of medieval heresies. Manteuffel devoted to it a book as well as several detailed studies. He dealt above all with the origination of heresies, taking the example of adherents of voluntary poverty and seeking to find out how the dividing lines between orthodoxy and heterodoxy are formed and where they run.[55] In the opinion of the author, both these notions were of a relative character; the judgements of the Church concerning views and actions qualified as heretical were determined above all by pragmatic considerations. Voluntary poverty as an individual aspiration presented no threat to church structure; however, when it assumed the form of a collective and mass-scale phenomenon, it became dangerous and was treated with considerable severity. Manteuffel also began research – which was interrupted by his death – on medieval heterodoxy. It resulted in two interesting studies, on Pierre de Jean Olivi and on the chiliastic beliefs of Joachim of Fiore.[56] The problems of the dividing lines between orthodoxy and heterodoxy were also dealt with by Stanisław Trawkowski in his thorough study on the origins of the Prémontré movements and on the evolution of the character of the Premonstratensians in the various countries of Europe.[57] Against the background of this evolution, the author outlined the changing attitude of the order towards the problem of women; these are among the more interesting findings of his work. Following up, as it were, Manteuffel's conclusions on the role of Cistercians in the political designs of the papacy, Trawkowski showed the dependence of the Premonstratensians' internal evolution upon the requirements of papal policy and the intended papal reforms. Also devoted to problems of heresy is Stanisław Bylina's book on the social programmes and ideas of the Italian humiliates, the béguines of southern France and the Rhine beghards.[58] Analysing the agenda of poverty of these groups, the author strove to grasp the common elements and the differences of social contestation in medieval heterodoxy. Particularly interesting is the part of the book devoted to the begging beghards in the Rhinelands towards the end of the thirteenth and in the fourteenth century – in the findings concerning both the social composition of the group and the character of the elite in their social and ethical programme. Many scholars, especially in Wrocław's historical centre, have grappled with the problems of Hussitism, above all the question of the Hussite influence in Poland and the nationality aspects of the movement; however, new light was also shed upon certain problems of the ideology of Hussitism.[59]

Finally I should note here Jerzy Kłoczowski's important and original attempt to give a synthetical exposition of the history of groups living in communities in Western Christendom from the decline of antiquity to the fifteenth century.[60] It is, in fact, an exposition of the history of Christianity as seen through the actions, the social and ethical programmes and the social values of its most active and leading groups. The author traced the beliefs of social groups and the types of Christian religiousness in connection with the fact that agriculture was gaining in importance in Western European society in the early Middle Ages, and that the process of transformation was connected with the development of urban civilization in the first half of the second millennium. Closing his study on the threshold of the great Reformation movements, the author showed the medieval premises of the far-reaching process of individualization of religious life.

There are no original works of a synthetical character in the vast field of the history of medieval European culture, yet the number of detailed studies and new proposals has been quite considerable. I should point, first of all, to the problems of conflict of traditional cultures with Christianity which have aroused growing interest in European medieval studies. Stanisław Piekarczyk first took up the problems of religion in early medieval Scandinavia on the threshold of Christianization,[61] detecting in particular the ideologies of the various social groups, and then devoted a comprehensive work to a confrontation of Christian and pagan patterns of culture and conduct among the Germans (in the fifth to the eighth century).[62] In this latter study, investigating the relations between the barbarian world and Christendom, the author considered the degree of attractiveness of Christianity to peoples who were the object of catechizing and proceeded to a revaluation – sometimes with excessive *parti pris* – of old Germanic tradition and Germanic polytheism. He pointed to the usefulness of Christianization to those in authority and to the upper groups of society, and showed at the same time the barbarization of Christianity in those centuries as the condition of the social spread of the new religion. Edward Potkowski took up research in the heritage of pagan beliefs in Germany in a later period; the subject of his monograph is the problem of the 'living ghost': the attitude of German society in the Middle Ages towards the presence of the dead in the world of the living.[63] Using narrative material from twelfth- and thirteenth-century collections of tales, legends and *exempla* (especially those of Caesarius of Heisterbach, Thomas of Cantimpré and Walter Map), the author investigated how contemporary Christian beliefs treated posthumous life and confronted contemporary eschatology with the doctrine of the Church and with theology. Finally, I should mention here Jerzy Strzelczyk's thorough monograph devoted to Gervase of Tilbury[64] and in particular to his geographical works (where he hypothetically ascribed to Gervase the famous *mappa mundi* from Ebstorf), Ignacy Zarębski's studies on early Italian humanism and its reception in Poland,[65] and the numerous detailed works relating to the problems of medieval culture and ideology.[66]

Krzysztof Pomian's work on the conception of history and the attitude towards the past in medieval thought, from Augustine to Ockham and Petrarch, belongs to the sphere of theology and philosophy.[67] Investigating interrelations between history and philosophy, the author tried to establish the peculiar features of the medieval understanding of history. Pomian argued that in the Middle Ages the past was the object of faith and not of seeking historical truth; this determined basically the historian's research procedures. In the course of the twelfth and thirteenth centuries this conception underwent important transformations which found expression in the activation of the historian's attitude: he relinquishes his former role of a mirror reflecting the account of the past and assumes a critical attitude.

The problems of medieval philosophy are widely represented in Polish research.[68] Polish medievalists, centred around Stefan Świeżawski and Jan Legowicz, conducted parallel research in the history of Polish and European medieval philosophy. I do not propose to give here an account of these studies;[69] merely to point out the diversity of directions of research: it includes works on Thomism, on the notion of beauty in the thought of the thirteenth century, on Averroism, on the philosophical school of Bologna and on the psychological doctrine of Albertism and Thomism in the fifteenth century.[70]

Questions of medieval intellectual culture have also been dealt with in many aspects, above all in relation to investigations concerning Poland's place in European culture, the reception of ideas, patterns and institutions. Thus Brygida Kürbis and Marian Plezia, in their studies on Polish historiography, treated problems of Western European patterns and investigated the mechanisms of transformation in the course of cultural reception.[71] Adam Vetulani, in connection with his research on the origins of Cracow University, outlined the foundations of universities and their policies in Central Europe in the fourteenth century in Prague, Cracow and Vienna.[72] Polish historians of art have achieved much in the field of studies of art and culture in medieval Europe. Apart from a large number of detailed studies where the analysis of an iconographic record often leads to more general problems of medieval culture,[73] I should cite here an original attempt to present a comprehensive exposition of the history of art in the Middle Ages; its first volume was Piotr Skubiszewski's work on Carolingian and pre-Romanesque painting.[74] The same historian devoted a separate study to the theme of power in Ottonian art;[75] examining the political content of figurative compositions in which effigies of emperors appear, the author reached the conclusion that the Ottonian monarchy carried on in this way an offensive propaganda of its political programme. Problems of medieval architecture have also been the subject of works of various kinds, with textbooks and encyclopedias appearing alongside original works of research. Worth citing here is the outline of medieval theory of architecture attempted by Maria Łodyńska-Kosińska. Likewise, Krystyna Secomska's book on French painting of the fifteenth and sixteenth centuries combined the qualities of reliable information with aptly selected analyses.[76] Among attempts at synthetical presentations of medieval art, Jan Białostocki's study on the late Gothic deserves to be mentioned: the author strove to define the peculiar and distinctive features of that period of European art.[77]

This review of Polish research on the general history of the Middle Ages shows its wide range in the chronological, geographical and thematic sense. Particularly noticeable has been a certain concentration of interest on crucial social and economic problems and on the broadly conceived history of culture (including the history of political culture). It is on these paths of research that Polish medieval studies have a chance of showing the originality of their historical thought.

Notes

1 A comprehensive list and review of such works does not exist. Cursory accounts have been made in papers presenting the progress of research, such as, e.g. H. Łowmiański, 'Les recherches sur l'histoire du Moyen Age jusqu'à la fin du XVᵉ siècle au cours des vingt années de la République Populaire de Pologne', in *La Pologne au XIIᵉ Congrès des Sciences Historiques à Vienne*, Warsaw 1965, pp. 195–201. A bibliography of this research – far from complete, though – is contained in *La Pologne au XIIIᵉ Congrès des Sciences Historiques à Moscou*, Warsaw, 1970, vol. II, pp. 57–66.

2 T. Manteuffel, *Średniowiecze powszechne: próba syntezy* [General medieval history: attempt at a synthesis], Warsaw, 1958; *Historia powszechna: Średniowiecze* [General history: the Middle Ages], Warsaw, 1965. Manteuffel has expounded his conception of general history in the article: 'O historii powszechnej słów parę' [A few words on general history], in *Studia Historica w 35-lecie pracy naukowej H. Łowmiańskiego*, Warsaw, 1958.

3 B. Zientara, *Historia powszechna średniowiecza* [General history of the Middle Ages], Warsaw, 1968, 2/1974.

4 The following works should be cited here, above all: K. Koranyi, *Powszechna historia państwa i prawa* [General history of state and law], vols II/I and III, Warsaw, 1963–6; M. Sczaniecki, *Powszechna historia państwa i prawa* [General history of state and law], Warsaw, 1973; W. Tatarkiewicz, *Historia filozofii* [History of philosophy], vol. I, Warsaw, 1970, and *Estetyka średniowieczna* [Medieval aesthetics], Warsaw, 1962.

5 S. Inglot, *Historia społeczna i gospodarcza średniowiecza* [Social and economic history of the Middle Ages], Wrocław 1949; B. Geremek, K. Piesowicz, *Ludzie, towary, pieniądze* [People, goods, money], Warsaw, 1968.

6 J. Baszkiewicz, *Myśl polityczna wieków średnich* [The political thought of the Middle Ages], Warsaw, 1970.

7 A. Gieysztor, *Zarys dziejów pisma łacińskiego* [Outline history of Latin paleography], Warsaw, 1973. The same author presented

separately the problems of reforms of writing in the eighth century, in 'Problem karolińskiej reformy pisma' [The problem of the Carolingian reform of the alphabet], *Archeologia*, V, 1952–3 (1955), pp. 155–77.

8 One might cite here, by way of example: K. Tymieniecki, *Dzieje Niemiec do początku ery nowożytnej* [History of Germany up to the beginning of the modern era], Poznań, 1948; K. Górski and W. Czapliński, *Historia Danii* [History of Denmark], Wrocław, 1965. A separate place, between general history and the history of Poland, is held by research in the history of the Teutonic order and its state in Prussia; in this field, the basic works by K. Górski and by M. Biskup should be noted; cf. K. Górski, *L'Ordine teutonico*, Turin, 1971.

9 G. Labuda, *Pierwsze państwo słowiańskie – państwo Samona* [The first Slav state – the state of Samo], Poznań, 1949.

10 S. Kętrzyński, 'Karol Wielki i Bolesław Chrobry' [Charlemagne and Boleslaus the Brave], *Przegląd Historyczny*, XXXVI, 1946, pp. 19–25; J. Nalepa, 'Wyprawa Franków na Wieletów w 789 r.' [The expedition of the Franks against the Velets in 789], *Slavia Antiqua*, IV, 1953, pp. 210–30; M. H. Serejski, *Karol Wielki na tle swoich czasów* [Charlemagne and his times], Warsaw, 1959, 'Karol Wielki cesarzem wbrew woli' [Charlemagne made emperor against his will?], in *Mediaevalia*, Warsaw, 1960, pp. 21–7.

11 H. Łowmiański, *Studia nad początkami społeczeństwa i państwa litewskiego* [Studies in the origins of the Lithuanian state and society], vols I–II, Vilnius 1931–2.

12 H. Łowmiański, *Podstawy gospodarcze formowania się państw słowiańskich* [Economic bases of the formation of Slav states], Warsaw, 1953; cf. by the same author, 'La genèse des états slaves et ses bases sociales et économiques', in *La Pologne au X* Congrès International des Sciences Historiques à Rome*, Warsaw, 1955, pp. 29–53. The author explicates his theories but also modifies them in his fundamental work *Początki Polski* [The origins of Poland], Warsaw, 1964; five volumes of this work have appeared so far.

13 M. Małowist, 'Z problematyki dziejów gospodarczych strefy bałtyckiej we wczesnym średniowieczu' [From the problems of the economic history of the Baltic zone in the early Middle Ages], *Roczniki Dziejów Społecznych i Gospodarczych*, X, 1948, pp. 81–120.

14 S. Piekarczyk, 'Studia nad rozwojem struktury społeczno-gospodarczej wczesnośredniowiecznej Szwecji' [Studies in the evolution of the social and economic structure of early medieval Sweden], Warsaw, 1962.

15 G. Labuda, 'Tendances d'intégration et de désintégration dans le Royaume Teutonique du X* au XIII* siècle', in *L'Europe aux IX*–XI* siècles* ... , pp. 77–91.

16 W. Hensel, *Słowiańszczyzna wczesnośredniowieczna: zarys kultury*

materialnej [The early medieval Slav world: an outline of material culture], Warsaw, 3/1965; *Archeologia o początkach miast słowiańskich* [Archeology on the origins of Slav towns], Wrocław, 1963; and *Méthodes et perspectives de recherches sur les centres ruraux et urbains chez les Slaves (VIᵉ–XIIIᵉ s.)*, Warsaw, 1962.

17 A. Gieysztor, '*Les origines de la ville slave*', in *Settimane di Studio del Centro Italiano di Studi sull'alto Medioevo*, VI, Spoleto, 1959, pp. 279–303; and 'Les structures économiques en pays slaves à l'aube du Moyen Age jusqu'au XIᵉ siècle et l'échange monétaire', in ibid., VIII, Spoleto, 1961, pp. 455–84.

18 Cf. Polish papers presented in *I Międzynarodowy Kongres Archeologii Słowiańskiej 1965* [1st International Congress of Slav Archeology 1965], vols I–VI, Warsaw, 1968; see in particular S. Tabaczyński's interesting paper 'Struktury gospodarcze środkowoeuropejskich społeczeństw barbarazyńskich' [The economic structures of Central-European barbarian societies], II, pp. 76–101.

19 *Lexicon antiquitatum Slavicarum: summarium historiae cultus humanitatis Slavorum*, Wrocław, 1961–.

20 G. Labuda, *Fragmenty dziejów Słowiańszczyzny Zachodniej* [Fragments of the history of Western Slavs], vols I–II, Poznań, 1960–4.

21 K. Modzelewski, 'Le vicende della pars dominica nei beni fondiarii del monastero di San Zaccaria di Venezia (sec. X–XIV)', *Bolletino dell' Istituto della Storia della Società e dello Stato Veneziano*, IV, 1962, and V, 1963; and 'Z dziejów wsi wczesnofeudalnej: Północnowłoski system dworski i jego upadek' [From the history of the early medieval countryside: the north Italian manorial system and its decline], *Kwartalnik Historyczny*, 70, 1963, pp. 797–822.

22 B. Zientara, *Kryzys agrarny w Marchii Wkrzańskiej w XIV w.* [The agrarian crisis in the Uckermarck in the fourteenth century], Warsaw, 1961 (Ger. trans., Weimar, 1967). For structural transformations of the countryside in the late Middle Ages, cf. also A. Mączak's short study: 'Z problematyki kryzysu wielkiej własności ziemskiej w Anglii XIV–XV w.' [Some critical problems of big landed property in England in the fourteenth to fifteenth centuries], in *Wieki średnie*, Warsaw, 1962, pp. 227–37.

23 M. Małowist, 'Zagadnienie kryzysu feudalnego w XIV i XV w. w świetle najnowszych badań' [The problem of the crisis of feudalism in the fourteenth and fifteenth centuries in the light of recent research], *Kwartalnik Historyczny*, LX, 1953, pp. 86–106; and *Studia z dziejów rzemiosła w okresie kryzysu feudalizmu w Zachodniej Europie w XIV wieku* [Studies in the history of crafts in the period of the crisis of feudalism in Western Europe in the fourteenth century], Warsaw, 1954. Cf. also B. Zientara, 'Zagadnienie depresji rolnictwa w XIV–XV wieku w świetle najnowszej literatury' [The problem of depression in agriculture in the fourteenth and fifteenth centuries in the light of recent literature], *Przegląd Historyczny*, LI, 1960, pp. 262–73.

24 B. Geremek, *Najemna siła robocza w rzemiośle Paryża XII–XV w. Studium o średniowiecznym rynku siły roboczej* [Wage-earners in Paris crafts and trades in the twelfth to fifteenth centuries: a study of the medieval labour market], Warsaw, 1962 (Fr. trans., Paris, 1968; It. trans., Florence, 1974). The author dealt with wider problems of wage-earners, in his paper 'Les salariés et le salariat dans les villes au cours du bas Moyen Age', in *Troisième conférence internationale d'histoire économique*, Munich, 1965; Paris-La Haye, 1968.

25 B. Geremek, 'Les migrations des compagnons au bas Moyen Age', *Studia Historiae Oeconomicae*, V, 1970, pp. 61–79.

26 T. Rosłanowski, 'Średniowieczne górnictwo i kuźnictwo westfalskie oraz ich wpływ na gospodarczy i osadniczy rozwój regionu w XI–XIV w.' [Medieval mining and smithcraft in Westphalia and their impact on the economic growth and settlement of the region in the eleventh to fourteenth centuries], *Studia z dziejów górnictwa i hutnictwa*, XI, 1967, pp. 113–41.

27 R. Kiersnowski, *Wielka reforma monetarna XIII–XIV w.* [The great monetary reform of the thirteenth and fourteenth centuries], Warsaw, 1969.

28 The bibliography of these works is to be found in the collective volume *Społeczeństwo – Gospodarka – Kultura* [Society – economy – culture], Warsaw, 1974; some of them are included in M. Małowist, *Croissance et régression en Europe (XIVᵉ–XVIIᵉ siècles)*, Paris, 1973.

29 H. Samsonowicz, *Późne średniowiecze miast nadbałtyckich* [Baltic cities in the late Middle Ages], Warsaw, 1968. Cf. also the reviews of Polish research in the history of the Baltic: L. Leciejewicz, 'Sea problems in research into early medieval Poland', *Acta Poloniae Historica*, XXIII, 1971, pp. 136–49, and H. Samsonowicz, 'Recherches polonaises sur l'histoire de la Baltique au déclin du Moyen Age (XIVᵉ–XVᵉ siècle)', ibid., pp. 150–61.

30 E. Cieślak, 'Z zagadnień historii prawa morskiego na Bałtyku i Morzu Północnym' [From the problems of the history of maritime law in the Baltic and the North Sea], *Przegląd Zachodni*, 1961, 1–2, pp. 89–101, 'Reglamentacja handlu rybami przez Związek Miast Hanzeatyckich w XIV i XV w.' [Regulation of the fishing tade by the league of Hanseatic towns in the fourteenth and fifteenth centuries], ibid., 1952, 5–6, pp. 432–59; S. Matysik, 'Zagadnienie zimowej przerwy w bałtyckiej żegludze Hanzy w XIV i XV w.' [The problem of the winter pause in the Baltic navigation of the Hanse in the fourteenth and fifteenth centuries], *Zapiski Towarzystwa Naukowego w Toruniu*, XVI, 'Ze studiów nad współwłasnością statków morskich w żegludze bałtyckiej w XIV–XV wieku' [Studies on the property of sea-going ships in Baltic shipping of the fourteenth to fifteenth centuries], *Czasopismo Prawno-Historyczne*, XIV, 1961, pp. 35–82, and *Prawo nadbrzeżne – Ius naufragii* [Coastal law – Ius naufragii], Toruń, 1950.

31 H. Samsonowicz, 'Uwagi nad średniowiecznym patrycjatem miejskim w Europie' [Observations on the medieval urban patriciate in Europe], *Przegląd Historyczny*, XLIX, 1958, pp. 574–84.

32 T. Rosłanowski, *Recherches sur la vie urbaine et en particulier sur le patriciat dans les villes de la moyenne Rhénanie septentrionale*, Warsaw, 1964.

33 B. Geremek, *Ludzie marginesu w średniowiecznym Paryżu* [People on the social margins in medieval Paris], Wrocław, 1971 (Fr. trans. Paris, 1975); and 'La lutte contre le vagabondage à Paris aux XIVᵉ et XVᵉ siècles', in *Ricerche storiche ed economiche in memoria di Corrado Barbagallo*, Naples, 1970, II, pp. 211–36.

34 The problems of late medieval social movements were also taken up by T. Cieślak, on the example of Hanseatic towns: *Walki ustrojowe w Gdańsku, Toruniu oraz w niektórych miastach hanzeatyckich w XV w. [Political struggles in Gdańsk, Toruń and some Hanseatic towns in the fifteenth century]*, Gdańsk, 1960.

35 H. Samsonowicz, 'Zagadnienia demografii historycznej regionu Hanzy w XIV–XV w.' [Problems of the historical demography of the Hanseatic region in the fourteenth to fifteenth centuries], *Zapiski Historyczne*, XXVIII, 1963, pp. 523–55 (cf. the summary in *Hansische Geschichtsblätter*, 1964); B. Geremek, 'Paris la plus grande ville de l'Occident médiéval?' *Acta Poloniae Historica*, XVIII, 1968, pp. 18–37.

36 A. Rutkowska-Płachcińska, *Gospodarka i zasięg oddziaływania miasta średniowiecznego: Salon-de-Provence w połowie XIV w.* [The economy and range of influence of a medieval town: Salon-de-Provence in the middle of the fourteenth century], Wrocław, 1969. This study, like the work (not yet published) by D. Poppe: *Struktura gospodarcza burgum prowansalskiego w XIV w. – Reillanne, Basses-Alpes* [The economic structure of a provençal burg in the fourteenth century – Reillanne, Basses-Alpes], originated from the research conducted by the Centre des Etudes Méditerranéennes in Aix-en-Provence.

37 H. Samsonowicz, *Życie miasta średniowiecznego* [The life of a medieval town], Warsaw, 1970.

38 M. Małowist, *Wschód i Zachód Europy w XIII–XVI wieku* [The east and west of Europe in the thirteenth to sixteenth centuries], Warsaw, 1973.

39 J. Bardach, 'Historia praw słowiańskich: przedmiot i metody badawcze' [History of Slav laws: the subject and methods of research], *Kwartalnik Historyczny*, 70, 1963, pp. 255–85.

40 J. Matuszewski, *Studia nad prawem rugijskim* [Studies in the law of Rügen], Poznań, 1947.

41 I. Malinowska, 'Ustrój komuny Bolonii w XV wieku' [The political system of the commune of Bologna in the fifteenth century], *Czasopismo Prawno-Historyczne*, XIII, 1961, pp. 47–107, and *L'ordinamento del comune de Bologna nel quattrocento*, Milan,

1966; I. Malinowska-Kwiatkowska, *Prawo prywatne w usta-
wodawstwie Królestwa Sycylii, 1140–1231* [Private law in the legislation of the kingdom of Sicily, 1140–1231], Wrocław, 1973.

42 M. Staszków, *Komuna w doktrynie prawnej XII–XIV w.* [The commune in the legal doctrine of the twelfth to fourteenth centuries],
Wrocław, 1968.

43 W. M. Bartel, *Ochrona wolności osobistej na tle rozwoju państ-
wowości anglosaskiej Brytanii – do roku 1066* [Protection of personal liberty and the evolution of statehood of Anglo-Saxon Britain
up to 1066], Cracow, 1965.

44 Cf. in particular T. Manteuffel, 'Problem feudalizmu polskiego'
[The problem of Polish feudalism], *Przegląd Historyczny*, XXXVII,
1948, pp. 62–71, and 'On Polish feudalism', *Mediaevalia et
Humanistica*, XVI, 1964, p. 94ff.

45 M. Sczaniecki, *Essai sur les fiefs-rentes*, Paris, 1946.

46 K. Baran, 'Stosunek wasalny w świetle praw i literatury anglo-sas-
kiej Brytanii' [Vassal relationship in the light of the laws and literature of Anglo-Saxon Britain], *Czasopismo Prawno-Historyczne*,
XXII, 2, 1970, pp. 1–29; S. Russocki, 'Le rôle de la "fidelitas" et du
"beneficium" dans la formation des états slaves', *Acta Poloniae
Historica*, XXVI, 1971, pp. 171–88.

47 A. Vetulani, 'Le Décret de Gratien et les premiers décrétalistes à la
lumière d'une source nouvelle', *Studia Gratiana*, VII, 1959,
pp. 209–313.

48 K. Górski, 'Die Anfänge des Ständewesens im Nord- und Ostmittel
Europa im Mittelalter', *Anciens pays et assemblées d'états*, XL
1966, p. 45ff, and 'Les débuts de la représentation de la "communi-
tas nobilium" dans les assemblées d'états de l'Est européen', ibid.,
XLVIII, 1968, pp. 39–55.

49 S. Russocki, 'Narodziny zgromadzeń stanowych' [The birth of state
assemblies], *Przegląd Historyczny*, LIX, 1968, p. 214ff;
Protoparlamentaryzm Czech do początku XV wieku [Proto-parlia-
mentarism in Bohemia up to the beginning of the fifteenth century],
Warsaw, 1973; and 'Les assemblées pré-parlementaires en Europe
centrale', *Acta Poloniae Historica*, XXX, 1974.

50 S. Russocki, 'Opór władcom i prawo oporu u Słowian w wiekach
średnich' [Resistance to rulers and the right of resistance among
Slavs in the Middle Ages], *Czasopismo Prawno-Historyczne*, XX,
1968, pp. 117–52, and 'Średniowieczne synody prowincjonalne a
zgromadzenia przedstanowe' [Medieval provincial synods and pre-
state assemblies], ibid., XVII, 1, 1965, pp. 39–71.

51 J. Baszkiewicz, *Państwo suwerenne w feudalnej doktrynie politycznej do początków XIV w.* [*Sovereignty of state in feudal political
doctrine up to the beginning of the fourteenth century*], Warsaw,
1964.

52 A. Gieysztor, *Ze studiów nad genezą wypraw krzyżowych: encyk-
lika Sergiusza IV* [From studies on the origins of the crusades: the

encyclical of Sergius IV], Warsaw, 1948 (Eng. trans. *Mediaevalia et Humanistica*, V, 1948, pp. 3–23, and V, 1950, pp. 3–34).

53 T. Manteuffel, 'Zakony kościoła katolickiego do połowy XIV wieku' [Orders of the Catholic Church up to the middle of the fourteenth century], in *Szkice z dziejów papiestwa* [Essays on the history of the papacy], Warsaw, 1958, pp. 1–43.

54 T. Manteuffel, *Papiestwo i cystersi ze szczególnym uwzględnieniem ich roli w Polsce na przełomie XII i XIII w.* [The papacy and the Cistercians, with special regard to their role in Poland at the turn of the twelfth to thirteenth century], Warsaw, 1955; cf. by the same author, 'La mission balte de l'ordre de Citeaux', in *La Pologne au Xe Congrès . . .* , pp. 107–23.

55 T. Manteuffel, *Narodziny herezji: wyznawcy dobrowolnego ubóstwa w średniowieczu* [The birth of heresy: adherents of voluntary poverty in the Middle Ages], Warsaw, 1963 (Ger. trans., Graz, 1968; Fr. trans., Paris, 1970; It. trans., Florence, 1975).

56 T. Manteuffel, 'Piotr syn Jana Olivi: święty czy herezjarcha?' [Pierre, son of Jean Olivi: a saint or a Heresiarch?], *Przegląd Historyczny*, LV, 1964, pp. 392–404, and 'W oczekiwaniu ery wolności i pokoju: historiozofia Joachima z Fiore' [In expectation of an era of freedom and peace: the philosophy of history of Joachim of Fiore], ibid., LX, 1969, pp. 233–56.

57 S. Trawkowski, *Między herezją a ortodoksją: rola społeczna premonstratensów w XII w.* [Between heresy and orthodoxy: the social role of the Premonstratensians in the twelfth century], Warsaw, 1964.

58 S. Bylina, *Wizje społeczne w herezjach średniowiecznych: humiliaci, begini, begardzi* [Social visions in medieval heresies: the humiliates, the béguines, the beghards], Wrocław, 1973.

59 R. Heck and E. Maleczyńska, *Ruch husycki w Czechach i w Polsce* [The Hussite movement in Bohemia and Poland], Wrocław, 1953; E. Maleczyńska, *Ruch husycki w Czechach i w Polsce* [The Hussite movement in Bohemia and Poland], Warsaw, 1959, and 'Ze studiów nad hasłami narodowościowymi w źródłach doby husyckiej' [From studies on nationality ideas in the sources of the Hussite era], *Przegląd Historyczny*, XLIII, 1952, pp. 60–82; S. Bylina, *Wpływy Konrada Waldhausena na ziemiach polskich w drugiej połowie XIV i w pierwszej połowie XV wieku* [The influence of Konrad Waldhausen in Polish territories in the second half of the fourteenth and the first half of the fifteenth century], Wrocław, 1966, 'Elementy chiliastyczne w poglądach Jana Żeliwskiego' [Chiliastic elements in the views of Jan Żeliwski], *Przegląd Historyczny*, LXIII, 1972, pp. 241–52; R. Heck, 'Świadomość narodowa i państwowa w Czechach i w Polsce w XV wieku' [National and state consciousness in Bohemia and Poland in the fifteenth century], in *Pamiętnik X Powszechnego Zjazdu Historyków Polskich w Lublinie*, Warsaw, 1968, pp. 126–51, and *Tabor a kandydatura*

jagiellońska w Czechach, 1438–1444 [Tabor and the Jagiellonian candidature in Bohemia, 1438–1444], Wrocław, 1964.
60 J. Kłoczowski, *Wspólnoty chrześcijańskie* [Christian communities], Cracow, 1964.
61 S. Piekarczyk, *O społeczeństwie i religii w Skandynawii VIII–XI w.* [On society and religion in Scandinavia in the eighth to the eleventh centuries], Warsaw, 1963.
62 S. Piekarczyk, *Chrześcijaństwo i barbarzyńcy* [Christianity and the barbarians], Warsaw, 1968.
63 E. Potkowski, *Dziedzictwo wierzeń pogańskich w średniowiecznych Niemczech: defuncti vivi* [The heritage of pagan beliefs in medieval Germany, defuncti vivi], Warsaw, 1973.
64 J. Strzelczyk, *Gerwazy z Tilbury: studium z dziejów uczoności geograficznej w średniowieczu* [Gervase of Tilbury: a study from the history of geographical erudition in the Middle Ages], Wrocław, 1970.
65 I. Zarębski, 'Il Boccaccio nel primo umanesimo polacco', in *Studi sul Boccaccio*, ed. V. Branca, III, Florence, 1965, pp. 247–94.
66 Cf. A. Gieysztor, 'La légende de Saint Alexis en Occident: un idéal de la pauvreté', in *Études sur l'histoire de la pauvreté*, Paris, 1974, pp. 125–39; B. Geremek, 'Św. Antonin z Florencji o żebrakach i jałmużnie' [St Antonio of Florence on beggars and alms], in *Wieki średnie*, Warsaw, 1962, pp. 239–47; B. Lapis, 'Jana z Salisbury rozumienie zadań historiografii' [John of Salisbury's interpretation of the tasks of historiography], *Commentationes*, XV, 1971; K. Górski, 'Le roi-saint: un problème d'idéologie féodale', *Annales ESC*, 24ᵉ année, 1969, pp. 370–6.
67 K. Pomian, *Przeszłość jako przedmiot wiary: historia i filozofia w myśli średniowiecza* [The past as the object of faith: history and philosophy in the thought of the Middle Ages], Warsaw, 1968.
68 The results of this research are presented in three periodicals: *Mediaevalia Philosophica Polonorum* (in foreign languages), *Studia Mediewistyczne* and *Materiały i Studia Zakładu Historii Filozofii Starożytnej i Średniowiecznej*.
69 Cf. reviews of research: W. Seńko, 'Aperçu sur les recherches concernant la philosophie médiévale en Pologne', *Mediaevalia Philosophica Polonorum*, I, 1958; S. Świeżawski, 'Aperçu sur les recherches des médiévistes polonais dans le domaine de l'histoire de la philosophie', in *Die Metaphysik im Mittelalter*, Cologne, 1961.
70 W. Stróżewski, 'Próba systematyzacji określeń piękna występujących w tekstach św. Tomasza' [An attempt to systematize the definitions of beauty appearing in St Thomas's texts], *Roczniki Filozoficzne*, VI, 1958, pp. 19–51, and 'O kształtowaniu się doktryn estetycznych w XIII wieku' [On the formation of aesthetical doctrines in the thirteenth century], in *Średniowiecze: studia o kulturze*, Warsaw, 1961, pp. 9–49; Z. Kuksewicz, *Averroïsme polonais au XIXᵉ siècle*, Wrocław, 1965, *De Siger de Brabant à Jacques de Plaisance: la*

théorie de l'intellect chez les averroïstes latins des XIIIe et XIVe siè-cles, Wrocław, 1968, *Awerroizm łaciński XIII wieku* [Latin Averroism of the thirteenth century], Warsaw, 1971, and *Albertyzm i Tomizm w XV wieku w Krakowie i Kolonii* [Albertism and Thomism in the fifteenth century in Cracow and Cologne], Wrocław, 1973. An interesting work on medieval philosophy is J. B. Korolec, *Filozofia moralna Jana Burydana* [The moral philosophy of John Buridan], Wrocław, 1973.

71 B. Kürbisówna, 'Motywy makrobiańskie w Kronice mistrza Wincentego a szkoła Chartres' [Macrobian motifs in Master Vincent's chronicle and the school of Chartres], *Commentationes*, XVII, 1972, pp. 67–80; M. Plezia, *Kronika Galla na tle historiografii XII w.* [The chronicle of Gallus against the background of twelfth-century historiography], Cracow, 1947, and *Od Arystotelesa do 'Złotej legendy'* [From Aristotle to the 'Legenda Aurea'], Warsaw, 1962.

72 A. Vetulani, 'Urban V wobec nowo zakładanych uniwersytetów środkowoeuropejskich' [The attitude of Urban V towards the newly established Central-European universities], in *Pastori et magistro*, Lublin, 1966, pp. 203–28; 'Cracovie, Vienne et Pecs: trois fondations universitaires', in *Les universités européennes du XIVe au XVIIIe siècle*, Geneva, 1967, pp. 56–9; *Początki najstarszych wszechnic środkowoeuropejskich* [The origins of the oldest Central-European universities], Wrocław, 1970.

73 Cf. e.g. L. Kalinowski, *Geneza Piety średniowiecznej* [The origin of the medieval pietà], *Prace Komisji Historii Sztuki*, X, 1952; T. Dobrzeniecki, 'Legenda średniowieczna w piśmiennictwie i sztuce: chrystofania Marii' [The medieval legend in literature and art: the christophany of Mary], in *Średniowiecze: studia o kulturze*, II, Wrocław, 1965, pp. 7–131; P. Skubiszewski, 'Problemy alegorii średniowiecznej: o myśleniu alegorycznym w średniowieczu' [Problems of medieval allegory: on allegorical thinking in the Middle Ages], in *Granice sztuki*, Warsaw, 1972, pp. 49–57; Z. Waźbiński, 'Akt klasyczny w sztuce średniowiecznej' [The classical nude in medieval art], *Biuletyn Historii Sztuki*, 1966, p. 67.

74 P. Skubiszewski, *Malarstwo karolińskie i przedromańskie* [Carolingian and pre-Romanesque painting], Warsaw, 1973.

75 P. Skubiszewski, 'W służbie cesarza, w służbie króla: temat władzy w sztuce ottońskiej' [In the emperor's service, in the king's service: the problem of power in Ottonian art], in *Funkcja dzieła sztuki*, Warsaw, 1972, pp. 17–72.

76 M. Łodyńska-Kosińska, *Architektoniczna 'scientia' gotyku: szkice z zakresu teorii architektury w średniowieczu* [The architectural 'Scientia' of the Gothic: essays from the theory of architecture in the Middle Ages], Warsaw, 1964; K. Secomska, *Mistrzowie i książęta* [Masters and princes], Warsaw, 1972.

77 J. Białostocki, *Późny gotyk* [Late Gothic], Warsaw, 1965, pp. 17–82.

2

The Exemplum and the Spread of Culture in the Middle Ages

Contemporary studies in the history of culture reveal a renewed interest on the part of historians in the value of literature as a source of historical testimony. This is connected with the directions which such studies have recently tended to follow, and with two such directions in particular. The first, influenced by the achievements of social and economic history, is the historian's reawakened interest in mass phenomena: recent studies in the history of culture have encompassed the problem of how culture functions, how it is created and received, and how to measure its social spread and significance. The second, influenced by the development of psychology, both social psychology and psychoanalysis, as well as by the epistemological transformations which have affected ethnology, is the increasing attention devoted by the cultural historian to processes and phenomena beyond the scope of classical 'conscious' history: to subconscious phenomena as they are revealed in stereotypes of social behaviour, social attitudes and sensibilities. For both these trends, and especially for the latter, literature is a vast and essential source. Literature, especially of the kind which lacks lofty artistic pretensions and, aiming lower, reaches a wide and socially diverse audience, allows us to follow the evolution of culture and cultural models on a mass scale, to observe behavioural models and social attitudes, and to gain an insight into emotional reactions and value judgements.

The renewed interest among medieval historians in preachers and the *exempla*, or anecdotes, which they used to illustrate their preaching is connected to a more general shift in methodology. The first critical studies and collections of medieval *exempla* began to appear at the beginning of the nineteenth century, when romantic interest in the Middle Ages was at its height.

Monographs, collections and catalogues of sources[1] and comparative essays on the subject continued to appear at an increasing rate in the decades which followed. This period also saw the first attempts to consider the problem of the medieval *exemplum* as a whole; notable among these was a study by the Dutch scholar C. G. de Vooys of the role of legend and the *exemplum* in medieval Dutch literature,[2] the work of J. A. Mosher on the *exemplum* in English literature,[3] and, most exhaustive and best documented of all, a study by J. T. Welter,[4] who also began the monumental task of editing a *Thesaurus Exemplorum*.[5] Unfortunately, despite the interest in the subject, neither the editions of basic sources of *exempla* nor the studies of their function and content were of a standard to satisfy the demands of modern scholarship, or to serve as the basis for a broader study of medieval culture.[6] Collections of *exempla* of crucial significance are still awaiting their scholarly edition; even in Lecoy de la Marche's partial edition of the *exempla* collected by Etienne de Bourbon,[7] essential works, rejected by the editor as marginal, are omitted. The two anthologies of *exempla* edited by the German historian of folklore Joseph Klapper[8] and based on Silesian manuscript sources are of minimal value for historical research, for they treat the *exempla* in isolation from one another, without considering their functioning and their transformations as a whole, and disrupt their structural unity.

More recently, the American historian Frederic C. Tubach published a compendium of medieval *exempla*[9] which, despite the justified criticism it evoked, constitutes a basis for systematic research. More recently still, Jacques Le Goff and Jean-Claude Schmitt have been engaged in an eagerly awaited study of thirteenth-century *exempla* and their connection with traditional medieval culture, and have also promised a scholarly edition of the collection of Etienne de Bourbon.

The very definition of the *exemplum* as a distinct genre is problematic: every historian proposes a different one of his own.

The conceptual range of the term has been most broadly defined by Welter, who sees the *exemplum* as a story or an anecdote, a fable, a moral tale or a description which can be used to make a doctrinal, moral or religious point.[10] On such a definition, the *exemplum* would include all past and present narrative and description. Such broadness of definition, however, testifies only to a certain inability to master the diversity of the seemingly elementary form of narration which the *exemplum* represents. The German historian of folklore Rudolf Schenda is inclined to define the *exemplum* as 'eine didaktische Proposition mit moralisierender Tendenz', or as 'ein unterhaltsam vorgetragenes Lehrstück, das die Sittlichkeit fördern will',[11] but this definition is too restrictive in attributing the *exemplum* to medieval paraenesis. Perhaps Crane's old definition is still the most useful. Crane pointed out that ecclesiastical writers used the term *exemplum* in two senses: in the general sense of an example, and in the more restrictive sense of an 'illustrative story'. He attributed this second sense to the anecdotes contained in the sermons of Jacques de Vitry and to all short anecdotes in general.

Any definition of the *exemplum* as a genre, however, contains two aspects which should be noted. The first, and most important, of these is its strong link to oral discourse, and particularly to the sermon. This can be seen in the structure of the written narrative, which appears to reproduce the texture of a speech in the course of which elements of moral instruction are emphasized at strategic points.[12] The second is the fact that the narrative deals with human behaviour and its motivation, but does so within the context of the relationship between God and man, encompassing sin and salvation, miracles and punishment, and the philosophy of divine grace.[13]

The difficulties encountered in any attempt to arrive at a definition of the *exemplum* as a genre are also connected to considerable divergence of opinion concerning its evolution and its social and literary role. During the first centuries of its expansion the Church, in its efforts to propagate the true faith, sought to stir the spirit and touch the imagination of the faithful – the secular and regular clergy as well as the masses – with something more than the rather too hermetic writings of the Church Fathers; legend and the *exemplum* were well suited to the role. The Bible, the Lives of the Saints and the Church Fathers, and, later, the first homilies (chief among them being the writings of Gregory the Great), constituted the basics for this. From the *Vitae Patrum* of the fourth and fifth centuries to Honorius Augustodunensis in the twelfth, the *exemplum* evolved as a way of expounding the principles of Christian ethics.[14] Frederic Tubach,[15] who uses the term *protoexemplum* when referring to this period, points out the uniformity of the moral model contained in the 'illustrative stories' of that time. This uniformity resulted from the way in which the action of the narrative was structured around references to the struggle between good and evil, and from the eschatological nature of the stories, in which social realities and the organization of life on earth seemed to play no role. The anecdote which Jacques de Vitry quotes from the *Vitae Patrum* is a good example of this type of fable: a woman tries to incite a hermit to sin with her; the hermit leads her into the marketplace, but she is ashamed to sin in full view of the crowd; whereupon the hermit says to her that he is less ashamed to sin in the sight of men than in the desert in the sight of God and the angels.[16]

The thirteenth century saw a fundamental development in the structure and content of the *exemplum*. The constant appeal to a metaphysical absolute as an essential point of reference in any discussion of ethical perfection was abandoned, and the rigorous opposition between the temporal world and the divine order gave way to a complex narrative about human destiny, a narrative in which individual psychology and the social context were taken into account. The figures who peopled this narrative were no longer mere personifications of good and evil; good and bad human behaviour, human wisdom and folly, knowledge and skill now constituted the material from which moral lessons were drawn. Another anecdote collected by Jacques de Vitry is of just this type. A woman accuses a young man of rape; he denies the charge. The judge sentences him to a fine of ten marks in silver, and when the woman, delighted, departs with the money, the judge orders the young man to follow her and take the money back. But she screams so loudly and defends herself so fiercely that the young man is unable to wrest the money from her. The judge then recalls the woman and orders her to restore the man's money to him because, he says, if she had defended her purity with as much determination as she displayed in defending her money, it would not have been possible to rape her in the first place.[17] Here, the moral lesson, or the moralizing aspect of the story, is no longer an inherent part of the narrative, but must be added on; one of the functions of such a story was also to amuse and to entertain, and it was up to the preacher to provide the allegorical interpretation which would allow him to use it as a vehicle for his moral teachings.

Welter saw symptoms of the *exemplum*'s decline in the diminishing output of original *exempla*, in an increasing reliance on old material, much of it profane, which was modified and reworked, and in the expansion of the narrative element at the expense of doctrinal teachings. Both religious education and preaching were affected by this decline.[18] In his view, the symptoms of this 'decadence' did not become striking until the fifteenth century, the close of the Middle Ages. According to Tubach, whose theory is much more radical, the decline of the *exemplum* had already begun in the thirteenth century, when the *protoexempla*, which expressed the sum of religious norms, gave way to a heterogeneous mass of narratives which together made up a *speculum mundi*: 'The exemplum became a mirror of life, an organic part of a social context and a vessel for literary and folkloristic imagination.'[19]

There are two respects in which one might be wary of such a view of the evolution of the *exemplum*. First of all, there seems to be no immediately obvious justification for distinguishing between the two phases of the *exemplum*'s development; the product of literary and folkloristic imagination, as well as the reflection of social realities, can equally be found in the minor literary genres of the early Middle Ages (although of course the social realities and folkloric tradition were different from those of the late Middle Ages). Conversely, those severe constructions which so starkly laid down the basics of Christian ethics and which Tubach attributes to the *protoexemplum* can also be found in the literature of the late Middle Ages. Furthermore, the moralizing function of simple tales did not disappear with the coming of the late Middle Ages. What did change was their literary significance and their place in literature. But a close study of the circulation, publication and readership of *exempla* in the post-medieval period and in the centuries that followed, up to the baroque era, will reveal their persistence not only as a distinct literary form but also as a certain set of scenes and ideas.[20] What changed was their function and the way in which they circulated. At first their spread was largely oral, and if they were transcribed it was chiefly in order that they might be put to oral use, in the telling of stories, or preaching, or reading aloud.[21] With the growing role of the book in the spread of culture they increasingly came to be read rather than listened to. For this Gutenberg's revolution was to a large extent responsible, but fourteenth- and fifteenth-century collections of manuscript *exempla* were also destined to be read, and even after the seventeenth century the *Magnum Speculum Exemplorum* was circulated in manuscript form in its Russian translation. This change can also be seen as a passage from a collective audience (at a sermon or, in monasteries, a reading aloud of *hodie legenda est vita*,[22] for example) to an individual readership.

The crucial change took place in the course of the twelfth and thirteenth centuries. It should be considered separately rather than as part of the formal development of the literary genre. The flowering of Cistercian literature and, later, that of the mendicant orders owed much to Eastern traditions of narrative which were gradually seeping into the West. But the key event was the transformation, at the turn of the twelfth and thirteenth centuries, of the main structures of Western Christianity,[23] formulated at the Fourth Lateran Council.

Preaching to the masses was supposed to be the basic tool of religious education. Expounding the truths of the faith was supposed to encourage people to put into practice the moral imperatives and ethical models presented to them by the preacher. Thus the parables used had to deal with a number of different situations and attitudes; they were intended to act as an instrument of teaching by praising certain human attitudes while condemning others, or by dramatizing more abstract considerations with the aid of allegory. Sometimes the moral lesson was just attached at the end of a simple story. In collections of sermons, *exempla* were included as arguments in the presentation of the subject; sometimes several *exempla*, occasionally even ten or more, could be found in a single sermon. At the same time, in the thirteenth century, collections of *exempla* for the use of preachers began to appear, obviously geared to a specific type of narrative. The two great mendicant orders vied with each other in the production of such collections: the Dominicans had Étienne de Bourbon's

Tractatus de diversis materiis praedicabilibus, which contained
nearly three thousand *exempla*; Humbert de Romans' *De abun-
dantia exemplorum*, also known as *De dono timoris*; and an
alphabetically arranged compilation by Martin of Opawa. The
Franciscans had Jean de Galles and his *Breviloquium de vir-
tutibus* and the *Liber exemplorum* by an anonymous English
author. In the collection of Jean de Galles, the arrangement of
exempla is subordinated to the duties of the faithful, defined
'according to the variety of their status' (*secundum varietatem
statuum eorum*); this type of compilation, adapted to the
demands of preaching *ad varios status*, was a common product
of medieval scribes.[24] Many collections of *exempla* were arranged
alphabetically, or by subject-matter, or by the sources from
which they were drawn (biblical *exempla*, for instance, and the
exempla found in the works of St Augustine, are arranged in this
way); some collections of *exempla* contained explanations of the
allegory or the moral of the parables (the famous treatise on
chess by the Italian Dominican Jacobus de Cessolis contained
such additions).[25] An alphabetical arrangement of the material,
adopted by the Venetian Franciscan Paulinus Minorita (circa
1344) for his *Satyrica Historia*, shows how the systematic and
progressive creation of an instrument of teaching can come to
encompass an increasingly broad range of narrative material.[26]

The role of *exempla* in the spread of culture in the Slavic countries has never been the object of any systematic study, although
historians, and literary historians in particular, have often
approached the topic in their research.[27] What interested them
particularly was the extent to which medieval *exempla* served as
a source of narrative material in the first stages of the development of literature in national tongues; for it was indeed a vast
and rich source, and drawn on abundantly. This is borne out not
only by the translations, some of them better than others, which
were published in the sixteenth century but also, indirectly,
by the influence which these medieval stories had on sixteenth-
century writers.

It was not only through the written word that medieval *exempla* were spread; the pulpit, too, played an important role in their
transmission. The widespread knowledge that existed of medieval
themes and stories was owing to the sermons of parish preachers,

as the work of Mikołaj Rey can testify. Hence the importance of medieval *exempla* for an understanding of Polish culture, which has a long tradition. Research into mass culture in the Middle Ages is greatly impoverished by the absence of any registers or lists of sermons, and by the lack of studies, critical editions or research on the role of the collections of sermons and *exempla* in medieval Polish libraries.

Research on the role of *exempla* in the spread of culture should involve three stages: firstly, the original work; secondly, the narrative material in collections of *exempla* dealing with Polish territory; and thirdly, the use to which *exempla* were put in different genres of medieval literature. The problem is too vast to be dealt with here, but a brief outline of what is involved is appropriate.

The *Promptuarium exemplorum* of Martin of Opawa[28] is the only one of the whole generation of thirteenth-century collections of *exempla* which has its origins in the ecclesiastical circles of the Slavic countries. Martin, known as 'the Pole', was so famous in Europe through his chronicles of popes and emperors that his name became a sort of technical term, synonymous with 'historian'; and yet no study of his work has so far been attempted.[29]

Among the various works attributed to Martin, the collection of sermons entitled *De tempore et de sanctis* is one, at least, about the authorship of which there can be no doubt. Martin, who was known as a eminent preacher,[30] collected 321 sermons, to which he added, as a sort of appendix or a separate compilation, a collection of over two hundred *exempla*, to be used by preachers as a source for their own compilations. Martin's collection of sermons was reprinted several times after the first edition of 1484, printed in Strasbourg,[31] and enjoyed a solid popularity. The collection of *exempla* known as the *Promptuarium exemplorum* was profoundly influenced by the collections of Étienne de Bourbon and Humbert de Romans, both in the arrangement of the material and in its selection. In its arrangement it diverges hardly at all from Étienne de Bourbon's collection (there are separate chapters on the conception and birth of the Virgin Mary), and only a very few of the *exempla* have been drawn from other sources. Because of this lack of original material in Martin's collection,[32] there would be little point in examining the arguments contained in it for signs of a connection with the problems of the author's home region. Martin was a theologian with close ties to the Curia, of which he may even have been the preacher; he seems very prudent in his choice of *exempla*, rejecting those whose origin he considered doubtful as well as those where the narrative assumed a central role at the expense of the religious content. For this reason, Martin's collection should be considered in conjunction with the other collections of *exempla* from the second half of the thirteenth century: it is in the Roman Curia's clear preference for the devotional *exemplum* that one can discern a favourable attitude, on the part of some of its influential elements, towards the initiatives taken in that regard by the two mendicant orders.

Martin's is the only extant collection of *exempla* which can be said to have links, albeit indirect ones, with the Slavic regions. In the fourteenth century, however, manuscripts containing copies of *exempla* of diverse provenance and forms circulated widely. The *Gesta Romanorum* collection, whose popularity in Poland and Bohemia in the late Middle Ages was only a prelude to the successful career it was to enjoy in the sixteenth century, played a particular role here. In this collection, the narrative is already beginning to attain a certain literary autonomy; it has ceased to be merely a tool to be used by the preacher as a basis for his sermons. But, like the narrative arguments of sermons and in conjunction with them, it also served to organize the imagination in certain ways, and to provide stereotyped points of reference with the aid of which value judgements could be made and morals tested. A similar but smaller collection of 35 *exempla* is contained in a manuscript in the library of Olomouc known as 'Stories from Olomouc'.[33] Here, the *exempla* are mixed up together with the literary prose of the late Middle Ages, and alongside historical and geographical works.

Nevertheless, the emergence of the *exemplum* as an autonomous form of literature does not seem to offer sufficient grounds for speaking of the complete secularization of the genre.[34] Ecclesiastical, and particularly monastic, circles still seem to be involved in the composition, collection and copying of these works, for which they themselves still made up the principal audience. The introduction of arguments that were more intimately linked to people's daily lives was perfectly in line with the programme of Christian teaching of the time.

Existing alongside these collections was a large number of other literary works in which *exempla* appeared in profusion. Recently a catalogue was drawn up of *exempla* in Czech literature of the period before Jan Hus; they played an important role as explanatory and illustrative arguments in educational literature, philosophical treatises and satirical works. Satires on artisans, for example, made use of some very imaginative examples with specific social references.[35] Nevertheless, the literature of the pulpit clearly remained the most fertile ground for collections of *exempla*. This has not yet been well demonstrated in the case of Bohemia, where Waldhausen cites few *exempla*, and where Hussite preaching was opposed to their use. The *Linea salutis* and the *Exemplar salutis*, two collections of sermons by John Sylvanus, otherwise known as Jerome of Prague, confessor to the Polish king Jagiełło, contain no narrative material; *exempla* were only put in by Polish copyists.[36] The Polish literature of the pulpit is exceedingly rich in them.

At the beginning of the fourteenth century, Peregrinus of Opole,[37] an extremely interesting writer who made use of anecdotal material in the composition of his sermons, was using anecdotes taken from daily life and even from natural history (for example, his sermon on St Bartholomew included stories about the habits of serpents) alongside examples drawn from the Holy Scriptures. From the end of the fourteenth century onwards, the literature of the pulpit was produced in Poland at an increasing rate;[38] some of it was original, but mostly it drew on the better-known collections of European sermons.[39] Brückner's studies have demonstrated the richness of these compilations – for that is what most of them were, whether the material was original or not – in their anecdotes and their descriptions of events and local customs. The most varied and diverse of these works were collections known as codices; some of these were composed entirely of sermons,[40] while others contained different types of religious literature brought together in one collection. It is these codices which must be analysed for an understanding of the content of religious teaching at the time. The *Penitentiary of the Holy Cross*, a collection dating from the middle of the fifteenth century,[41] contains, alongside various treatises on confession, penitence, sin and the commandments, titles such as *Miracula bona et utilia* (fo. 153–74), *De quaedam regine* (fo. 157, v.), and *De tentacione dyaboli.* The *exempla* which appear in these collections of sermons should also be detailed and listed. In the codices, as in the *Penitentiary of the Holy Cross,* they occupy an independent place of their own; both in general and in thematically arranged collections, they appear as instruments of preaching.[42]

The abundant manuscript sources to be found in ecclesiastical libraries in Silesia have already been the object of studies by specialists in medieval *exempla*; it was on these sources that J. Klapper's anthologies of *exempla* were based. One of the codices in the Dominican monastery in Wrocław, probably recopied in the mid-fourteenth century, contains, alongside a number of theological treatises, short sermons and religious texts, an ample collection of *exempla*, and it was this collection that constituted the principal source for Klapper's work.[43] In addition to this collection, a relatively old one on Polish territory, the Silesian sources contain several others. The characteristic feature of collections of *exempla* compiled by copyists from Silesia and Poland's eastern regions is that they contain no anecdotal material of a local nature. In sermons, elements of local folklore appeared in descriptions of witchcraft and superstitions which the preacher condemned, or in the course of enumerating the circumstances in which communion could not be received. Some very interesting material concerning the struggle that was waged against folklore and superstition is contained in a collection of sermons copied (not, as Brückner claims, compiled) by Piotr de Miłosław;[44] this collection has yet to be studied. Themes of a local nature were also provided by hagiographies of local saints. *Exempla*, on the other hand, seem to have constituted a distinct corpus, distinguished by the fact that they were based on written works, and therefore not subject to any form of oral transmission.

Why this was so is a question which cannot be answered without a more detailed analysis than is possible here.[45] It would seem, however, to be associated with the more general problem of the attitude of the Church towards popular culture. There is a fairly free flow of popular stories and arguments in European collections of *exempla*, and this expressed the Church's tendency to use them as instruments to internalize Christian values. In order to do this, however, the Church needed great ideological and organizational powers at its disposal; and in Polish territory, where evangelization was more recent and the apparatus of religious education weaker, this was not yet the case. Folklore was treated as a residue of paganism, and as such it was completely alien and hostile territory. This hostility to folklore, so visible in Polish preaching, did not prevent the Church from adopting the syncretism of its missionary period (apparent in such gestures as its incorporation of traditional festivals into the church calendar, the Christianization of magical practices and so forth); but it did preclude a fuller incorporation of the oral cultural tradition.

It should be stressed that, in addition to elites, whose role in the oral transmission of culture is attested to in literary sources, the Church, and in particular the monastic orders, also played an important role in this regard. The content of this transmission was obviously religious, but it consisted of simple stories about miracles, unusual events, ghosts and other wonders. One might consider these oral traditions as the folklore of a specific community or social environment – in this case the community of the Church, which could diffuse such folklore on a mass scale.

In the 1920s Kazimierz Dobrowolski had already seen the importance for the history of Polish medieval culture of the stories in the collection of Caesar of Heisterbach.[46] Four of these stories (I. 36; III. 3; III. 6; and III. 13) are situated *in Polonia*; their subjects are, respectively, the cruel prince, the simple lay brother who knew only the Ave Maria, the leprous princess, and the miracle of the Jewish boy of Wrocław. An analysis of the possible origins of these stories shows that other, older versions of them had existed, and from this one might surmise that setting them explicitly in Poland was a literary technique intended to make them more credible and realistic by providing a specific place and date for the narrative. However, the collection does mention, as sources for these stories, some Polish Cistercian monks on their way to the Rhineland and to the German Cistercian Gottfried of Altenberg, who is said to have visited Polish Cistercian monasteries. We may suppose, then, with Dobrowolski, that the stories did originate on Polish territory, mainly in Silesia, and that they were told in Cistercian monasteries in Silesia or Greater Poland.

These sorts of 'legends', whether written or oral,[47] made up from scratch or borrowed and transformed, were a constant part of monastic life. They made the rounds of different monasteries, circulating by mouth, before being copied into the pages of manuscripts. They also constituted the basic material of hagiographical literature.[48] Tales of miracles often contain stories from sermons and collections of *exempla*, transformed and adapted according to the circumstances.[49] Thus one can see how the scribes, in copying collections of sermons and *exempla*, were creating tools both for the use of church communities and for the purpose of religious education and propaganda, for which they were responsible; the demands of the Church, as well as the needs of preachers, had to be satisfied, and the elaboration of *exempla* with more complex narrative structures also provided for the needs of the monastic community. This can be seen in the collection of stories compiled by a Polish Franciscan, brother Seweryn, in the early part of the sixteenth century.[50] He drew numerous *exempla* from the Little Flowers of St Francis, and adapted them according to the amount of paper available to him. What is significant is that he drew these stories not from his reading but from the oral tradition, basing them on what he had heard during his travels in Italy. Thus printing had not yet supplanted the intimate link between the telling of stories and their transcription by the pen of a scribe.

Research into the folklore and ethnography of *exempla* has led to their classification by themes and types, but the results, at least up to now, have been less than fruitful; they compare badly with similar attempts at classifying the fable, for example. One might say that, if *exempla* have found their Aarne and Thompson in Tubach's *Index exemplorum*, they are still awaiting their Propp: someone who would establish the relationship between the characters and the forces at work in the *exemplum*, draw up a schema of the narrative argument and study the rules and directions of the *exemplum*'s transformations. The variations in the results obtained so far are owing not only to insufficient analysis and a diversity of criteria, but also to the diversity of genres represented by all the *exempla*.[51]

The more recent the compilation of *exempla*, the more easily it lends itself to literary historical analysis; the arguments of the narrative reappear throughout various collections, and the stories are copied with a certain amount of original literary imagination.

Let us take, as an example, the stories contained in the *Speculum exemplorum*, a fairly late collection dating from the fifteenth century.[52] Table 2.1 lists their origins.

Table 2.1   The origins of the stories in the *Speculum exemplorum*

Distinctio	*Source*	*Number*	*%*
I	Gregory the Great and Petrus Damianus	112	9
II	Church Fathers	250	20
III	Bede and the history of the Cistercians	66	5
IV	Vincent de Beauvais	82	6
V	Thomas de Cantimpré	136	11
VI	Caesar of Heisterbach	103	8
VII	Lives of the Saints	106 }	21
VIII	Lives of the Saints	163 }	
IX	*Ex diversis*	218	17
X	*Noviter conscripta*	30	2

The collection of stories contained in *Distinctio X* is of particular interest,[53] for it represents the personal contribution of the compiler, and incorporates his own testimony on the events of his time.[54] He was almost certainly a Dutchman,[55] with connections both to the Augustinian monastery of Windesheim and to the *devotio moderna* movement. This twofold connection has left its mark both on the content of the stories and on the choice of their geographical setting. Their dates, on the other hand, do not seem to have been of great interest to the author: in one story (X. 4), he says of an event that it 'took place about ten years ago, after dusk'; in another (X. 11), that it happened not long after the death of Geert Groot (i.e., after 1378). In all the other stories, events happen 'in the past', but the narrative always seems to convey the impression that the past referred to is a fairly recent one. The author tries to make the events he describes more credible and realistic by invoking direct knowledge of them and a personal acquaintance with the characters involved (X. 18 and 25); this is also a way of drawing attention to the contemporary nature of the stories. He concentrates more on situating the action of the stories in a particular location; ten of the stories take place in Holland, and eight in German towns. Half of the stories are about the clergy, for the most part monks rather than regular priests.

This prompts an examination of the sources of information for this group of new *exempla*. In two cases the author invokes his reading: 'I read in a German book' (X. 14), 'I read in a certain book' (X. 15); and in both cases the stories are markedly more elaborate, from the literary point of view, than others in the collection. In the other cases, there is an original ring to the transcription, regardless of whether or not the author made use of written sources. One might say, simplifying slightly, that transcription was a way of recording monastic folklore, of setting down all the tales told about various wonders. It is significant that monastic brothers and servants also make an appearance in the stories (X. 5, 12 and 13); they are simple, uneducated men, susceptible, in the atmosphere of a religious community, to visions and ecstatic states. It is worth giving one example here.

A certain monastery of the diocese of Münster found itself in conflict with its neighbours, who were peasants, about pigs foraging in the forest. A lay brother was responsible for making sure that the pigs did not stray beyond the limits of the monastery's pastures; but he suffered terribly from the burden of this task, for it prevented him from participating in religious offices for long periods of time. He therefore spoke to the pigs and asked them not to stray beyond the prescribed limits, and then took himself off to the monastery. But despite all the malicious efforts of the peasants, the pigs did not go beyond the prescribed limits.

Here the miracle is a very simple one, and takes place within the context of ordinary, everyday life. The story is indeed in the tradition of the Little Flowers of St Francis, but it is of the kind told in monastic kitchens rather than in refectories. Such stories about everyday problems, in contemporary settings, were more than just rationalizations of the miraculous tales of folklore; by describing miraculous events in people's everyday lives, they were proof of the constant intervention of God and of the devil in all human affairs.

One of the stories concerns events which took place in 1453 in Wrocław,[56] during the fast which followed the festival of the Exaltation of the Holy Cross (X. 2). The Jews were said to have profaned the host, and as a result the entire Jewish community of the town was destroyed. About a hundred and fifty people were said to have been burnt at the stake, the rest having converted to Christianity. There is no doubt that the conflict itself is a historical fact, connected with John of Capistrano's stay in Wrocław;[57] his preaching, together with tales told by monks journeying from monastery to monastery, contributed to the spread of information about the Wrocław events throughout Europe, and the story was among the most famous of the accounts which circulated by word of mouth in the Middle Ages.[58] A certain continuity may be observed in the tendency to situate Eucharistic miracles in Wrocław. An account of the Eucharistic miracle and the Jewish boy can already be found in Caesar of Heisterbach's *VIII libri miraculorum* (*in Polonia contigit, quod dicturus sum, in civitate, quae vocatur Breslavi*, III. 13), situated in Wrocław.[59] It is one of several stories which Gottfried of Altenberg and other Cistercians must have brought back from Polish monasteries, which explains its presence in Heisterbach's collection.[60]

We can see from all this how long and complex were the paths along which these miraculous accounts wound their way into circulation, thanks to the constant wanderings of religious brothers from monastery to monastery. Indeed, monastic communities seem to have been both the crucible in which popular stories and themes from mass culture were melted down and the centre from which they spread.

We have no original compilations of *exempla* from Polish medieval literature comparable with French or German collections. But Heisterbach's collection, along with Polish works of hagiography, bear out the fact that such accounts arose out of and functioned within the oral tradition, and were seldom written down. One such account, transcribed in Poland, was the famous story of the Abbot of Wachock, who was snatched away in 1456 by 'a devil of horrible aspect in the form of a very ugly negress'.[61] This account, whose author was Michael of Kleparz, abbot of the Benedictine monastery of the Holy Cross at Łysa Góra, is in fact a satirical pamphlet aimed at the Cistercian abbot Mikołaj Rziga, eloquently illustrating one of his sermons on profligacy. We know too little about the two abbots to be able to say what conflict set them against each other and what was the source of their hostility. There are no grounds for supposing that Michael of Kleparz made use of stories being passed around by word of mouth.[62] We do, on the other hand, have grounds for supposing that such accounts were rapidly absorbed into the popular tradition. The Benedictine abbot was writing about a contemporary event (indeed, he actually says '*nunc*'); his readers, therefore, perceived the work of the devil as being *hic et nunc*, all around them, in their own day.[63]

The *exempla* and the collections of *exempla* we have been considering here are all late works, but all that we know about their origins and about the mechanisms governing their construction can equally well be applied to earlier collections. Thus we can say that it was above all in monasteries that stories with a particular kind of theme were circulated, from library to refectory to kitchen, giving a sort of brew in which culture from 'book-learning' was mixed up with the oral spread of information. In thirteenth-century collections of *exempla*, the transcription of oral traditions seems more visible than in later compilations, and folklore plays a much greater role; and it also seems legitimate to assume a sort of 'taming' of folklore in the course of this work, for the better dissemination of Christian culture. The lack of transcriptions of this kind concerning Poland may be owing not only to the slow development of literature in medieval Poland but also to a much more strongly negative attitude towards folklore, which tended to be rejected rather than integrated and tamed.

The question of the genetic link between *exempla* and the oral tradition does not exhaust the subject of their relationship to folklore. For the history of culture it is perhaps the second aspect of this relationship – the spread of *exempla*, their functioning and the extent of their presence within the culture – that is the more important. This is not the place to attempt to establish or justify the claim that the themes which run through the oral tradition were drawn largely from 'bookish', or written, culture; suffice it to say that, in the balance of influence between the written and the popular tradition, the former was constantly evening the score. In nineteenth-century collections of folklore, echoes can sometimes be found of stories which Jacques de Vitry or Caesar of Heisterbach had drawn from the oral tradition. The themes woven into the sermons of popular preachers and used by the Church to illustrate religious teaching were also the source of much popular culture (and literary culture, too, as the example of Rej shows); they circulated by word of mouth at mills, fairs, inns and pilgrimage sites, the traditional centres for the spread of popular oral culture.

The role of *exempla* as illustrations to religious teaching should also be understood in its most literal sense. It is difficult for a historian to judge how men in centuries past saw the world; perception was also subject to historical change, however slow it might have been and however tenuous and uncertain the testimony we have about it. It seems, however, that in the Middle Ages people tended to react more strongly to visual than to aural stimuli; reading apart, it was through pictures that religious teaching was carried to the masses, and the stories they heard were meant as pictures: they were intended to stimulate the imagination. They were not only aids in explaining the abstract truths of religious teaching; they were illustrative in the literal sense, in that they were meant to evoke images in the minds of the listeners, and act upon their imaginations. This is still, to a certain extent, how mass culture functions today.

The thematic order in which *exempla* were arranged corresponded to the principal themes of religious teaching. Stories and anecdotes were no less important an aspect of religious teaching than explanations of moral theology and the truths of the faith, for they constituted the conceptual building-blocks of individual and collective mental constructions.

Without attempting a review of all the themes and situations contained in this material, it is worth taking a closer look at the ideas suggested by *exempla* which have the supernatural as their theme. Humbert de Romans taught that the commandments contained the following ideas: *deus, angelus, homo, caelum, diabolus, infernum, praecepta, consilia, sacramenta, scriptura, virtutes, vitia;*[64] and these were, accordingly, the themes with which his *exempla* were concerned. But while the truths of the faith about God and heaven, the sacraments and divine service were explained primarily with the aid of examples taken from Scripture and patristic literature, the problems of reward and punishment, divine intervention in human affairs and the way in which human ends and designs may be fulfilled were best illustrated through stories.[65] Such stories, by putting these problems into relief and giving them concrete and dramatic shape, illustrated the relationship between men, angels and the devil.

The popular view of the role of angels encompassed far more than classical church dogma,[66] which limited them to singing the praises of God; in these stories their primary function is as men's guardians, who reveal the secrets of the future and provide help in times of need. They also inspire fear, not only during the struggle for the souls of the dying or in the apocalyptic context of the Last Judgement, but also in their role as guardians. In a story from the *Speculum exemplorum*, set in Zwolle, a young boy of great beauty accompanies a group of friends to an evening of debauchery, but then does his best to dissuade them from evil deeds. This annoys them, and they force him to go to a prostitute. Once there, he gives her money but does not sin, instead persuading her to abandon her life of sin. He then returns to his friends, who are convinced that he has done what they had demanded. On his way home he is stopped in the street by a figure dressed in black and surrounded by a halo of light, who strikes him to the ground with a great blow: it is his guardian angel, who, on God's orders, wants to set him back on the path of righteousness and preserve him from bad company. Although the angel seems severe and unjust, it is nevertheless clear in this case that he wishes to protect the young man. Elsewhere, however, the angel might act as the vengeful arm of divine justice: for instance, he kills a boy because, from the day of his birth, his parents had renounced their generosity and stopped giving alms.[67] In another case, the bloody vengeance meted out by an angel astonishes a pious Anchorite, who cannot understand how an angel can punish for actions which are to take place in the future.[68]

But the place of honour in these stories is reserved for the devil and the infernal powers. The devil, as he is presented in the *exempla*, appears to be characterized by a model inventory of diabolical actions and features. What is perhaps more interesting still, however, is his duality, and the ambivalence and fluidity with which he is portrayed; this kind of characterization is typical of folklore in general, of its values and its judgements.[69] The devil[70] is handsome[71] and ugly, young and old, elegant and repulsive; these contradictory descriptions might well be intended to emphasize the extent to which the devil is dangerous and perverse, and able to assume different guises. The devil always appears to be acting for men's good. Here he is, in one story, appearing to a group of undisciplined and ill-behaved pupils in the form of their master, three days dead, and whipping them soundly;[72] elsewhere, he warns a man who intends to commit an evil deed (he cries 'pfoui' three times).[73] In yet another story, a cobbler from Mayence curses the priest who encouraged people to wear pointed shoes, but the curse is turned back upon him: the devil falls upon him in the street and beats and abuses him.[74]

In an *exemplum* about the usurer of Assisi, noted down by the Polish Franciscan Seweryn during his trip to Italy, the devil – *quidam demon . . . in humana forma* – appears as a messenger of God. The usurer has been buried outside the doors of the basilica of Assisi, because, although he received the sacraments before he died, he did not return the fruits of his usury; as a result of the devil's efforts, the usurer *regecit Corpus Christi in calium*, whereupon the devil snatches his body from the tomb.[75] The words in which the devil addresses the sacristan are significant: 'Ego sum demon, qui ex precepto Dei in hac forma ad te veni.'

The portrayal of the devil in Polish art and literature deserves some serious research, as does the more general problem of the extent and causes of the phenomenon of satanism in the late Middle Ages; and the dualism of the devil's nature as he is depicted in folklore is certainly worthy of being studied in detail. But it is also interesting to note that the Church, in its teaching, opposed the attribution of extraordinary powers to the devil, and discouraged the tendency to blame the devil for all evils. In a collection of sermons written around 1407 there is an anecdote about a servant who had left her mistress and then returned, saying that she had been tempted by the devil; whereupon the devil, who had been following these events from the beginning and was now listening in his corner, cried out that it wasn't true.[76] While the pulpit was certainly a powerful means of spreading knowledge about the devil, and the place from which the struggle against satanism was waged, it was also a means of combating the exaggerated picture which the masses had formed of the infernal powers.

A constant element of religious teaching in the Middle Ages was the struggle against magical practices, which the Church treated as superstitions; and here, too, anecdotes often served as illustrations and concrete arguments. Such stories, however, also contained interesting information about religious practices of a magical character. The manuscript of Szczyrzyce, of which Kazimierz Dobrowolski made a study many years ago,[77] contains four stories, edited by the Polish Cistercian Jan Szarlat, about the miraculous powers of the words *et verbum caro factum est*. These words allegedly had the power to exorcise the demons from the possessed and to chase away the devil when he had ensnared the faithful; a monk who failed to genuflect or to display the appropriate reverence (*nec aliquam reverenciam faceret*) at these words received a blow from the devil. This testifies to the faith people had in the magical power of words. An *exemplum* in a Silesian sermon[78] from around 1470 is significant in this regard: a physician called Thomas, able and pious (*peritissimus et valde devotus*), and full of reverence for his master and patron, was wont to treat his patients with the aid of the following formula: *Dominus meus et deus meus sanet te*. A story in another Silesian manuscript throws light on the controversial nature of the name Thomas:[79] a certain *rusticus* decided, 'in accordance with the doctrine of Pope Celestine', to choose a patron for himself from among the Apostles. He drew lots, for such was the prevailing custom, and when he saw that the saint's image which he had drawn was that of St Thomas – *cartula cum nomine sancti Thomae* – he cast it away with loathing; but he continued to draw the same image every time he tried, again and again. Finally his parish priest sent him on a pilgrimage to Jerusalem. During the voyage the ship encountered a storm, and lots were drawn (*sortes committunt*) to see whose fault it was that the ship should be exposed to such perils. The *rusticus* was found to be the guilty one, and it was decided, in order to obtain God's help, to throw him into the sea; it was then that his life was saved by St Thomas.

This story shows, in a particularly striking way, not only the 'magical' way of thinking (the attitude towards the magical properties of names) evident in didactic religious stories of a popular nature, but also the general presence of magical practices in religion in the late Middle Ages. The drawing of lots for the saint's name was also in accordance with popular magical practices.

When the stories were not taken from Scripture and were located outside scriptural space and time, they had to be made credible, and references had to be inserted to a specific place and time in which they were set. The year, on the other hand, was rarely indicated; more often only a general reference was made to history, as in the case of the *Gesta Romanorum*, or to the present, mention being made of the narrator's own memory of the events or of the testimony of witnesses. The process of making the stories credible was important for preachers, but it also played a role in other types of literature where the *exemplum* appeared, for example in historiography.[80] The line between historical narrative and literary argument was a very fluid one. An interesting example of this fluidity may be found in the history of the division of William the Conqueror's inheritance, recounted in an English chronicle, the *Continuation of Wace*:[81] the king asks each of his sons what bird he would like to be; one replies that he would like to be a falcon, another an eagle, and the third a starling. The king then proceeds to divide up the heritage in accordance with these choices and the reasons given for them. This story became part of the arsenal of anecdotes used by English preachers; it can also be found in the two collections of *exempla* edited by Gobi and Bromyard. The tentative analysis of this anecdote undertaken by Archer Taylor[82] has revealed considerable differences between the various transcriptions: the overall structure had been retained, but the constituent elements had been modified. These differences would appear to suggest that the story had a continuing life of its own through oral transmission. Taylor's analysis also suggests that the story originated from a tale which was used as a source both in the historiography and in the literature of various countries (in one thirteenth-century version by Berthold of Holle Grane, the three sons are the sons of the king of Bohemia, Austria and Bavaria; they are vying for the hand of a princess, and the three birds are the starling, the falcon and the crane). Thus the historical legend is intimately intertwined with the literary fable, and the two blur into each other. What is significant here is the link between the written and the oral transmission of *exempla*.

The *exemplum* was an instrument of religious education, and especially of preaching. In the practice of Christianity as defined by the Fourth Lateran Council, it was a way of transmitting the truths of the faith and the principles of Christian behaviour to the masses. The historian attempting to analyse the way in which it functioned will therefore come up against a number of fundamental obstacles, for he will have to study popular culture, the common culture of the masses, while all the documents at his disposal concern the culture of the elites. Our knowledge of *exempla* comes from manuscripts in the libraries of medieval monasteries which were transcribed by men of the pen; the use of manuscripts was for a long time restricted to the elite – indeed, for a long time it was restricted to monasteries. *Exempla* were passed on from one collection to another and borrowed by authors from one another and by preachers for their sermons. Their reach was therefore limited; but one should remember that medieval *exempla* were transmitted orally, and that it was to sermons, lectures, prayers and being read aloud, rather than to the written word, that they mainly owed their diffusion in medieval culture.

This, then, is how we are able to study *exempla* as a phenomenon of mass culture, even though neither the form in which they have been preserved – and by this I mean not only the simplified structure of the fables into which they were woven but also the language of the transcriptions – nor the number of extant manuscript books can attest to their nature as a mass phenomenon.

The typological diversity of *exempla* is immense: there are legends and oriental tales, stories of miracles and fables from antiquity, tales from monasteries, anecdotes, biblical stories, myths and observations about natural history.[83] When listened to, they were intended to illustrate, to serve as examples, and to inculcate a certain form of behaviour, in accordance with the function of legend in Jolles' categorization of 'simple forms'.[84] This was a role they were to retain for a considerable length of time, for they continued to serve as sources for baroque preaching and modern religious literature.[85]

Insofar as another of their important functions, in the socio-technical sense, was to break up the monotony of sermons about religious doctrine, *exempla* were also meant to amuse. Indeed, in the course of the late Middle Ages they were increasingly associated with amusement, and the functioning and treatment of written collections of *exempla* encouraged this trend: autonomous collections of *exempla* came to be regarded not only as didactic texts or vehicles for conveying information but as forms of diversion. And as the anecdotal and facetious aspects of these collections gained in emphasis, *exempla* sometimes lost their religious associations entirely and became secularized. The evolution of the genre was characterized by the gradual autonomy accorded to the narrative itself, at the expense of the moral message, and by an increasing emphasis on information pertaining to social mores; Edward Petru cites the collection of stories from Olomouc[86] as an illustration of this tendency. But this process of secularization manifested itself in various ways, and was not everywhere the same.[87] Secularized stories continued to be disseminated in clerical circles. Caesar of Heisterbach tells of a sermon by the abbot Gerwardus, at which he himself was present, during which many monks and many of the laity slept soundly; presently the abbot paused and said, 'Listen, brothers, for I shall now tell you something new and interesting. Once upon a time there was a king called Arthur ...'[88] Having thus succeeded in waking everyone, the abbot was able to continue with his sermon. This testimony sheds some light on the kinds of interests which gave rise both to medieval liturgical drama and to the increased role of narration in monastic literature. Julian Krzyżanowski has advanced the theory that the *Gesta Romanorum*, a late collection of *exempla*, was intended primarily for monks, to be read aloud in the refectory or individually, and that its aim was both to instruct and to amuse.[89] But these secularized stories retained their role as an instrument of preaching, which has always been built around anecdotes and continued to be one of the main methods of spreading religious teaching.

Because of the polarization of *exempla* on the problem of sin, which religious teaching tried to combat through realistic descriptions and a striking metaphysics, they can be seen as a sort of medieval 'counter-culture'. The vast problem of the medieval eschatological imagination, and in particular the role of the devil and the torments of hell, still awaits study. *Exempla* played an important role in the formation of this imagination, certainly no less important than iconography. In addition, among the vast number of questions involved in research on *exempla*, the question of how their negative content was transmitted is extremely important. Cautionary tales about evil and descriptions of diabolical monstrosities – the 'spicy' aspects of this illustrative form of teaching about hell and the devil – were not only intended to combat real sin and occult practices and beliefs; they also contributed to the spread of information about condemned practices and beliefs and about social life in other parts of the Christian world. Thus, because the *exemplum* contained elements drawn from popular culture as well as from ecclesiastical circles, on which that culture in turn also drew, we may, by studying how it functioned, shed some light on the sensibilities and imagination of the masses among which it was spread.

Notes

1 Cf. T. Crane, 'Medieval sermon-books and stories', *Proceedings of the American Philosophical Society*, 21, 1883–4, pp. 49–78; 'Medieval sermon-books and stories and their study since 1883', ibid., 56, 1917, pp. 369–402, and in *Reallexicon der deutschen Literatur*, ed. V. Neumann and J. Klapper, I. Berlin, 1958, pp. 413–17. For the bibliography, see R. Alsheimer, *Das Magnum Speculum Exemplorum als Ausgangpunkt populärer Erzählertraditionen – Studien zu seiner Wirkungsgeschichte in Polen und Russland*, Frankfurt, 1971.

2 C. G. de Vooys, *Middelnederlandsche Legenden en exemplen: bijdrage tot de kennis van de prozaliteratur en het volksgeloof der Middeleeuwen*, s'Gravenhage, 1900.

3 J. A. Mosher, *The Exemplum in the Early Religious and Didactic Literature in England*, New York, 1911.

4 J. T. Welter, *L'exemplum dans la littérature religieuse et didactique du Moyen Age*, Paris, 1927.

5 He accomplished it only in part: see J. T. Welter, 'Un recueil d' "Exempla" du XIIIe siècle', *Etudes franciscaines*, 30, 1913, pp. 646–65; *Le Speculum Laicorum*, Paris, 1914; *La Tabula Exemplorum*, Paris, 1926; 'Un nouveau recueil franciscain d'Exempla de la fin du XIIIe siècle', *Etudes franciscaines*, 47, 1930, pp. 432–76, and 595–629.

6 This is how Rudolf Schenda put it at the 1967 congress of folklorists: 'Anläufe, Ansätze, kein einheitliches Streben, kein gemeinsames Wissen, um einer klar umrissenen Gegenstand'. Cf. R. Schenda, 'Stand und Aufgaben der Exemplaforschung', *Fabula*, 10, 1969, p. 77.

7 A. Lecoy de la Marche, *Anécdotes historiques: légendes et apologues tirés du recueil inédit d'Etienne de Bourbon*, Paris, 1877.

8 *Erzählungen des Mittelalters in deutschen Ubersetzung und lateinischen Urtext*, ed. J. Klapper, Breslau, 1914 (Wort und Brauch, 12); J. Klapper, *Exempla aus Handschriften des Mittelalters*, Heidelberg, 1911.

9 F. C. Tubach, *Index Exemplorum*, Helsinki, 1969; and N. D. Oppel, 'Zur neueren Exemplaforschung', *Deutsches Archiv für Erforschung des Mittelalters*, 28, 1972, pp. 240–3.

10 J. T. Welter, *L'exemplum . . .*, p. 1.

11 Ibid., p. 2.

12 R. Schenda, op. cit., p. 81.

13 *The Exempla or Illustrative Stories from the 'Sermones Vulgares' of Jacques de Vitry*, ed. T. F. Crane, London, 1890, p. xviii (Publications of the Folklore Society, 261).

14 Cf. S. Battaglia, 'L'essemplo medievale', *Filologia Romanza*, 6, 1959, pp. 45–82.

15 F. C. Tubach, 'Exempla in the decline', *Traditio*, 18, 1962, pp. 407–17; 'Strukturanalytische Probleme: das Mittelalterische Exemplum', *Hessische Blätter für Volkstunde*, 59, 1968, pp. 25–9.

16 T. F. Crane, op. cit., pp. 108 and 256; cf. *Patalogia Latina*, vol. 73, col. 327.

17 T. F. Crane, op. cit., p. 107, n. 255.

18 J. T. Welter, op. cit., pp. 454–5.

19 F. C. Tubach, op. cit., p. 417.

20 G. Kuttner, 'Wesen und Formen der deutschen Schwandeliteratur des 16. Jahrhunderts', *Germanistische Studien*, 152, 1934; E. Moser-Rath, 'Erzähler auf der Kanzel: zu form und Funktion des barocken Prädigtmärleins', *Fabula*, 2, 1959, pp. 1–26.

21 Collections of stories of this kind sometimes circulated among Italian humanists without ever being printed. One example of such a collection is Teseo Pini's *Speculum cerretanorum*, published recently for the first time under the title *Il libro dei vagabondi*, ed. P. Camporesi, Turin, 1973.

22 Cf. J. Krzyżanowski, 'Legend in Literatur und Folklore', *Fabula*, 9, 1967, pp. 111–17.

23 Cf. J. Kłoczowski, 'Kryzysy i reformy w chrześcijaństwie zachodnim XLV–XVI wieku', *Znak*, 205–6, 1971, p. 852.

24 A compilation of this type was studied by A. Hilka: 'Neue Beiträge zur Erzählungsliteratur des Mittelalters', *Jahresbericht der Schlesischen Gesellschaft für Vaterländische Kultur*, 90, 1912; this article escaped the attention of J. T. Welter when he himself came to study this compilation; cf. J. T. Welter, *L'exemplum ...*, pp. 236–44.

25 J. T. Welter (op. cit.) lists an impressive number of such collections.

26 A. D. von den Brincken, 'Tabula alphabetica', *Festschrift für Hermann Heimpel*, 2, Göttingen, 1972, pp. 900–23.

27 The analytical studies and editions by Julian Krzyżanowski should be mentioned here; cf. in particular *Romans polski XVI wieku*, Warsaw, 1962, and *Proza polska wczesnego Renesansu*, Warsaw, 1954. There is an interesting overview of these problems in T. Kruszewska-Michałowska's 'Narodziny i rozwój nowelistyki w literaturze staropolskiej', *Studia z dawnej literatury czeskiej, słowackiej i polskiej*, Warsaw and Prague, 1963, pp. 267–599.

28 The bibliography may be found in K. Langosch, *Verfasserlexicon*, 3, Berlin, 1943, pp. 282–9, and *Nowy Korbut*, 2, Warsaw, 1964, pp. 504–5.

29 Cf. J. Umiński, 'Pochodzenie i kariera Marcina Polaka', *Collectanea Theologica*, 24, 1953, pp. 163–88. For critical remarks on the identification of Martin of Opawa with Martin of Sandomierz see

J. Kłoczowski, *Dominikanie polscy na Śląsku*, Lublin, 1956, p. 140ff, and 'Marcin Polak', *Polski Słownik Biograficzny*, 19, pp. 559–61.

30 S. Baracz, *Rys dziejów zakonu dominikańskiego w Polsce*, Lvov, 1861, 2, pp. 5–15; B. Vydra, *Polska stredoveka literatura kazatelska*, Prague, 1928, p. 84ff.

31 *Sermones Martini ordinis praedicatorum penitentiarii domini papae ... promptuario exemplorum*, Argentinae MCCCCLXXXIIII. For a succinct analysis of this collection, cf. J. T. Welter, op. cit., p. 228ff.

32 J. Krzyżanowski stresses the originality of the *Promptuarium exemplorum* as a collection of independent examples where the purely literary aspect ends up being given more prominence than the moral message (cf. *Romans Polski ...*, p. 106), but in fact this seems applicable less to Martin's collection than to other collections of the time. The title of the collection must be properly studied.

33 *Olomoucké povidky*, ed. E. Petru, Prague, 1957.

34 E. Petru, *Vyvoj ceskoho exempla v dobe predhusitske*, Prague, 1966, p. 109.

35 Ibid., pp. 49–86.

36 Biblioteka Narodowa, MS IV 3018, f. 1–85 – Exemplar, f. 86–165, IV 3019 f. 35–129 v.

37 J. Wolny, 'Łaciński zbiór kazań Peregryna z Opola i ich związek z tzw. "Kazaniami gnieźniejskimi" ', *Średniowiecze: studia o kulturze*, I, Warsaw, 1961, pp. 172–238; 'Incipity z 127 kazań Peregryna', *Polonica w średniowiecznych rękopisach bibliotek monachijskich*, Wrocław, 1969, pp. 175–84.

38 A. Brückner, 'Kazania średniowieczne', *Biblioteka Warszawska*, I, 1891, pp. 241–58, and II, 1892, pp. 445–71; 'Kazania średniowieczne', *Rozprawy Wydziału Filologicznego Akademii Umiejatności*, 24–5, Cracow, 1895; *Literatura religijna w Polsce średniowiecznej*, I, Warsaw, 1902, pp. 13–38.

39 Cf. J. Wolny's study of religious education and preaching in *Dzieje teologii katolickiej w Polsce*, ed. Marian Rechowicz, I, Lublin, 1974, pp. 149–209, and 273–308.

40 For example, those in the library of the University of Wrocław: MS I.O. 123 (*Sermones varii cum exemplis*, with a vast amount of hagiographical material), and MS I.O. 134 (*Sermones collecti per fratrem Stanislaum Geyszeler*, which contain abundant narrative texts).

41 Biblioteka Narodowa, MS II, 3015; M. Hornowska, H. Zdzitowiecka-Jasieńska, *Zbióry rękopiśmienne w Polsce średniowiecznej*, Warsaw, 1947, p. 333.

42 Biblioteka Narodowa, MS IV, 3019, which contains two collections of *exempla*, in alphabetical order: *Naturalia bona et utilia ad predicacionem* (fo. 190–208), and *Liber figurarum cum exemplis naturalibus* (fo. 208–279).

43 Library of the University of Wrocław, MS I, F. 115, fo. 160–206; cf. J. Klapper, *Die Erzählungen* . . ., n. 1–164.

44 J. Wolny, 'Materiały do historii wagantów w Polsce średniowiecznej', *Biuletyn Biblioteki Jagiellońskiej*, 19, 1969, p. 81.

45 It is difficult to take seriously Klapper's claim (*Erzählungen* . . ., p. 14) that this shows that the German population in the second period of colonization were no longer sufficiently naive, nor had enough '*sagenbildende Kraft*' to incorporate their own stories into fourteenth- and fifteenth-century collections of *exempla*.

46 K. Dobrowolski, 'Przyczynki do dziejów średniowiecznej kultury polskiej z rękopisu szczyrzyckiego', *Studia staropolskie: księga ku czci A. Brücknera*, Cracow, 1928, p. 337ff.

47 Cf. J. Krzyżanowski, *Legend in Literatur* . . ., p. 159, n. 22.

48 K. Dobrowolski, 'Żywot św. Jacka: ze studiów nad polską hagiografią średniowieczną', *Rocznik Krakowski*, 20, 1926, p. 31ff.

49 Cf. D. Borawska, *Z dziejów jednej legendy*, Warsaw, 1950, p. 43ff.

50 *Z opowiadań średniowiecznych*, ed. H. Kowalewicz, Warsaw, 1974 (*Silva Medii et Recentioris Aevi*, 3).

51 *Reallexicon der deutschen Literaturgeschichte*, I. Berlin, 1958, p. 414.

52 *Editio princeps*, Deventer, 1481; there were over thirty editions up to the middle of the fifteenth century. I have used the 1487 Strasbourg edition.

53 *Incipit decima et ultima distinctio Speculi exemplorum in qua habentur exempla quae aut verissima relatione didici, aut in libris theutonicis scripta inveni vel ipse facta cognovi.*

54 An attempt – not particularly successful – to analyse this part of the *Speculum* by J. Matuschak, in an essay entitled *Das Speculum exemplorum als Quelle volkstümlicher Glaubensvorstellungen des Spätmittelalters*, Siegburg, 1967 (*Quellen und Studien zur Volkskunde*, 8).

55 The *Speculum exemplorum* is most commonly attributed to the Cistercian Gilles the Goldsmith (Aegidius Aurifaber). Cf. Matuschak, op. cit., p. 10, for an examination of the arguments. B. Kruitwagen, in his 'Speculum exemplorum', *Bijdragen voor de geschiedenis van het Bisdom van Haarlem*, 29, 1905, p. 359, puts forward the name of Herman von Ludingakerk.

56 *In Wratislavia quae theutonica Breslau nuncupata est et in regione Bohemiae sita.*

57 L. Oelsner, 'Schlesische Urkunden zur Geschichte der Juden im Mittelalter', *Archiv für Kunde Österreichischer Geschichtsquellen*, 31, 1864; *Scriptores rerum silesicarum*, 7, n. 5; *Monumenta Poloniae Historica*, 3, pp. 785–9, and 4, pp. 1–5. This event and the various accounts of it need to be studied in greater detail for the light they shed on the spread of information. In a Polish collection of sermons from the fifteenth century, there is an account of anti-Jewish events in Silesia in 1453 and, alongside a description of the 'Jewish conspiracy', some remarks about the inefficacy of John of

Capistrano's actions taken against the Jews in Cracow (Biblioteka Narodowa, MS IV, 3021, fo. 223 v.).

58 Cf. P. Browe, 'Die Hostienschändungen der Juden im Mittelalter', *Römanische Quartelschrift für christliche Altertumskunde und Kirchengeschichte*, 34, 1926, pp. 167–97.

59 This was a widespread view in the Middle Ages. For another version, cf. J. Klapper, *Erzählungen* . . ., p. 278 n. 58, (with bibliography).

60 K. Dobrowolski, *Przyczynki* . . ., p. 337ff.

61 First published by W. Ketrzyński in *Monumenta Poloniae Historica*, 6, pp. 558–89, and more recently by H. Kowalewicz, *Z opowiadań średniowiecznych*, pp. 7–23.

62 Cf. S. Thompson, *Motif Index of Folk-Literature*, Bloomington, IN, 1955–8, G. 303.3, 1, 6, 'The devil as a black man', and Q. 457.

63 H. Kowalewicz advances the theory that there was a real event behind the story, to wit, the kidnapping of the abbot of Wachock by a group of masked men, identified as devils (ibid., p. 8), but this kind of positivist interpretation does not seem convincing.

64 Humbert de Romans, *De officio praedicatoris*, in *Liber de eruditione praedicatorum*, ed. J. J. Berthier, Rome, 1889, p. 370.

65 Cf. M. Günter, *Psychologie der Legende*, Freiburg, 1949, p. 7.

66 J. Matuschak, op. cit., p. 22ff.

67 J. Klapper, *Erzählungen* . . ., p. 321, n. 110.

68 Ibid., pp. 411–14, n. 211.

69 Cf. J. Le Goff, 'Culture cléricale et traditions folkloriques dans la civilisation mérovingienne', in *Niveaux de culture et groupes sociaux*, Paris, La Haye, 1971, pp. 21–32.

70 Cf. F. C. Tubach, *Index exemplorum*, 1550. For the *Speculum exemplorum*, cf. J. Matuschak, op. cit., pp. 37–45.

71 Cf. J. Klapper, *Erzählungen* . . ., pp. 396–400, n. 194.

72 *Speculum exemplorum*, V, 42 (Thomas de Cantimpré, *De proprietate apium*).

73 Ibid., V, 67.

74 Ibid., X, 27.

75 H. Kowalewicz, op. cit., pp. 63–4.

76 A. Brückner, 'Kazania średniowieczne', *Biblioteka Warszawska*, 1, 1892, p. 455.

77 K. Dobrowolski, op. cit., p. 348; J. Klapper, *Erzählungen* . . ., p. 324, n. 119, and *Tabula exemplorum*, pp. 20–1, n. 64–5.

78 J. Klapper, *Exempla*, p. 60, n. 75, (*Collectio variorum sermonum*, Library of the University of Wrocław, MS I.F. 740, from a monastery at Zagan, 1470).

79 Ibid., pp. 58–60, n. 74, (*Sermones de tempore et sanctis*, Library of the University of Wrocław, MS I. F 759, from the Franciscan monastery of Jawor, middle of the fifteenth century).

80 Cf. B. Kürbis on the subject, in *Mistrza Wincentego Kronika Polaków*, Warsaw, 1974, p. 58ff and *passim*.

81 Francisque-Michel, *Chroniques anglo-normandes*, I, Rouen, 1836, p. 182ff.

82 A. Taylor, 'What Bird Would You Choose to Be? A medieval tale', *Fabula*, 7, 1965, pp. 97–114.

83 Cf. F. C. Tubach, 'Strukturanalytische Probleme: das mittelalterliche Exemplum', *Hessische Blätter für Volkskunde*, 59, 1968, pp. 25–9.

84 A. Jolles, *Einfache Formen*, Halle, 1929 (2/1956).

85 Cf. E. Moser-Rath, *Prädigtmärklein der Barokzeit: Exempel, Sage, Schwank und Fabel in geistlichen Quellen des oberdeutschen Ratones*, Berlin, 1964; R. Alsheimer, op. cit.

86 E. Petru, ed., op. cit., p. 109ff.

87 Cf. H. Bausinger, 'Exemplum und Beispiel', *Hessische Blätter für Volkskunde*, 59, 1968, p. 35.

88 R. Ganszyniec, 'Trzy dziełka Cezaryusza z Heisterbachu o Matce Boskiej', *Spraw. Tow. Nauk. we Lvov*, 3, 1923, p. 61.

89 J. Krzyżanowski, *Romans polski wieku XVI*, Warsaw, 1962, p. 109.

3

The Common Bond and the Feeling of Community in Medieval Europe

The concept of Europe has aroused the interest of European thinkers in various ways.[1] The civilizing and political development of other continents, European expansion beyond the borders of the home continent and a sense of threat to political systems or civilization are all factors that have provoked the drive towards an affirmation of European consciousness and a search for the historical roots of European unity. The activities of super-state and supranational relations after both world wars have intensified thinking on the subject of the essence of 'Europeanness', and led to a tendency towards a preoccupation with the historical fate of European community.

When we embark on an outline of supranational community ties in Europe during the Middle Ages we cross the paths of researchers into the concept of Europe; considerable areas of this subject have not yet been properly identified. Among the specific weaknesses of the present state of the literature are an occidentalist research perspective[2] and a failure to appreciate individual structural features in the medieval period. Within the framework of the existing research – more often expressed by means of programmes than of practical analysis – the position of the Middle Ages cannot be understood by itself. Doubts sometimes arise as to whether it is possible to talk of medieval Europe at all, bearing in mind that within these two concepts lies an inner contradiction. This does not prevent synthetic attempts to study the

Middle Ages being labelled in this way.[3]

The European idea did not receive particular affirmation during the Middle Ages, nor was the concept of Europe firmly recognized then. What is more, the modern expansion of the European idea began in opposition to medieval universalisms; it was sometimes also linked with the processes of intellectual secularization that occurred in the humanist period.

The significance of the research into community ties and European consciousness in the Middle Ages is obvious. The faint traces of the European concept that occur in medieval vocabulary enable us to grasp the nature and essence of the idea as it was at the very beginning, when it was establishing itself in the terminology of the period. In order to understand this we have above all to study community ties in medieval Europe and their repercussions on the social consciousness, and also to confront this picture with the geographical concept of Europe. Ancient tradition[4] demands that we observe the functional duality of the concept of Europe, as a geographical definition of a certain part of the world and as a picture of a civilization.

Research to date has not led to complete agreement on the connection between the place of Europe in ancient geographical knowledge and the myth of the rape of Europe; the opinion favoured is that the myth constitutes a typical eponymic transposition, that mythical Europe is simply an eponym of a part of the world. Connections between the geographical and the fictional semantic domain of the European concept go back even further in ancient tradition because Europe is understood as a cultural system and a community with a collective fate. The xenophobic juxtaposition of Europe – an area of freedom – and Asia – an area of despotism[5] – had to function for the next millennium in various contexts as a condition of the European programme in which the demand for supranational political union acquired an ideological and civil dimension.

We must agree with Arnold Toynbee that the opposition of Asia and Europe functioned largely on the basis of ignorance and consequent extravagant images.[6] One particular exegesis demonstrates that the term 'Europe' occurred in ancient writings with various geographical meanings, while in the medieval period it was given no cultural significance. It would be difficult to overestimate the importance of historical semantic research for a modern history of culture, although we must be aware of its obvious limitations. The more widespread and commonplace the use of words and ideas which form the subject of analysis, the more important the research. It would, however, be absurd for the terminology and conceptual apparatus of contemporary research to be dependent on the extent to which the terms or ideas were used in the period to which this research applies.

In referring to the ancient tradition of understanding Europe as a part of the world and as a civilization, as a geographical term, and as a historical and cultural concept, we fail to settle the question of the degree to which such an understanding of the term was disseminated in ancient times or, *a fortiori*, subsequently; we define the terms of the investigation according to the rigours of contemporary historiography and the interests of our times. There is no hidden danger of anachronism or presentism here: the researcher's task is to define the roots of a cultural community contemporary with us, since the processes that have led to the creation of this community in historical reality and to the formation of a collective consciousness have become subjects of interest. Retrogression, lying heavily on such a research question, in effect enriches our view of the past, on the obvious condition that the results obtained would subsequently be inscribed within the context of the processes and phenomena of the period being investigated. In other words, the research phenomenon has to be 'considered'; its meaning in social reality and in the collective consciousness of its times must be defined. In posing the question about the existence of a common European bond in the Middle Ages, we must consider it against the background of the universalistic structures that existed at that time; we must also aim to define the degree to which the people of the Middle Ages were aware of this bond.

We have to be aware, too, of the danger, which still exists, of an occidentalist view of Europe, following Ranke's expiatory conception in his research on Europe which identifies the continent with the Germanic-Roman world.[7] This leads not only to the elimination of the Slav peoples from the European horizon but also to a fundamental distortion of the picture of European civilization, which is reduced to a single model ignoring the fact that pluralism is one of its constituent features.

THE ROMAN INHERITANCE AND IMPERIAL UNITY

The civil and socio-political European community formed itself around varying cultural traditions, amid changes in evolutionary dynamics and within processes of a discontinuous nature. The cultural inheritance of the ancient world, which functioned as a creative force for European unity, constantly renewing itself, was linked with the Mediterranean region, whereas continental structures and centres played a fundamental role in the development of medieval Europe. We could say that medieval Europe was growing at the pace of the disintegration and collapse of unity in a world the economic, political and cultural life of which was defined by the *Mare Internum*. We consequently identify the medieval beginnings of Europe with the seizure of the wealth of Mediterranean civilization by the peoples of the continent.

This process, set in motion by the Romanization of the transalpine territories, was accomplished in the flow of expansion of Western Christianity, which undertook to continue the Roman imperial tradition; Pope Gregory VII announced nevertheless that 'quibus imperavit Augustus, imperavit Christus'. The people of the Middle Ages were aware of the connection between *romanitas* and *christianitas*; this conviction is apparent also in historiosophical treatises and the works of historiographers and in the formulations of documents.[8] Caesar's conquest of Gaul – as Leopold von Ranke wrote a century ago – gave rise to a new configuration of the West which assumed its true shape in the course of Christian synthesis, linking the ancient world, Christianity and the young barbarian peoples.[9] The basic structures and centres of this synthesis lay outside the Mediterranean Basin.

In the great debates initiated by the genetic processes of medieval societies, the temporal horizon of the European community was delineated in various ways. Alfons Dopsch, in opposing the theory of a radical turning-point between the ancient and the medieval periods, revealed the continuous nature of Europe's cultural development from Caesar's times till after the death of Charlemagne.[10] The significance of the Mediterranean Sea for ties between the communities of the ancient world in this form receded into the background, since its influence could not be felt in the social system and the organization of agrarian life.

The great historiographic argument of the nineteenth century between the 'Germanic' and 'Roman' theses on the interpretation of the genesis of European societies, being a transposition of European nationalist feelings at that time, withdrew into the background. Dopsch's proposals were intellectually very fertile; dozens of works followed the path of the great master. It is enough to recall their importance in the works inspired by Marcelli Handelsman at a Warsaw seminar on the Merovingian and Carolingian periods.[11] Attempts to refute or topple Dopsch's theories predominated both because of their overhurried and tendentious generalization and because of the evolutionary way in which the historical process was understood. The effacing of the medieval turning-point in the birth of Europe, which is of interest to us, was also a topic for discussion and criticism. Attempts were made to restrict the picture of continuing development to economic relations in civil development, perceiving mainly the differences and disjunctions which lay at the foundations of the formation of medieval Europe.

The eminent Belgian historian Henri Pirenne took a different stance.[12] He believed that the structure of the ancient world was fundamentally Mediterranean in nature, and so he directed his attention to the *Mare Internum*. In his history of Europe during the Middle Ages, which he prepared in a German prisoner-of-war camp during the First World War, he wrote:

> For hundreds of years Europe has gravitated towards the Mediterranean Sea. Civilization spread across her, different parts of her communicated with each other across her. Communal life was basically the same on all her shores; the same religion prevailed, customs and ideas were the same or very similar. The Germanic invasion made no fundamental changes to this situation. Despite everything, we can say that during the second half of the seventh century Europe still constituted Mediterranean unity, just as during the days of the Roman Empire.[13]

The turning-point did not come until the Arab invasions, which severed any exchanges between North and South, East and West. As a result of the invasions Mediterranean unity was rendered non-existent and Arabs settled by the *Mare Nostrum*. Contacts between the European continent and the East were broken. Distanced from the Mediterranean Sea, thrown on her own resources, under threat in the coastal regions of Italy, Provence and Catalonia, and remembering that the Arab invasion in 711 had held Visigoth Spain in subjugation for a long time and was checked with difficulty during the 740s, medieval Europe removed all centres of influence, and of political and cultural supremacy, from South to North. The Arab invasion defined the direction in which medieval Europe was to develop, northwards into the heart of the continent, leading to the break-up of the ancient *Orbis Romanus* and the closure of the Mediterranean Sea to the peoples of Europe. The new European centre lay between the Loire and the Rhine; here it was that the Carolingian empire developed. And so: 'Without Mohammed, Charlemagne would have been inconceivable.'[14]

The basic points of Pirenne's theory did not escape criticism. The first polemical voices showed that the continuing presence of oriental merchants in Italy and Gaul even after the eighth century, the flourishing great international trade linking West and East in the Merovingian period, or the destructive results of Arab expansion for the economic life of the European continent and its connections with the East should not be overestimated.[15] Maurice Lombard went the furthest in this criticism: he demonstrated that not only did the Arab invasions not prevent the development of great trade but in fact they became a powerful stimulus to its prosperity, providing the West with the minerals it lacked for trade with the East and increasing the circulation of precious metals in Europe.[16] At the basis therefore of the flowering of Europe and the affirmation of the West's economic supremacy lay an enlivening of trade-currency circulation and an influx of minerals after the Arab expansion.

Of all the arguments about the beginnings of the Middle Ages and the genesis of European societies we are interested only in the question of Mediterranean and European unity. In the same context we should also consider the nature of the Carolingian structure. It is obvious that the confrontation of the barbarian world and the socio-economic and cultural structures of the territories of the Roman succession that had taken place in the early Middle Ages, and especially during the Carolingian period, are of vital significance for the whole 'European millennium'. The community that had been formed during the early Middle Ages found its organizing strength in the ideological, cultural and political unity of Latin Christianity, although the ethnic and linguistic binding agent of the German and Roman community fulfilled a vital role in this. The Carolingian empire is an important place of observation precisely because processes of civilizing syncretism took place within its borders, because an institutional-state edifice had been raised that was breaking down ethnic differences, and finally because its collapse would create a field of play for these differences, forming the bases for the development of a modern 'Europe of nations', a community of different peoples, countries and states.

Europe is given a fairly important place in Carolingian political terminology. Over thirty references to Europe in written sources of the Carolingian era, set out by Marian H. Serejski in his study of the idea of Carolingian unity,[17] can be treated as evidence of this term's significance in the writings of the time, and certainly in the consciousness of Carolingian intellectual and political elites. It is difficult to regard this as a straightforward acceptance of an ancient literary tradition resulting from the relationship of medieval culture to the ancient world.[18] The Carolingian empire affirmed its unity in European terminology. The particular role of the Franks, which would be given a messianic character by the papacy's appeal to the Frankish leaders for help and protection,[19] greatly widens the scope and importance of the term 'Franks', just as the scope of the term 'Romans' also increased; the word 'Francia', in the hand of a monk in St Gall, has to define all the countries of Christendom to the west of Asia.[20]

Under the emperor's rule the Carolingian empire united three parts of Europe: Italia, Gallia and Germania,[21] hence the need for a universalistic definition of the extent of Charlemagne's political power. Europe fulfilled the role of the concept well: of an instrument of political propaganda and rhetoric, creating a geographical and civil definition for Carolingian hegemony and the Carolingian world (*orbis, mundus*) which was understood as a comprehensive political structure, on the lines of the *Orbis Romanus*, and therefore as one of the political powers that existed on earth. As a result, definitions of *Europae venerandus apex, Europae veneranda pharus* or also *rex pater Europae* issue from the pens of Charlemagne's chroniclers and panegyrists.[22]

The fact that at the close of the ninth century the *Annales*

Fuldenses identified Europe with Charlemagne's possessions is of even greater significance.[23] This does not only provide evidence that this association was preserved in tradition; it also indicates that the concept of Europe did not exist independently in the post-Carolingian period. Borrowed from the vocabulary of geographical erudition it became a political term, connected with a short-lived imperial reign and later with all attempts to revive it. It failed to acquire cultural substance. Was that because no socio-cultural community tie had been formed?

The concept of Europe occurs several times in the writings of Alcuin, one of the most representative figures of the Carolingian elite.[24] Most important is the context of a letter written in 790 (addressed to the Anglo-Saxon teacher Colcu).[25] While describing the general political situation, he maintains that the Church was enjoying peace and was growing in strength in the 'European countries' (*in partibus Europae*) after the conversion of the Saxons and Friesians. The victories over the Slavs and Avars, the frustration of the Greeks' intentions to expand in southern Italy, the victories over the Saracens in Spain – these are all included among the Church's successes. Alcuin indicates that there is a black mark in this picture, however: the Saracens' were expanding their territories, and they held the whole of Africa and a very large part of Asia in their hands. It is highly significant that the identification of Europe and the Church was made at this point. All Charlemagne's victories are recognized as victories for the Church and for Christianity. Victory over the Byzantines is also included in this context. Frankish, or Christian, Europe is contrasted with Saracen Africa and (to a large extent) Asia. In this way the traditional map *orbis terrarum* acquires religious substance, and the concept of Europe, Africa and Asia is given a socio-cultural sense.

The significance of this way of understanding those geographical terms must not be overestimated. In another of his letters, in which he makes a typical medieval 'enumeration', Alcuin notes in reply to the question 'of what are there three?' that there are three parts to the world: Europe, Africa and India (which is used as a synonym here for Asia).[26] This would seem to be a typical context: within geographical terminology, in the simplest scheme of knowledge about the world, in the canon of scholastic knowledge. Application of the term to Carolingian reality suited the universalistic or imperial ambitions of the Frankish ruler; in an interesting letter written by a certain priest to Charlemagne, and sent immediately after he took power, we find the qualification that he ruled over Europe.[27] As used by clerks, court officials and church scribes this erudite term is a useful instrument of pane-gyric, government propaganda and polemics in relation to the true depositaries of the tradition of unity. The concept of Europe acquired political meaning in the Carolingian era, serving the for-mation of imperial ideology[28] in the West: the Eastern empire did not need to appeal to this concept because it had inherited the 'world' aspirations of the Roman empire.

Charlemagne's position as emperor was constantly affirmed in relation to Byzantium as that of one who continued the Roman succession. The 'European' rhetoric of those who eulogized the emperor of the West therefore was largely polemical in respect of Byzantium. This was not a new or original feature in that situa-tion. It showed how the Frankish ruler's circle embraced the anti-Grecism of the Latin Church, which had been going on for hundreds of years and was on the increase. The papacy was the centre in which awareness of the separateness of the Latin West was crystallized;[29] the *imperium occidentale* was a factor in the growth of the Latin Church's separateness,[30] and its expression and security. Long before the eleventh-century schism, the col-lapse of Christianity and the formation of a separate cultural structure for the Latin West, which would consider the hostile, foreign world of the East to include both Christian Byzantium and the Muslim Arab world, was a *fait accompli*.

If we look back at the formation of European ties we recognize this as an essential voyage for the inheritance of the Carolingian community. In the Romano-German edifice Charlemagne's power, uniting Italia, Gallia and Germania, and also making an opening towards the Slav world,[31] thence entering the sphere of Byzantine influences and destroying Avar power, created the con-ditions under which the Slavs could be incorporated into the Western community.[32] The Carolingian empire provided the inducement for creating a cultural community considerably more lasting than the actual political structure.

Independently of the fact that the cultural development of the Carolingian and post-Carolingian period drew abundantly on the East, as much from the Greeks as from the Arabs, awareness of the Western community manifested itself above all in a sense of being distinct from the East.[33] In both its positive and its negative programme Christianity was to be the substance and the true binding agent. The Christian character of Byzantium did not interfere with this at all; the Greek Christians appeared to the people of the West to be renegades. But at the same time there was great controversy about the perpetuation of the imperial idea, the natural home of which was the 'second Rome' – Constantinople.[34]

Byzantium declared itself the heir and perpetuator of the Roman empire, and at the same time claimed superior authority over the whole Christian community. The entire union of state and Church in Byzantium favoured the cohesion of this doctrine, the universalism of which did not need to resort to geographical nomenclature. A well-known piece of Byzantine-Roman polemics, which occurred when Pope Leo IV, on rejecting the mantle sent to him by the patriarch of Constantinople, announced his superior sovereign authority over Christianity in Europe,[35] is highly significant. The polemical, refutatory nature of the papal declaration is very clear here. It is a statement or proposition for the division of spheres of influence: Europe is made over to Rome and, presumably, Asia is left to Byzantium.

Byzantine universalism did not accept these divisions and retained the doctrine of unity in the sphere of Roman succession. The symbolism of the activities and actions of the Byzantine emperors was ostentatiously universalistic, denying or scorning the institutions of the Western empire. This universalism found expression in the specific hierarchy of rank at the Byzantine court, which ascribed to every ruler a particular rung of the ladder, the highest of which was reserved for the Byzantine emperor alone. This nomenclature was increasingly poorly suited to reality, and it became the language of court etiquette in the service of diplomatic protocol. Courtiers knew how to greet a particular ruler at court according to the importance of his state and the nature of its connections with the empire; but there were fewer occasions for the use of such ceremonial because Byzantium's influences had diminished and its universalistic aspirations had melted away. The political horizon of the Byzantine empire was becoming increasingly unambiguously limited to Eastern areas.[36] Only there do we find the foundations of the real efforts made by the Byzantine emperors to achieve unity. In relations with the European West, even when the direct interests of the Byzantine emperor, such as Norman expansion in Italy, were concerned, it is difficult to talk of a realization of imperial hegemony. Episodically thoughts would recur of political unity between East and West under Byzantine rule, which would in practice mean the supremacy of the papacy over the West, but there were no economic, institutional or civil foundations for such unity.

The astonishment of Liudprand of Cremona at the hostility he experienced from the Byzantines in 968 during his second visit to Constantinople, when he went there as Otto I's emissary, is further evidence of the difference in civilization between East and West.[37] Coming from a family connected with Lombard-Byzantine politics and knowing Greek well, the Bishop of Cremona was painfully aware that he was being treated as a barbarian in the capital of the emperor of the East, and his master, the Roman emperor, was considered a usurper. In the actual text there are doubtless many exaggerations and a few court plots aimed at the recipient, but it is an account which furnishes evidence of the fundamental lack of familiarity between the East and the West.[38] And ideas of imperial universalism found no lasting support in the actual extent of the political and civil influences of the Eastern empire. The fluctuating state of the prestige of the Byzantine *basileus* and the cohesion of his empire did not promote unity. The structure of the Church was not a unifying structure either; the autocephalic tendency in the development of Eastern Christianity's institutions prevailed over the Church's authority in Byzantium.

In the case of Eastern universalism the Church was harnessed to imperial doctrine. In the West universalism was a subject of conflict between the secular and spiritual powers. The *renovatio imperii* carried out in the tenth century sanctioned the ambitions of the Saxon dynasty to take over the Carolingian imperial tradition and to build a political structure based on imperial hegemony.[39] Without trying at this point to describe the complicated question of the renewal of the empire, and its later fate, we ought to mention just one of its aspects: the place and extent of awareness of the unity of the Carolingian inheritance.

Germany's imperial hegemony was based on a close connection with the internal unity of the Germans.[40] Sometimes, it is true, these processes diverged: a concentration of attention on imperial interests on the Apennine peninsula did not favour internal German unity. The symbolic prestige of the Roman emperor, however, had above all to serve the integration of the German kingdom and the establishment of successive dynasties – Saxon, Salic or Swabian (Hohenstaufen) – in the circumstances of Roman hegemony in relation to the German princes and magnates. The universalistic programme of the German emperors found its basic reference and conditions in the politics and internal situation of *Regnum Teutonicum*, and in the politics of expansion it carried out. The directions of this expansion varied. Temptation came constantly from the South, broken and powerful Lombardy, towards which the south German princes, and then Henry I the Fowler (919–936), directed their appetites; the imperial politics of the Ottonians met these plans and desires halfway.[41] The politics of Eastern expansion made themselves known increasingly powerfully: the imperial idea, the religious substance of which was the defence and spread of Christianity at the cost of 'barbarians' and 'bad Christians', gave them justification and ideological sanction.

In affirmation of imperial intentions we would have noticed that Germany's political interests, for which imperial ideology was only the instrument, were uppermost, and that reference to Roman heritage as an argument for universal hegemony was by nature only verbal. The way in which Liudprand answered the *basileus*' invective: 'you are not Romans at all, but Lombards', is significant. Otto I's emissary replied that the Lombards, that is, the Franks, Saxons, Lotharingians, Swabians and Burgundians, so despised the Romans that when they wanted to insult their enemies they called them Romans, in anger, associating the name with infamy, weakness, miserliness, immorality and deceit.[42] Federico Chabod perceives a confrontation between Germanic and Roman awareness in this account;[43] in interpreting this we should take into account the fact that the name Roman was used here as a synonym for Byzantine, 'Romea', and that the pejorative 'Roman' accordingly referred to the increasing antipathy between 'Latins' and 'Greeks'. The Ottonian panegyrists and the chancellery experts of the Saxon dynasty, however, referred back unambiguously to the Roman nomenclature[44] and emphasized the 'Roman' character of the rule of the Ottonians; the Roman element became an integral part of the German imperial idea in the Middle Ages. A feasible arrangement of political forces, however, prevailed over the formulae of doctrine.[45] Excessive involvement in Apennine matters on the part of the emperors – both Otto III and Frederick II – at once had an adverse effect on the cohesion of the German kingdom and weakened it.

Otto III's case[46] was particularly significant. He was firmly involved in the programme of *Renovatio Imperii Romanorum*, which recalled a combined ancient and Carolingian tradition. He thought of building a community of Christian peoples which would revive the former greatness of the Roman *Imperium*, giving Rome to the heads of this community – the pope and the emperor – as its capital.[47] He was deceiving himself by thinking that the centre of gravity of the restored empire could be brought back to Italy, and he was unable to find any support among the German magnates. The empire, of which Germania apparently was to have been a constituent part similar to Gallia, Italia and Sclavonia,[48] was a concept foreign to the German princes; the idea of the *imperium* was to serve the interests of the German kingdom. For this reason Bruno of Querfurt writes with sarcasm of the pleasure that Otto found in Rome, where he wanted to remain and which he intended *ioco puerili* to return to its former greatness: 'with extremely futile effort he tried to revive the dead spark of ancient Rome.'[49]

The fundamental significance of the Carolingian legacy is evident in the development of the German imperial idea, in which threads of Roman tradition, German affirmation and Christian mission were intertwined.[50] This concerned above all the way in which the Carolingian legend functioned as binding agent for imperial ideology,[51] but in effect it applied to the place of imperial universalism in European history. The universalism of the Roman empire of the German people created new super-state ties to a small extent, and rather episodically. In the perspective of European unity that interests us, imperial universalism demonstrated the long memories of Carolingian unity, as well as a certain need for the hierarchical political structure which seemed to result unavoidably from the Christian mission ascribed to all monarchic power, and a sense of the solidarity of the political interests of all Christendom.

A deep-seated particularism characterized the economic and

ethno-political reality of the Christian world at that time; it was impossible then in practice to realize a universalistic imperial model either of the Ottonians or of the Staufs. A gulf existed between the exuberantly developed doctrine of 'world rule' and reality.[52] The unifying functions of imperial universalism were insignificant; doctrine above all served the aims of strengthening the internal German state and its expansive intentions.[53]

The conflict between imperial and papal universalism did not in fact exceed the limits outlined here. The papacy, with its universalistic intentions, had stronger support than the empire in its vast organizational structure and centralized apparatus. When announcing doctrine, the popes, full of their papal power *super gentes et regna*, demanded to be a step ahead of the emperors in Christian political society.[54] In fact the dispute was really power over the world, over the political unity of Christendom, and in this sense, bearing in mind how artificial a subject it was – since medieval Christianity did not create political unity – we can say that the political universalism of the papacy remained in the world of ideas and doctrinal programmes.

The real political triumphs of the papacy concerned Italy itself. At the height of its powers the papacy managed to create a system of political dependency in the rest of the Christian sphere among its rulers: at the time of Innocent III[55] the head of the Roman Church appeared in the role of arbitrator and master of Christian rulers, and he acquired direct feudal supremacy over kings and princes. The conflict between the papacy and the empire had the countries of the empire *sensu largo* (that is, including the empire's claims to supremacy over Christian countries) as territorial reference, and the subject of conflict was power over Western Christendom understood as empire. Innocent III exceeded these limits: he was actively interested in the countries of Central-East Europe, he meddled in Poland and Hungary, but he also went into the Balkan peninsula, acquired temporary supremacy over Bulgaria, and drew Bosnia and Serbia into the sphere of Roman influence and subordination to the pope.

In the most developed theocratic programmes the secular state was subjugated to God's state, the attributes of emperor were ascribed to the pope and it was the Church that was recognized as the *Imperium Romanum*.[56] Theological effort went towards justifying the political essence of the Church, which combined spiritual and secular elements. Thomas Aquinas, when considering indulgence rights, analysed the concept of the Church as *congregatio* and maintained that it was a collective body and also a political community, for it was the people (*populus*).[57] The Church also had to combine the practical performances of both powers. The traditional juxtaposition of 'priest' and 'soldier' would in this way be controlled. Among the titles of Gregory IX we read the following: 'vicar of almighty God, emperor of the heavens'. The universal Christian state *was* the Church.[58] This, however, was only a postulative doctrine, in deep discord with reality.

The idea of imperial unity – from the Carolingian structure to the dispute between emperor and pope about leadership in the *res publica christiana* – frequently altered its substance and its political and territorial references, and referred to various social powers. In the social imagination of the feudal era, marked by hierarchism and dependency, it was the crowning of political structures and the natural regulation of political order in the Christian community as *sui generis* 'of international society'.[59] It was important not only for doctrine, for the learned discourses of theologians and jurists; it influenced the consciousness of the political elites, it shaped a certain system of signs coded in political symbolism, common to all European Christianity,[60] and it made sure that the super-party idea of 'unity' endured as a lost reality or a programme reality, as 'recollections' in the collective memory, as legends, as possibilities. The tendencies of the development of political reality in medieval Europe did not, however, lead to imperial unity, but to the strengthening of sovereignty in national states. 'Roman' unity was realized to a wider extent in the cultural community *christianitas*.

CHRISTIANITAS AS A CULTURAL COMMUNITY

Christianitas as a fundamental concept uniting medieval Europe was not the realization of a universal mission on the part of Christianity, that *ordinatio ad unum* of the whole world in which the *humanum genus*, without exceptions, would have to find a place for itself.[61] It was a naturally religious and political structure that emphasized the extent of Rome's hegemony, the range of its influences and laws. It also differed from the concept of a Church[62] whose 'metaphysically unifying awareness'[63] supported a certain hierarchical order and above all allowed for the participation of members of the clergy in government. The concept of *christianitas* covered secular political reality and collective spiritual life at the same time. Roman power – which on the threshold of the second millennium seemed to have acquired two heads, with the pope and the emperor at the forefront – had to rest not only on the unity and cooperation of the institution but also on the common bond of the basic framework of religious life, on unity of cult, liturgy and collective forms of concern for salvation. Catholic unity was, after all, a product of the harsh battle for hegemony over beliefs and the collective mentality; the community of *christianitas* appeared in comparable relation to the victory of pagan beliefs and directions recognized as heterodox.[64]

A study of the conversion of the European peoples, a comparative history of which has not yet been written, reveals how awareness of the community of Western Christianity functioned. The religious *instrumentarium* of accepting a new faith was quite rudimentary, at least on a mass scale. The lives of the holy missionaries pointed to a more or less developed programme of Christianization, but always with the emphasis on the nature of the cult, on religious custom, and not on the truths of the faith.[65] We can recognize that the description in the life of Otto, Bishop of Bamberg, of the Christianization of western Pomerania is an account of a rich programme of conversion:[66] churches had to be built to serve God, according to Christian custom (*more Christianorum*) everyone was to fast on Friday and keep Sunday, the saints had to be honoured appropriately, Lent had to be observed, children had to be baptized on Easter Saturday and god-parents chosen for them, marriage between god-parents or relatives was not to be tolerated, and the dead could not be buried in forests or fields but in cemeteries, as Christian custom would have it (*sicut mos est omnium Christianorum*). Finally, Otto taught the people of Pomerania that they were not allowed to build temples to pagan gods, perform magic in any form or maintain contact with pagans; they were also required to attend church to make confession or call a priest to the house for that purpose and to undergo canonic penance in specific instances, and after childbirth women were supposed to obtain a blessing in church.

This inventory of practices permitted and forbidden demonstrates that conversion meant above all the abandonment of past habits and the acceptance of new ones, with particular emphasis on the external aspects of religious practices. This statement does not mean that collective conversions diminished in importance. The result, however, was that Christianization meant that the *mos Christianorum* spread and the customs and behaviour of various ethnic groups adapted to a combined canon of customs[67] that gave the Christian West a certain internal unity.

The concept of *christianitas*, finding support in a real community of culture and custom, expressed the state of a collective consciousness the social range of which was expanding during the Middle Ages. Papal universalism and the Crusade movement benefited from this concept as an effective instrument of propaganda. It did not exist only in the political field and the writings of the papal archives, or among learned jurists and theologians, publicists and poets. The cultural community was formed thanks to a unity of linguistic communication created by the universal function of Latin in Western Christianity, and thanks to a basic concurrence of liturgy, ritual and church building, the conformity of the basic rhythm of time as marked by Sundays and the principal annual holy days, and the comprehension of space and its sacred organization (such as inside churches, and in the inhabited and natural landscape). Even when conversion to Christianity was not deep-seated or total, when traditional beliefs lived alongside Christian practices and the doctrinal truths of the new faith had been poorly absorbed or even disseminated, collective conversion or membership of the Roman Church formed the basis of ties of culture and custom.

The migrations and changes taking place in the heart of the church elite strengthened these integrating processes in Western Christendom. Many of the clergy, especially those of higher rank, travelled to other countries, not only as part of their missionary duties, but as part of the normal practice of church life. The apostle of Germania, Archbishop of Mainz (from 747), St Boniface – one of the great builders of unity in *christianitas* – was after all an Anglo-Saxon, like Alcuin, adviser to Charlemagne, and Abbot of Tours from 796.[68]

While local clergy were being attracted to converted Poland, church hierarchies and monastic societies were constantly being strengthened by incomers from other countries: French, Germans, Italians. The Płock bishopric, founded during the reign of Bolesław the Bold, brought its dignitaries from France and Liège; in the twelfth century its bishops were as follows: Alexander of Malonne from the Liège region, Werner of Burgundy or perhaps of southern Germany, Wit, probably from a Polish knightly family, and then another foreigner, Lupus, believed to be of French origin.[69]

There were too few people in some countries, and too many in others, who were technically educated to perform church and state duties and to teach and carry out other intellectual functions, and this situation caused people to migrate, thereby contributing to the unification of the intellectual culture of Christendom.[70] The circulation of manuscripts and liturgical books, and of encyclopedic, scientific and literary works, fulfilled a similar role. In this way the material of medieval intellectual culture and the instruments of cult, erudition and writing converged, just as representational forms, preserved in the fine and decorative arts, were being circulated together with the movement of works of art and the migration of artists.

This affected the church and court elites above all: it was they who participated in these exchanges and benefited from them; they too played the fullest part in the cultural community of Christendom and were aware of it. This common substance of Christian culture was not shut away behind the walls of monasteries and cathedrals; even when popular preaching was poorly developed the spectacle of the liturgy was received by the masses, and church architecture, sculpture and painting was widely seen.[71] We could say that, when there was mass dissemination, cultural transfer became superficial and impoverished and less and less of its substance was understood and absorbed. The fact remained, however, that the community of intellectual culture and the considerable convergence of artistic culture within the sphere of Latin Christianity had a substantial influence on the masses and repercussions in the collective mind of a community of varying ethnic make-up and custom.

The element that strengthened these processes whereby an awareness of community bonds was formed was the great collective action of the Christian world, which involved 'political societies' above all, but in their wake the wider social spheres as well. These were the Crusades.

Research into the history of the Crusades, their aims and achievements, their national and social make-up, has revealed enormously varied situations.[72] Without going into the differences of each expedition, however, we can consider their overall significance. Ideas of unity in the Christian world, and of its common interests and activities, have crystallized around the subject of recapturing the holy places of Christendom. There was rivalry between the papacy and the empire during the course of the Crusades on the question of pre-eminence in governing the *res publica christiana*. The first expedition emerged at the turn of the eleventh century as a triumph for the papacy, to which the initiative of the movement, and then also its leadership, belonged, but the Crusades of the thirteenth century remained beyond the reach of papal supremacy; the great national powers of the Christian West affirmed themselves as guardians of the interests of Christianity and were in competition with each other in this role.[73]

These disputes apart, the idea of the crusade did exist; it was articulated in various ways in theological discourse and legal doctrine, but it also influenced the minds and emotions of the wider masses.[74] What is more, it was precisely at the mass level that this idea spread widely, and in reality. Some of the exhortations of the papacy met with indifference more than once among the rulers; political calculations were always involved. France's King Louis VII was ready to give up one-twentieth of his income, but did not risk participating in the expedition because he was afraid of what Henry II of England would do on the Continent; Frederick Barbarossa delayed supporting the crusader initiative of Alexander III because he preferred it to look as though the crusade was an imperial initiative; and there were many other similar examples. On the other hand the enthusiasm for the Crusades among the wider masses, and their zeal, remained unextinguished for a very long time.

After the first expeditions the idea of the Crusades seemed to gather force, independently of the disasters that befell the Latin state in the Holy Land, and the Crusaders; the crusade 'became a normal form of spiritual life in the Christian West'.[75] The pope's appeals to join the crusade were addressed first of all to knights who owned no land at home and men who possessed the skills of war.[76] These responded strongly, not only because they were tempted by hopes of high adventure or were attracted to leave the homelands in which they felt trapped, but also because the ideal of an 'order of knights' was being realized in the idea of the crusade. Failures in war and fortune weakened the enthusiasm of those groups for distant travel; the actual idea of armed service in the interests of Christian community retained its significance by creating a sense of supranational ties among the knights, and by spurring them on to participate in crusades on European soil.

The papal appeals aroused the enthusiasm above all of the masses in town and country; in their eschatological and apocalyptic fervour they joined the expeditions, disrupted organized military preparations and broke free of organization and order. The historian of the Crusades is forced to place a low value on the effectiveness of these people's fervour, but at the level of collective emotion it is difficult not to perceive the vital significance of these movements in the process whereby the collective consciousness of the Christian community was being formed. Intensified religious experience went hand in hand with social identification on a group macro-scale, within the wider framework of *christianitas*. Antisemitic disturbances, a series of pogroms, the significant places of enlistment in the folk crusades and their routes, are also evidence of these processes of collective identification; among the various motivations for these acts of hatred the predominant feature was enmity towards 'foreigners'.[77] A sense of 'familiarity', shaped according to the traditional local ties typical of society, was carried in this way to the widest circle, to the Christian community.

We should not judge the fact that the crusade movement extinguished the antagonisms between Eastern and Western Christianity in the name of a common interest: the defence of the holy places of Christianity. Even before the scandal of the Fourth Crusade, which went to Byzantium instead of Palestine, and conquered and plundered the shining, rich metropolis, there was considerable antagonism between Rome and Byzantium after the seal recently set on the split of Christianity (1054).[78] In effect the crusade idea was directed against the East's traditional preponderance as regards purity of Christian doctrine. The Crusades were the exclusive act of the Christian West, affirmation of its unity in the service of Christianity.[79]

Oriental influences, active even before the Crusades, exerted very strong pressure on the culture, customs and religious life of Western Christendom during the course of this movement. Independently of this, however, the cultural difference of Western Christianity in relation to Byzantium emerges and is consolidated during the course of the Crusades. Even without the evidence of the Fourth Crusade, the progress of the expeditions and the chronicle and literary evidence of the crusade movement indicated that there was no place for Byzantium and Eastern Christianity in the concept of *christianitas*, which formed a community tie around the Christian faith.[80]

Finally, there is the important social aspect of the crusade movement, extending beyond psycho-religious motivations: the migrations of people. In socio-historical and economic research into the genesis of the Crusades a finger has been pointed at the changes taking place at that time in the family structures of the aristocracy and knighthood, changes connected with the great demographic push that occurred during the first centuries of the second millennium. The appearance of a growing number of young men (*iuvenes*) in knightly society, the younger sons of the aristocracy who were unable to find positions for themselves worthy of their upbringing, created tensions within local structures.[81] There is evidence of similar processes of the collapse of family structures and relative overpopulation among peasant societies in the more rapidly developing regions of the West. It has been suggested that the famous Children's Crusade of 1212 was a movement made up precisely of social elements uprooted from the countryside and connected with the migrations of young people from the country, which were on a massive scale during this period.[82] The vital forces of the knights' crusade were being extinguished, but the crusade idea had passed into peasant society, rendering itself independent even of feudal society and adapting itself to the antagonistic aims of the down-trodden classes.[83]

Of interest to us here is the fact that the transference of the idea of the Crusades from knightly society to the country people is linked with an increasingly intense *prise de conscience* among the Christian community. The migrations, independently of socio-economic reasons and motivations, acquired a religious motivation because they appealed to the solidarity of the Christian community. These migrations after all strengthened the real ties within the Christian community, just like the migrations of clergy and intellectuals already mentioned. Within the migrating groups, those ties that were not supported by traditional local or even linguistic and ethnic structures intensified. The migrations that had developed out of the crusader spirit continued in the wanderings of farmers and artisans: the extension of French settlements in the direction of the Pyrenean peninsula, Flemish colonization or the great wave of German settlement in Central-Eastern medieval Europe[84] occurred with reference to the unity of the Christian world, and the resulting confrontations and ethnic mixtures influenced the tying of the threads of European unity.

The crusade movement also had significant consequences for the shaping of Christianity as a political community.[85] We have already discussed this matter in connection with the development of the imperial idea; here we need mention only the fact that the political aspirations of the papacy were connected with the widespread movement to reform church institutions and activities, the reconstruction of monastery life and the standardization of the way of life in Latin Christendom. The movement of Cluniac reform and its wide geographic range was proof of this process of standardization of church structures in the Latin West.[86] The history of the monasteries in later centuries would continue this process.

We can also examine the period when Europe was threatened by the Mongol invasions as being among the phenomena that crystallized the bond of Christian community in social reality and in the collective consciousness. The evidence of chronicles and the diplomatic activities of the papacy and the European courts reveal the extent of the great fear that gripped the countries of the European West and East in the first half of the thirteenth century. *Timor Tartarorum* seems to have been a universal feeling; correspondence between European rulers before the Mongol offensive of 1240–1, and after it was extinguished, expressed the terror that had seized European opinion. The first illusions about David, the Christian king of the Tartars who liberated the Holy Land and conquered (or exterminated) the Saracens, were rapidly dissipated. Terrifying news about the devastation of Hungary and detailed accounts of the Mongols and their victories in the East, in Ruthenia, Hungary and Poland, created an atmosphere of threat.[87]

The mendicant orders played a special part in spreading the news about the Mongol danger and in summoning the Christian rulers to join forces. The pope and the emperor were expected to act to unite the people; rival and conflicting initiatives issued from these two centres of command. Christendom's internal conflicts were exposed to the full and began to prevail over the sense of threat. But the point of reference in all the actions taken was the need to defend the joint interests of the Christian world. At the First Council of Lyons in 1245 Innocent IV pointed to the *insolentia Saracenorum, schisma Graecorum* and *sevitia Tartarorum* as representing a great danger for Christianity:[88] it is precisely these three threats that could be considered the external elements which led to the auto-identification of *christianitas*.

Was the 'great terror' of the Tartars really so widespread? This is not an easy question to answer. The source accounts available to us come from the clerical world; they reveal the state of knowledge, the moods and emotions of that society, and of the courts and great offices of state and Church. We can assume that information of this type passed from the elite to the masses with ease, since information of the 'panic' type travels particularly effectively.[89] The legends and stories that have been created relating to the Mongol world and the defence of Christendom against the Tartar invasion are evidence of the extent to which the Christian world was collectively sensitive to the threat hanging over it. How long this feeling lasted, and how strong it really was, can be ascertained only in those regions through which the Mongol invaders passed or which were under direct threat. It was in those countries that the help expected from other Christian countries created a bond among the Christian community, and where the people found hope at a time of collective fear. In the Christian countries of the West, on the other hand, the 'great terror' was a transitory episode, and the internal conflicts between rulers, the ineffectiveness of the crusade initiatives and the lack of enthusiasm for joint action pointed to the weakness rather than the strength of community ties in Christendom.

The geographical frontiers of medieval *christianitas* seemed to be defined obviously and somewhat automatically by the extent of political and religious conversion which, in the tenth century, delineated the eastern and northern boundaries of the Christian world. Within lay the Scandinavian countries and Hungary, and the Slav countries in which the influences of Greek and Latin Christianity crossed paths. Both Churches took part in the conversion of the Slavs following the activities of Cyril and Methodius, who introduced Christianity in the manner of a typical medieval process of conversion, in which government and religion, state and Church, were closely linked one with the other, and whoever was in power decided whether the process had been a success or a failure.

The actions of such men of the Church as St Wojciech (Adalbert) have ensured the presence of Latin Christianity in the Slav world. International echoes of the martyrdom of St Wojciech, the various descriptions of his life and death and the interest of the pope and the emperor are conclusive proof of the place occupied by the conversion of the Slav world in the Christian consciousness of this period.[90] St Wojciech's stay in Rome, in the Greek-Latin monastery of San Alessio on the Aventine, was also significant, not only because it led the Polish émigré bishop into the world of Greek asceticism, ecclesiology and liturgy, but also because it linked him with Rome.[91] It is an example of the integration of western Slav social elites into the Christian community, for whom Rome remained the spiritual and symbolic capital.

But the authoritative, political nature of early medieval conversion meant that, in the area of culture and beliefs, its effect on the masses was limited and slow. For this reason it was thought for a long time that the Slavs were not only *gens inculta*, as Bartholomew of England writes in the second half of the thirteenth century,[92] but that they lived like animals – according to the Florentine encyclopedist Brunetto Latini at the end of that century[93] – like all people who live at the edge of the world. Even up to the middle of the thirteenth century the Slav world remained on the periphery in the consciousness of the Christian world, which meant that, despite the conversion of their rulers, the Slav people would have been quite reluctant to join them in the cultural sphere of *christianitas*. The degree of awareness of the Christian community varied considerably: it seemed to weaken the closer its frontiers.

When collective action was required, medieval *christianitas* showed itself to be poorly united. In the spiritual life of the community, unifying ritualistic and cultural structures were imposed on local traditions and customs. Examples of a worthy life coincided; accepted or idealized models and norms were similar, like those considered reprehensible. Patterns of holiness circulated throughout Christian society. An important unifying element was the universality of the law throughout all *christianitas* in relation to church matters, and also to the ever wider range of questions concerning human behaviour and interpersonal relations.[94]

The ethos of knightly life fed on the legend of Mediterranean struggles and on northern tradition, and although it sounded different in the words of the troubadours of Provence, in the songs of the German Minnesänger or in Polish epics and historiography, it retained the universal dimension of the model *miles Christi*. Institutional church structures also possessed unifying characteristics, giving all *christianitas* a comparable, internally similar character.[95] But the *res publica christiana* was emerging with growing strength as a family of independent nations. The traditional centres of universalistic programmes, the papacy and the empire, suffered a profound crisis. At times of trial, such as during the Crusades or when confronting the Mongol danger, it turned out that, even if they were not in conflict with the culture and spiritual unity of *christianitas*, they at any rate did not display this unity and did not serve it.[96] The late medieval idea of Europe took as its starting-point the particularity of political and cultural structures in Europe.

TOWARDS A COMMON EUROPEAN BOND

The basic European political structures originate from the processes that formed the national states in the ninth to the eleventh centuries. The entire subsequent 'European millennium' retained the divisions created at that time, with the great collective bonds between nations and states to the fore.[97] Local connections and blood ties constituted the strongest feelings in the social consciousness; an awareness of wider unions was built up on these two forms of association. *Christianitas* created a mood of confessional and civil community on a mass scale. An awareness of cultural, ethnic and regional changes gradually emerged, however, within the framework of the community. A fourteenth-century French author gave expression to this, stating that Europe had been settled by Christian nations 'of various faiths'.[98]

Imperial and papal universalism failed to shape a sense of political community in the mass consciousness, and the crisis of imperial reality in the thirteenth century revealed – at least in the minds of political and intellectual elites – a lack of unifying structures whose universalism would respect the sovereign freedom of the national states.[99] The anti-imperial and anti-papal polemics of the fourteenth century[100] destroyed the moral and philosophical bases of the universalistic programmes of the *imperium mundi*, which were irreconcilable with a tough form of state sovereignty. The success of the European concept, which became increasingly widely employed in the fifteenth century, could also be explained by this aspect of the matter: it was a universalistic concept that did not upset the sovereignty of specific states, gave no superior authority to any rank, and did not award a specific mission or supremacy to any nation or state.

The occurrence of the European concept in the political and colloquial terminology of the late Middle Ages has been analysed in detail more than once.[101] The result has been a vast lexical search which has revealed that the word 'Europe' was used increasingly frequently during the fourteenth and especially the fifteenth century, and that it lost the connotation of geographical erudition of previous centuries. The semantic and historical argument is of vital importance for the subject of interest to us here. The function of words, the lexical and situational context in which they occur, the informational and emotive content of concepts and terms, demonstrate the state of collective awareness and also the processes and changes occurring in it. Research of this kind into the collective consciousness, however, demands mass documentation and long series of publications, as well as investigation of the most colloquial lexical material. Both these conditions have been poorly fulfilled in the case of the European concept in the vocabulary of the fourteenth and fifteenth centuries.

It is true that this word appeared with increasing frequency.[102]

In church polemics of the Avignon period, in conciliarist writings the question of the Church's geographical boundaries was of extreme importance. The fact that Avignon was closer *a finibus modernis ecclesie catholice* and was more centrally situated than Rome in relation to actual Catholic borders was treated as an argument in favour of this southern French town remaining the papal capital. Europe was also identified with Christianity because Christian rulers held power in only a few countries outside Europe.[103] The conflicts that arose at the Council of Constance over the principles of organizing into nations[104] also encouraged reflection on the geographical framework of church activities, and 'Europe' emerged then as a natural term. In this respect the argument put forward in the English memorandum at the Council of Constance on the subject of the statute of specific nations at the council was revelationary.[105]

The author of the memorandum drew on geographical erudition, pointing out that the earth was divided into three parts, Asia, Africa and Europe, while Europe was divided into four powers or even kingdoms (*regna*): those of Rome, Constantinople, Ireland (then continued by the English monarchy) and Spain. The domains of obedience to the pope in Europe were also divided into four parts. The memorandum mentioned the following regions in turn, together with the Churches subject to the pope in Europe:[106] the eastern region, to which Hungary, Bohemia, Poland and Germany belonged, the western region, made up of France and Spain, the north, encompassing England, Wales, Scotland and Ireland (and the islands belonging to them) plus Denmark, Sweden and Norway, and finally the south, made up of Italy and those of the Greeks who remained in obedience to Rome, that is the Cypriots and Cretans.

In this exposition, weighed down by medieval erudition and its traditional numerical classifications, the horizon of Europe revealed here and dealt with in three interconnected divisions – geographical, political and ecclesiastical-religious – carries particular weight. The concept of Europe no longer functions here as an antiquarian geographical term but is given a political and, more importantly, a religious sense. The emphasis that Christianity is understood as obedience to Rome is limited only to Europe (*sola Europa modo est christiana*, says one of the Council memoranda);[107] it also leads to identification in the other direction, to the introduction of a sign of equality between Europe and Christianity. The concept of Europe also appears in this sense from the pen of one of the leading representatives of intellectual culture in the fifteenth century, Enea Silvio.[108]

In ascertaining the limited circulation of the European concept we have no basis for treating a change in the extent of its use as evidence of mass awareness. The range of observations, however, concerns the furnace in which the key concepts of social awareness are forged. These reached a more commonplace circulation from discourses and council memoranda, from the works of learned jurists and encyclopedists; in the sixteenth century the concept of Europe and the words derived from its name entered everyday language. The word's change of function was an important sign. Its context indicated that it referred to a certain internal cohesion of people and countries on the one hand, and on the other to the inclusion of this collectivity in the widening horizon of the world of which Europe is a part.

At this first level we are dealing above all with the myth of unity, as constructed by the political and intellectual elite. Unity in the Carolingian era was a layer, thin and feeble, like the great bartering exchanges, long-distance trade, and distant relations between monasteries and between courts at that time. During the centuries that followed those relations between groups of people, those exchanges of goods, thoughts and customs increased enormously, but they also brought their particular character to the surface. A considerably more solid structure arose, with longer lasting foundations but local horizons. Instead of the wonderful market of objects from the whole world near medieval Pavia there were local stalls and regional markets. Exchanges and personal contacts of this kind also defined the awareness of collective ties.

The development of economic life energized the exchange of goods along the land and river routes of the European continent and on all European sea coasts.[109] This exchange formed links between the far-flung corners of Europe. Differences in natural resources and in the degree of economic advance and asynchronism in the development of creative powers and in the evolution of social relations created far-reaching economic interdependence. This lay at the basis of the geographical division of work on the macro-scale, and therefore of regional and national specialization in certain types of production: the cloth trade in Flanders, mining in Central Europe or wheat and animal production in Poland, for example.

We should not overestimate the range of these specializations and the economic interdependence that went with them, especially where small-scale production of luxury goods was concerned. The general tendency was to aim for balance in the development of various branches of production within individual regions and countries. What is more, those international and inter-sphere economic links led to widespread consolidation of local, regional and national alliances; precisely this type of connection was to be seen in the organization of corporate life, in large-scale commerce, in merchants' travels and in the organization of markets. The wide horizon of connected interests had appeared at the level of town activities, but more in the form of competitive relations than of European solidarity.

Economic connections on an overall European scale were also given expression by a certain synchronism in the market situation. Economic indicators, movement in earnings and prices, the circulation of money and credit and, finally, the fundamental developmental trends of the agrarian economy indicate a common rhythm in economic life in late medieval Europe.[110] Research has pointed out the diversity of elements defining this 'pulsating' convergence in the European economy, among them climatic changes, the community of settlements on a continental scale and similarities in basic economic structures within the European sphere at this period. But an anachronism in the formation of specific spheres of European development was revealed with force in the changes that took place in the fourteenth and fifteenth centuries: when the West experienced a structural crisis in the fourteenth century it was the European East in fact that entered a dynamic period of its development.

Critical differences in the evolution of social structures in the countries of medieval Europe stood out, the consequences of asynchronism in economic development. The differences in production structures, and different specializations in the macroscale in the West (and South) and the East (and North), that were already obvious in the fourteenth and fifteenth centuries, and which were to define the modern era, were extended in differences of social development and of the arrangement of social forces in relations between town and country, and among gentry, peasantry and townspeople. But we can also observe certain common features which go beyond general similarities in the feudal condition, and these concern the role of the aristocracy and the gentry.

The significance of the aristocracy and the gentry in the social order provides a link between the histories of European societies up to the turn of the eighteenth century. Independently of their different foundations, and economic functions in specific developmental spheres, it fell to the gentry to occupy the foreground of the historical scene; it was they who secured power and prestige for themselves and occupied leading positions in state and Church.[111] Their life style and social attributes made their mark on the whole form of social life. The heraldic signs of affiliation and origin were a language that forged links on an overall European scale. The gentry manor house as a sociological model and as a type of 'domestic economy'[112] shaped the life of traditional societies up to the time of the industrial revolution, and was also reflected in the organization of the town house and even the peasant home. The model of the life of the knight and the landowner was a universal ethos which created a specific hierarchy of values for the entire social consciousness; all social levels would adapt to it, even when they pronounced themselves against it.

The model knight-cum-landowner that has grown out of a syncretic adaptation of the 'barbarian' ideals of a war-mongering life into the Christian concept of division of social roles and into economic reality would seem to paraphrase the entire evolution of European societies. It passed from one far-flung corner of Europe to another, together with the acculturation processes taking place during the Middle Ages, and retained its basic characteristics at the courts of the French kings and of the Dukes of Lithuania, so recently converted. Admittedly we can find certain similarities in the social situation outside Europe (Japanese analogies have already been pointed out in research into feudal institutions), but this does not alter the fact that the role of the nobility and its culture, as described in this way, constitutes a link between European societies.

We can also describe the specific roles of European towns and town culture in a similar way. In his sociology of the town Max

Weber outlined the basic differences between Islamic, Indian and Chinese towns, which formed a type of 'oriental' town, the towns of the ancient world buried in country surroundings and the towns of medieval Europe.[113] European urbanization has taken root in two distinct forms: first of all, in the development of networks of towns, which are the basis for the circulation of the blood of economic life and which form themselves into hierarchic structures, and secondly, in the separation of the town from the social landscape, in far-reaching differentiation between craft-cum-industrial and agricultural production, between town and country.[114] Towns would strive for autonomy as a consequence of their different situation; this would lead to the social emancipation of the townspeople and the formation of an urban ideology, that is, the articulation of the townspeople's separateness. The differences between Florence, Ghent and Poznań in demographic and spatial size, in the character and style of buildings and in the degree of wealth were enormous, but there remained some basic common elements: the primary importance of production and trade, the density of population, the specific organization of space and the urban centres, the corporate organization of social life, and specific privileges of town society.

In this way the outside observer can see vital common features in the social landscape of late medieval Europe. For the people of the Middle Ages these common features appeared to a limited extent. The wanderings of knights, court life, international tournaments, diplomatic activity, participation in crusades overseas or in Europe – including the Crusades in Prussia, organized by the Teutonic knights – formed the basis for knowledge of this community. Literature also made its contribution. In the towns the travels made by merchants, the migration of specialists and the wanderings of journeymen played a similar role. The techniques of trade and money circulation required a knowledge of the relations between various measures, currencies and prices on the European markets, a knowledge of different countries, towns and great firms. Town councils also communicated events and matters of common interest among themselves, independently of state boundaries. And these contacts were established within certain spheres of influence and relations, and relations subsequently within their framework became closer. In order to be aware of the limited contacts between specific European countries, suffice it to mention the bewildering impression that contact with Italy made on the French knights in the period of Italian expeditions at the close of the fifteenth century.

Medieval universalisms crumbled in the face of reality, but each of them left lasting traces in the collective consciousness in the form of certain systems of reference. Appropriate community ties were formed by processes initiated by the lower ranks, and by an increasing influx of news, objects and people. The most powerful and lasting legacy was undoubtedly that of the community of Latin Christianity, which made a certain view and understanding of the world and society universal on a vast scale, which possessed a common rhythm of time – the result of the syncretic construction of the church calendar – and the culture of which fed on similar or shared written material. In the intellectual domain we see a common mentality and sensitivity, visible in people's reactions and collective imaginations; the origins of these common features should not be restricted to the inspiration of the Church, to shared written or artistic sources, but should also be linked with the common elements of living and life style mentioned earlier.[115]

The European cultural community's specific *prise de conscience* occurred of course in medieval intellectual circles, above all in the universities. Medieval universities,[116] considered by thirteenth-century scholastic thought along with *sacerdotium* and *regnum*, to be a third ruling force in the world, remained closely connected with the universal mission of the Church; they cultivated the idea of a community of learning and thought. At the close of the Middle Ages the universities were connected increasingly closely with national monarchies – a situation also reflected in university geography and new university foundations – and took on a national character.[117] That service to the monarchy was expressed in concrete activities, in diplomatic undertakings, in the work of ecumenical councils and in polemical and historical writings. In this last area university, monastery and chancellery intellectual centres produced ethnographical treatises in which the origins of the people were entered into biblical genealogy, the history of peoples or tribes known from history, or historical events described by ancient chroniclers.[118]

It is significant that, in the structures of expositions on the subject of national histories of peoples living on the periphery of medieval Christianity, not only were there imaginary entries about their participation in historical events of the Greco-Roman world, but they were also included in the biblical genealogy of European peoples to whom the Bible (Genesis 9: 25–7) and patristic writing attributed common origins from Japhet.[119] There exists an awareness, evident in medieval writings and in school teaching, that behind the geographical concept of Europe there lies a certain reality, a certain community, and it is a community best understood by the people of this period because it is bound by origins and blood ties.

All collectivities acquire a particularly harsh self-knowledge or form an awareness of their differences on coming into contact, in a hostile or peaceful manner, with another community. At the close of the Middle Ages two vitally significant phenomena emerge: the Turkish danger and expansion towards other continents.

The 'great terror' of the Tartars in the thirteenth century, which we have mentioned, was a transitory phenomenon with limited scope, whereas Turkish expansion in the centuries that followed constituted a universal and total threat to the entire Christian world.

There was no comparable situation in European diplomacy. Both the papacy and the national monarchies sought contact with the Porte, and they deliberated the same Turkish problem from the internal European perspective of political arrangements and basic conflicts on the international political scene.[120] The political attitudes towards the Turkish question that stood out were primarily the function of the interests of specific states, and were expressed in the formation and intensification of national feeling.

Turkish expansion, coming ever closer to Europe, had certain unifying effects, however. In the political sphere there were attempts to unify the efforts of Christian rulers in order to meet Turkish expansion head on, and together. These attempts were initiated principally by the papacy in the traditional crusader spirit, but they were unsuccessful in bringing about any universal action, either at the end of the fourteenth or during the fifteenth century; the crusader idea no longer had any support in the Christian community, and dislike of the theocratic idea of a 'Christian monarchy', and of imperial universalism, meant that the papal crusade initiative held no appeal, and plans for a 'Christian league' fell apart.

The undertaking of the Bohemian King Jiři of Podiebrad, who in 1462 proposed a plan for an alliance of Christian rulers, was of considerably greater significance.[121] There were precedents for a plan of this kind,[122] but earlier proposals for a union of European monarchs had come from publicists and legislators, whereas this time the initiative came from one of the monarchs, influenced by a direct threat from a 'common enemy'. The initial formulations of that *Tractatus pacis totae Christianitati fiendae* indicated the miserable state of the Christian world at the time, once the *aurea provincia* and now in total disarray, and so weak that the Turks could extend their borders without reprisal, thereby seizing huge areas of Africa and Asia. Nothing could stop them any more: after occupying the Greek empire they started to take Christian provinces and kingdoms.[123]

The ambiguity of the concepts employed here is highly significant; first the geographical names of two parts of the world, then the Greek empire, then *christianitas*, which is identified solely with Europe. The initiative of internal peace for opposition to the external enemy is directed at the monarchs and establishes a solidarity of activities within the sovereign laws of each state; the Turkish danger is not therefore exploited as an argument for universalism. The failure of the plan put forward by Jiři of Podiebrad, who obtained the support of Mathias Korwin and Kazimierz Jagiellończyk but did not succeed in dispelling the mistrust of Louis XI, is evidence of particularism within Europe.

The Turkish question produced more profound, far-reaching results in the realm of social awareness. There was widespread interest in the Turks; historiographical works did not only record the actual course of events but also referred to the Turkish past; literature preserved evidence of the geographical and ethnographical interest in the Turks in the fifteenth century.[124] This went back after all to earlier accounts of the Turks. The invention of printing served the spread of knowledge about the Turks; tracts and descriptions of the Turkish danger appeared. In a fifteenth-century work we find the argument – repeated after the report made by the Venetian envoy Bernardo Giustiniani to the pope – that over a period of twenty-six years the perfidious Turk managed to defeat two empires (Byzantium and Trabzon), four kingdoms, twenty provinces and two hundred towns.[125] Accounts of Turkish customs mostly contained various *fabulae seu ficticia*, as Gyorgy of Hungary wrote in his own description of Turkish customs.[126] The author himself had reasons to demand that his evidence be believed. In 1436, as a 15- or 16-year-old boy, he was taken captive by the Turks and remained with them for over twenty years. He could therefore tell the European reader: 'how terrible, how dreadful is the sect of Turks.'[127]

The so-called *Memoirs of a Janissary* are similar in tone; this is a Turkish chronicle, written in the last years of the fifteenth century by Konstanty Michałowicz, a Serb from Ostrowica, who settled in Poland after eight years of service in the sultan's guard.[128] Written thirty years after the author's return to live among Christians, the chronicle is above all a work of political propaganda, intended to rouse people to Christian unity in the struggle against the Turks. A bitter tone towards pope and emperor, and also the Christian monarchs, emerged from Konstanty's experiences of agitation. He connects hope for crusade action mainly with Olbracht. His *Memoirs* are intended to bring about a crusade, and he combines information about the Turks with descriptions of their lawlessness.

More important than this agitation, however, is the fact that the reader is offered a certain description of customs, presented principally in contrast to Christian customs. We can treat this as evidence of Christian ethnocentricity, but it is obvious that a knowledge of new, exotic geographical and cultural areas intensifies the feeling of our own sense of being different and strengthens ties of solidarity. Both knowledge of the Turks and awareness of the danger of Turkish expansion create circumstances that support the development of a sense of community interests and ties linking countries in the European circle.

Expansion beyond Europe, and the associated progress of knowledge and geographical technique, also led to the development of a European awareness.[129] Only a few European countries took an active part in this expansion, but before any great discoveries the geographical horizon of medieval Europe changed fundamentally. A distant region which had long been the subject of tales recounted by medieval man,[130] who took mental possession of the area by investing it with certain qualities, gradually became known.

Travellers' tales can confirm this fairy-tale view: Marco Polo visited the vast areas of Asia and lived there a long time, but his account is above all a narration about the wonders of life and nature, about entirely different customs, which contemporary criticism 'places among fairy-tales' and which were received by the people at the time as fairy-tales both for what was invented and for what was true.[131] The effect of this complicated curiosity was in each case a growing sense of the difference and separateness of the peoples of Christian Europe in respect of other continents.

The techniques of sailing were being developed, and so a cartographical picture of overseas areas was necessary for the pocket maps and portolanos used increasingly universally from the fourteenth century. The name 'Europe' was entered on these maps as a concept in circulation;[132] there is no doubt that this was evidence of the place that the concept of Europe was beginning to occupy in the social consciousness, in knowledge of the world as a constellation of countries, religions and civilizations.[133] The concept taken from the inventory of school knowledge, both abstract and pedantic, such as grammatical and mnemotechnical rules, thereby took on a life of its own in this way, extended its conceptual range, and became an essential ingredient of the intellectual culture of the late Middle Ages.

The work of the leading humanist of the fifteenth century, Enea Silvio Piccolomini, later Pius II, is evidence of particular significance in this regard.[134] Pius II's active interest in the Turkish question and his efforts to find a way out of the danger are well known. In a famous letter to Mehmed II he proposed that he convert to Christianity, promising him in return the administration of 'all Greece, all Italy, all Europe', and perhaps even the Eastern empire.[135] He tried to bind the Christian rulers into alliances, pointing out that it was the duty of all Christianity, and not just of those bordering countries under direct threat, to conquer the Turks. But he also involved himself in the matter as a humanist; he read tracts about the Turks, and in his historical and geographical works the Turkish question seemed to provide one of the important incentives to finding out about the world at that time. This last task was served above all by the monumentally conceived *Cosmographia*.[136] The work was not realized in its entirety, but the treatise on Europe[137] is recognizable as a completed project.

In it Enea Silvio carried out a survey of European countries from the point of view of facts connected with them and worth remembering.[138] The order of the descriptions of specific countries is rather surprising: the treatise begins with Hungary, then discusses the countries of the Balkan peninsula, from where it passes to a description of the history and customs of the Turks;[139] as well as anti-Turkish battles and the heroes of these battles – Hunyadi and Skanderbeg – there follows a description of Poland, Lithuania, Livonia, Prussia, Saxony, Thuringia, three Scandinavian countries, Bohemia, Holland, France, Franconia, Bavaria, Alsace, Lorraine, England, Scotland, Spain and finally Italy. This last description, of Italy, is the fullest; it takes up 18 chapters out of 66. Besides Italy, the specific positions of the lands of the empire are clear. Both from the text and from the order of description – which does not seem to be the result of a pamphlet type of work – comes Enea Silvio's special interest in the border lands of the Christian world, for its frontier in retreat before the thrust of Turkish expansion.

The technique employed by Enea Silvio for presenting or understanding the area is very significant. A narrative with those *gesta memoratu digna* is constantly woven into the geographical description, in which there is evident concern for scientific accuracy and the precise use of terminology. Thus the area can be understood through the fictionalization of its description. Together with a humanistic elegance of discourse and respect for knowledge there is also a traditional feature, significant for the medieval mind; nor did the turn of the Renaissance break the continuity of this long cultural duration. This also had an effect on understanding the concept of Europe; in this way Europe was connected with a certain memory of the past, and acquired cultural substance.

Enea Silvio employed the concept of Europe widely and constantly. The adjectival form 'European', in contrast with 'Asiatic', also appeared from his pen;[140] he wrote about 'Europeans', a term which had a longer tradition but was rarely used. It is obvious that in humanistic Latin these words sounded better than the term *christianitas*; after all, Enea Silvio himself clearly emphasized the fact that he identified the concept of the Christian with that of the European (for example, in the foreword to his treatise on Europe).[141] But the need to emphasize this identification is evidence of the effort used to adapt the conceptual apparatus to the new reality.

The Turkish question which returned constantly in the works of Enea Silvio (he even mentioned anti-Turkish activities in his description of Spain) also occurred in the context of separating Europe from Asia, and of defining the borders of Europe. In the face of the Turkish threat a special role would be ascribed in the consciousness of Western people to the countries of the eastern frontiers of Europe.[142] Kallimach's voice on the subject of Poland as the only effective barrier against Turkish expansion in the Christian world would be taken up by Machiavelli and the leading representatives of sixteenth-century thought.[143]

The learned circles of the fifteenth century were aware that concepts in current use were not very precise. Lorenzo Valla, in his famous critical exposition on the gift of Constantine, considers also the fragment of a document in which Constantine apparently relinquishes towns and lands in the West to Silvester; while pointing out the stylistic and erudite awkwardness of the counterfeiter – the creator of the document – Valla then poses the significant question (XIX, 61): 'what are the borders of the West? Where do they begin? Where do they go? Are the terms West and East, South and North as certain and defined as Asia, Africa, Europe?'[144] The Italian humanist already ascribes a certain precision to these last names, accepting that the frontiers of the continents are known in geography. In relation to Europe, fifteenth-century thought stops, however, before the analogous question which Valla posed in relation to the West. The eastern frontier of Europe, which separated it from Asia, was ambiguous.

While describing the division of inhabited areas in Asia, Africa and Europe, Enea Silvio clearly demarcates the northern and southern borders of this last: it is marked out from the south by the expanse of the territories of Spain, Italy and the Peloponnese, from the north by the lands of Germany and Norway.[145] The geographical erudition of ancient times and the Middle Ages had no difficulty in defining the remaining borders of Europe. From the west it was the Atlantic, from the east it was the Don and the Meotyda Marshes (or the Sea of Azov).[146] When, however, a certain civil whole was seen as a geographical concept, when Europe was identified – as it was by Enea Silvio – as being one with

Christianity, then the problem of the borders became more complicated.

It was necessary above all to cope with the post-Byzantine succession. We have stressed that the community to which the prehistory of the European bond was ascribed was formed in definite opposition to Byzantium. The fall of the Eastern metropolis, however, alters the situation fundamentally. Enea Silvio does not hesitate in the face of the Turkish danger to link the Greek Church with Latin Christianity, not on the path of political systems but in the name of deep-seated solidarity.[147] Together with the fall of Constantinople the Christian community (*christianitas*) lost its eye and its arm,[148] while at the same time Pius II examined the territories of the Greek Church as representing part of the Christian community. In a letter to Mehmed II he wrote of the Christian East with obvious nonchalance, but he had the Nestorians and the like in Asia or Africa in mind, while Europe, as a synonym for Christianity, also occupied the legacy of the Greek Church.

This was certainly not just an ideological concession but also a certain political ploy by Rome, which had not desisted in its attempts to rebuild unity within the Church on the basis of introducing order to papal power. The treatment of Christian Europe as a fatherland was important above all for this thesis: this was the danger that threatened us 'in Europe, that is, in the fatherland, in our own home, in our habitat'.[149] The frontier of this fatherland was more concerned with faith (hence the minimalization of the importance of Christians in the East) and civilization than with geography and politics. The horizon of the Byzantine empire fitted into it; it was an important novelty in relation to earlier centuries.

But the eastern continental border of Europe had also to be delineated. This was connected with difficulties not only because of the weak state of geographical erudition at the time, or of a poor knowledge of Eastern Europe in ancient and medieval literature,[150] but also because of the varying fate of Christianity in this part of Europe. The vicissitudes of the Church's battle with Hussitism, the failure of Latin missions to Ruthenia*, the great Polish Crusades debate about the degree of Christianization of

* Ruthenia is used in this translation for the area sometimes called 'Rus'; similarly Ruthenian is used for 'Rus'ian'.

Lithuania and the authenticity of Jagiełło's conversion encouraged a certain mistrust towards the durability of links between that Slav Europe and the European or Christian community. The baptism of Lithuania was, however, a fact of fundamental value for the European consciousness, for it was in that way that the last European state was Christianized; not until that moment was it possible to confirm Europe's sense of identity with Christianity. The neophytism of the power of the Jagiellonian monarchs was in accord with the general character of Central-Eastern European cultural structures, and it could also become a favourable circumstance for the development of a sense of European bond. Was there room in this community, however, for Ruthenia?

Both the Polish-Lithuanian monarch and Hungary traditionally maintained relations with Ruthenia; the situation there remained constantly on the political horizon of these states and this part of Europe. A sense of the danger of the Turks among the people at that time, as we have mentioned, was combined with memories of the Mongol invasion, of which Ruthenia, a Christian country, was a victim in the fullest sense. The people of the late Middle Ages saw no obstacle in embracing the lands and people of Ruthenia in the name 'Europe' and in maintaining her traditional physical border on the Don,[151] even when the physical division was considered the same as the civil division. Sporadic attempts to define the Volga as a European border also took place in the fifteenth[152] and sixteenth centuries,[153] but they were not very successful. European *prise de conscience* was linked both with recognition of Europe's place in the world at that time and with the progress of knowledge about Europe itself: understanding the eastern frontiers of Europe was part of this process in which the European East ceased to be *terra ignota*.[154]

This frontier begins to be treated as a 'shield', and later as a 'bulwark' of Europe. The terms *scutum* and *antemurale* can also be applied to Hungary and to Jagiellonian Poland, especially after the battle of Warna. The lands of schismatic Ruthenia were not treated in this way in Western opinion; the Latin West tended to think of schismatics as being like 'Saracens' but, in the face of the expansion of the crescent, the cross played a demarcating role on the other side. Understanding the European East progressed in the footsteps of ancient geography, and especially those of Ptolemy, whose work underwent a renaissance in the late Middle

Ages.[155] Eastern Europe's place in the writings of Enea Silvio, and in the historico-geographical and cartographical works of Nicolas of Kuza, hailed from an ancient tradition. Following this tradition, the lands of 'Scythia' and 'Sarmatia' appeared in descriptions of the geographical and cultural community of Europe. The sign of the cross and inclusion in ancient tradition made room in the European awareness also for Ruthenia, that distant European East.

Ancient geographical and cartographical tradition divided Central and Eastern Europe between Germania and Saxonia, recognizing the Vistula as the border dividing the two countries.[156] Research into the concept of Sarmatia has revealed that it was apparently most successful from the second half of the fifteenth century,[157] at the same time as the expansion of the concept of Europe. In the works of chroniclers, historians, cosmographers and geographers there are numerous references to Sarmatia. It occurs in significant contexts in Jan Długosz.[158] When he said that the 'Ocean of the North', that is, the Baltic, was also called *Mare Sarmaticum*, he explained the latter name by saying that the Sarmatians, that is, the Poles, had lands and towns on its coast.[159] He also used the terms Sarmatian Alps and Sarmatian Mountains[160] to indicate the Carpathians. He frequently recognized the Sarmatians and the Poles as being one and the same. In addition he used the definition *Sarmacia Europica*, indicating, however – this is a very crucial remark in the history of geographical writing – that early writers and historiographers also defined both the Poles and the Ruthenians as Sarmatians, just as he called the mountains dividing the Poles and the Ruthenians from the Hungarians Sarmatian.[161]

Długosz's *Chorografia* takes as its starting-point a description of Europe in which the biblical genealogy of Japhet and an exposition on the separation that was taking place between specific peoples as regards language, laws, rites and beliefs[162] were combined with a geographical description of Europe, starting from the borders of the Don. In this geographical-cultural description of Europe the Slav world was introduced particularly tellingly, as it was given a place among the Japhets, and at the same time its distant origins, the famous deeds of its ancestors and its overall wealth were mentioned as being important.[163] The emphasis that Byzantium lay in Europe was also of significance;[164] this statement was clearly polemical in the context of the whole exposition which, after all, was intended and announced as being a description of Europe. The Ruthenian lands were also described in the *Chorografia* – to the extent to which they appeared on the political horizon of the Jagiellonian monarchy. Długosz gave the concept of Ruthenia above all an ethnic character, while he used 'Moscovia' more rarely and rather as a political concept.[165] It is crucial, however, that Długosz included the Ruthenian lands and peoples in the geographical contours and historical fates of Europe, in the history of the Japhets, among the heirs of Negno, just like the other Slav peoples,[166] and also in the history of Rome.[167]

In the intellectual work of Cracow University the subject of Europe and the European East was continually present. It certainly occupied some place in the university's teaching. The example of Jan of Głogów is of particular significance.[168] In the incunabula of Ptolemy's *Cosmography*, as published in Ulm in 1486, a note written by Jan of Głogów in 1494 has been preserved[169] (which Bujak recognized as an outline of a geography lecture at Cracow University),[170] and the same author certainly also wrote the treatise *Introductorium cosmographiae*, a commentary on Ptolemy.[171]

In his description of the parts of the world Jan resorted to comparisons to simplify his text in the tradition of medieval mnemotechnics. He compared Asia to a great and powerful bear, while he presented Europe in the form of a winged dragon: its head was reaching to the northernmost points (*cardines*) of the world, the throat represented Livonia, the wings were Hibernia and Albion, the legs were the Balkan and Apennine peninsulas, the trunk was Panonia with Datia, and the tail, Spain, *gultur Poloni et Lituani possidunt, femora Germani et Galli occupunt*. Such an image of Europe (medieval and modern cartography abounded also in images of Europe as a woman or as a queen) went beyond erudite pedantry; it could have been more widely known. A complete understanding of Europe – in which lie the countries of the Jagiellonian monarchy, Poland and Lithuania – is important here.

The concept of Sarmatia, which, in geographical writings of the time tended to increase its range, was extended to these countries, to the entire Jagiellonian monarchy, during the fifteenth century.[172] The aim of including Ruthenian lands in a description of Europe, clear in Długosz's *Chorographia*, did not prevail in geographical writings at that time. In one of Jan of Głogów's notes in Ptolemy's *Cosmographia* we find Moskovia identified with Asian Sarmatia,[173] and thus the separation of the lands of the state of Moscow from Europe. Without overrating the degree of universality of this opinion, however, we can recognize it as one of the prevailing directions among fifteenth-century litterati. The most crucial fact is that the ancient differentiation between European and Asian Sarmatia was identified with the border between Europe and Asia:[174] once more we can see the imposition of the ethno-cultural division on the geographical division. The extension of the range of the concept of Sarmatia and its distribution in cultural circles in the fifteenth and sixteenth centuries reflected the entry of Central-Eastern Europe into the European consciousness.

The treatise written by Maciej of Miechów in 1517 about Asian and European Sarmatia,[175] that 'first modern geography of the European East',[176] constitutes a summary of medieval knowledge in this area and an attempt to apply it to reality. A score of editions of the works of Maciej of Miechów, Italian, Polish and Dutch translations, and more than one German one, prove how important and popular was the work. The geographical treatise goes together with the ethnographical and historical description; and in this case we can also observe the fictionalization of space, significant for the mentality of the time. Maciej of Miechów abandoned identification of the Jagiellonian monarchy with European Sarmatia:[177] by marking the borders of the latter, in agreement with the ancient borders, on the Vistula and Don, he ascribed only the Ruthenians, Lithuanians and Samogitians or Muscovites to it; on the other hand he sited Asian Sarmatia, or Scythia, between the Don and the Caspian Sea, maintaining that it was ruled by the Tartars, who had expelled or conquered the previous inhabitants.

As distinct from Scythia or Tartary, Maciej of Miechów placed Ruthenia, Lithuania and Samogitia, and the state of Moscow, in the European circle. In the course of the description he continually employed comparisons with other European towns and rivers, especially those of Italy; he explained this in an obvious manner by the fact that the work had a Western addressee (and perhaps an Italian one in particular) whom this comparison enabled to imagine unknown countries. But these comparisons also introduced new countries to the cultural map of Europe. When describing the Grand Duchy of Lithuania Maciej noted that 'there are more animals in the forests than in any Christian country'; he compared Wilno with Cracow, Novgorod with Rome, Moscow with Florence and Prague.[178] In his description of Moskovia we can discern a different note. In his polemics with the opinions that had been held till then about this country he first of all adjusted the geographical imprecisions (which made him famous in humanistic learned circles), then he informed the reader about the alleged nomadism of the country's inhabitants[179] and, finally, communicated the fact that in Moscow 'there exists only one Ruthenian, or Slavonic, language', and also that the Greek rite predominated there, while the bishops were subject to the Patriarch of Constantinople, and only the Kazan Tartars were pagans, like their kinsmen in Asian Sarmatia.[180] In the description of the state of Moscow we do not come across any facts about the history or organization of the Church, as in the case of the remaining countries of European Sarmatia. This was perhaps the result not only of a lack of precise or verified facts on that matter, but also of a sense of how this region differed from the remaining lands of European Sarmatia.

We have spent some time with the geographical and ethnographical ideas of Długosz, Jan of Głogów and Maciej of Miechów in order to show above all how the question of Europe's separation from Asia, especially in its civil aspect, appeared and was accurately defined in the consciousness of the educated elite of Eastern Europe. In research into European unity in the Middle Ages the question of the place of Ruthenia and the state of Moscow was the subject of constant dispute.[181] The actual outline of this border, its foothold in the Urals, in accordance with the modern geography of Europe (which was not finally established until the nineteenth century, however), or also its westward progression, was a secondary matter. In effect the subject of the dispute was the genesis of 'Russia's break with Europe'.[182] Historical fate, international connections, the system of rules and basic cultural structures of Kievan Rus meant that its inclusion in the European circle of civilization was accepted without great opposition.[183] On the other hand processes for excluding that region from Europe were sometimes sought in the Mongolian conquests and also in the unifying actions of the Moscow princes. The marriage in 1472 of Ivan III to Zofia, the niece of the last Byzantine emperor and heiress to the splendours of the Paleologues, was treated as a powerful element in the rebuilding of the ideology of Moscow – the 'third Rome' – and evidence of the foreignness of the state of Moscow in relation to the European community, of which Rome was the centre.[184]

Leaving to one side the political actualization of this question and the presentist tendency in the analysis of the whole question of the eastern borders of European civilization, we can state that the quarrel was above all historiographical in character.[185] It concerned the question of which geographical and civil horizon modern and contemporary European awareness was referring to, which historical tradition it lived by and which one it perpetuated. Reflection on European unity in the Middle Ages must approach this problem in another way and should answer the question of the place occupied by the subject of the eastern frontiers of the European circle in the super-regional European links and elements of European awareness that were being formed during the late Middle Ages.

While following the universalistic communities that were being formed during the ten centuries of the Middle Ages, we have also noticed that they were reflected in the collective consciousness. These were above all programming structures, proposed in propaganda activities by elite societies, and not a collective sense of bonds and solidarity. This is connected of course with documentary difficulties such as the fact that we lack classical documentation of the social consciousness for the medieval period. Research into the social awareness of the people of the Middle Ages rarely allows us to ascertain the sense of great, super-local ties. For the existence of the people was entangled above all in local ties. The development of economic and social life in the last centuries of the Middle Ages led to extended international relations, to the formation of connections and regional structures. Medieval consciousness retains a local horizon, however. In the minds of the people of this period all connections appeared above all as blood ties and the bonds between neighbours. Small groups and the collective solidarities that suited them formed in both these areas. But family, village and parish did not limit the horizon of the social awareness of the period: wider ties – regional, national, supranational – were built up on them.

The most important thing is that it was precisely these small groups and small solidarities that were also the models for the bonds on the macro-scale. In the category of blood ties medieval historians discussed the historical fates of Europe; in the category of neighbourhood they made a morphological description of European geography. In such a form – that of a sense of blood tie and of bonds between neighbours – only then could European awareness forge a path for itself away from elite societies towards wider groups. It was, however, a process by which this awareness passed from intellectual elites to social elites, up to the turn of the Middle Ages; the masses remained only slightly under its influence. It was the shock of geographical discoveries, the acceleration of the circulation of information and writing thanks to the cultural revolution – print – the growth of trading exchanges and the international division of work that permitted this awareness to become more commonplace. The first two centuries of the modern period introduced the concept of Europe permanently into intellectual circulation and social consciousness.

Notes

1 There is an extensive bibliography of the subject *inter alia* in R. J. Sattler, *Europa, Geschichte und Aktualität des Begriffes*, Braunschweig, 1971.
2 Here we should mention the exceptional importance of O. Halecki's works on the history of European unity in which Central-Eastern Europe secures a place for itself in the debate on European history. Cf. O. Halecki, *Europa: Grenzen und Gliederung seiner Geschichte*, Darmstadt, 1957, p. xiii [list of his works].
3 Cf. R. S. Lopez, *Naissance de l'Europe*, Paris, 1962; H. Dannenbazer, *Die Entstehung Europas: von der Spätantike zum Mittelalter*, Stuttgart, 1959–63, vols I-II; G. Labuda, 'Powstanie Europy średniowiecznej' [The rise of medieval Europe], *Kwartalnik Historyczny*, LXXII, 1965, pp. 153–8.
4 R. H. Foerster outlines the political problem of the concept of Europe in antiquity in *Europa: Geschichte einer politischen Idee*, Munich, 1967, pp. 11–27; D. de Rougemont, *Vingt-huit siècles d'Europe*, Paris, 1961, pp. 9–27, looks at legends about Europe.

5 G. A. Momigliano, 'L'Europa come concetto politico presso Isocrate e gli Isocratei', *Rivista di filologia e d'istruzione classica*, LXI, 1933.

6 A. J. Toynbee, *A Study of History*, Oxford, 1954, vol. VIII, p. 708ff (appendix entitled ' "Asia" and "Europe": facts and fantasies').

7 L. von Ranke, *Geschichte der romanischen und germanischen Volker*, Berlin, 1825; cf. G. Barraclough, 'Introduction', in *Eastern and Western Europe in the Middle Ages*, London, 1970, p. 7ff.

8 W. Ullmann, *The Growth of Papal Government in the Middle Ages*, London, 1955, p. 276.

9 L. von Ranke, *Über die Epochen der neueren Geschichte*, Leipzig, 1888, p. 18.

10 A. Dopsch, *Wirtschaftliche und soziale Grundlagen der europäischen Kulturentwicklung aus der Zeit von Cäsar bis auf Karl den Grossen*, Vienna, 1918–20; Dopsch also gave a general review of his theories in 'Stan kultury wczesnego średniowiecza' [The state of culture in the early Middle Ages], *Przegląd Historyczny*, XXX, 1932, pp. 392–7.

11 Cf. M. Handelsman, 'Badania szkoły warszawskiej nad wczesnym średniowieczem' [Research by the Warsaw School into the early Middle Ages], in *Średniowiecze polskie i powszechne: wybór pisma* [The Middle Ages, Polish and universal: selected writings], Warsaw, 1966, pp. 342–8.

12 After the first exposition of his theses in two articles: 'Mahomet et Charlemagne', *Revue belge de philologie et d'histoire*, I, 1922, pp. 77–86, and 'Un contraste économique: Mérovingiens et Carolingiens', ibid., II, 1923, pp. 223–35, Henri Pirenne devoted his last book, *Mahomet et Charlemagne*, published posthumously in Paris in 1937, to them. Pirenne's theories excited considerable ongoing discussion; the principal elements and bibliography can be found in A. Rising, 'The fate of Henri Pirenne's thesis on the consequence of the Islamic expansion', *Classica et Mediaevalia*, XIII, 1952, pp. 87–130.

13 H. Pirenne, *Histoire de l'Europe des invasions au XVIe siècle*, Paris and Brussels, 1936, p. 22 (published posthumously, this book contains the first outline of the ideas which Pirenne developed in detailed studies after the war).

14 H. Pirenne, *Mahomet et Charlemagne*, p. 210. Archibald Lewis placed the chronological caesura similarly to Pirenne, ascribing to the Byzantine blockade (716–827), however, a role that was destructive for Mediterranean alliances; see A. R. Lewis, *Naval Power and Trade in the Mediterranean, AD 500–1100*, Princeton, 1951.

15 P. Lambrechts, 'Le commerce de "Syriens" en Gaule du Haut Empire de l'époque mérovingienne', *L'Antiquité classique*, VI, 1937, pp. 35–61, and 'Les thèses de Henri Pirenne', *Byzantion*, XIV, 1939, pp. 513–36; R. S. Lopez, 'Mohammed and Charlemagne: a review', *Saeculum*, XVIII, 1943, pp. 14–38.

16 M. Lombard, 'Les bases monétaires d'une suprématie économique: l'or musulman du VIIe au XIe siècle', *Annales: économies, sociétés, civilisations*, 2, 1947, pp. 143–60.

17 M. H. Serejski, *Idea jedności karolińskiej: studium nad genezą wspólnoty karolińskiej w średniowieczu* [The idea of Carolingian unity: a study of the genesis of the Carolingian community in the Middle Ages], Warsaw, 1937, p. 87.

18 As H. Gollwitzer suggests in 'Zur Wortgeschichte und Sinndeutung von 'Europe', *Saeculum*, II, 1951, p. 164.

19 M. H. Serejski, op. cit., p. 29; A. Gieysztor, *Władza Karola Wielkiego w opinii współczesnej* [Charlemagne's authority according to contemporary opinion], Warsaw, 1938, p. 29.

20 G. Kurth, *Etudes franques*, Paris and Brussels, 1919, vol. I: *Francia et Francus*.

21 *Monumenta Germaniae Historica* [MGH], *Scriptores* vol. XV, pt 1, p. 359; '. . . qui tres paestantiores Europae species solidum satis corpus, sceptrifero sibi dominatu, Dei propitio, subegit, Italiam videlicet Galliam et Germaniam . . .'

22 M. H. Serejski, op. cit., p. 87ff; H. Gollwitzer, op. cit., p. 165; D. de Rougemont, op. cit., p. 48.

23 *Annales Fuldenses*, ed. F. Kurze, Hanover, 1891, 'Scriptores Rerum Germanicarum', sub. 888.

24 Cf. A. Gieysztor, op. cit., p. 24ff for Alcuin's role in articulating Carolingian imperial ideology.

25 *Epistolae Carolini Aevi*, ed. E. Dummler, Berlin, 1895, vol. II (*MGH Epistolae*, IV), p. 32.

26 Ibid., p. 124: 'Totus orbis in tres dividitur partes, Europam, Africam et Indiam.'

27 Ibid., p. 503: '. . . quod te exaltavit in honorem regni Europe.' Cf. L. Halpen, *Charlemagne et l'Empire carolingien*, Paris, 1949, p. 208ff.

28 Cf. E. E. Stengel, 'Kaisertitel und Souveränitätsidee', *Deutsches Archiv für Geschichte des Mittelalters*, III, 1939, p. 25; E. Rosenstock and J. Wittig, *Das Alter der Kirche*, Berlin, 1927, vol. I, p. 461ff. In this work Rosenstock voices the opinion that during Charles's time Europe became a political concept, expressing a fully developed European awareness. R. H. Foerster opposes this extravagent statement, op. cit., p. 356.

29 R. Wallach, *Das abendländische Gemeinschaftsbewusstsein im Mittelalter*, Leipzig and Berlin, 1928 (*Beiträge zur Kulturgeschichte des Mittelalters und der Renaissance*, ed. W. Goetz, vol. 34); Y. Congar, 'Orient et Occident: quatre siècles de désunion et d'affrontement', *Istina*, II, 1968, pp. 131–52.

30 A. Dempf, *Sacrum Imperium*, Munich and Berlin, 1924, p. 155ff; W. Ohnsorge, *Das Zweikaiserprobleme im früheren Mittelalter*, Hildesheim, 1947.

31 G. Labuda, *Pierwsze państwo słowiańskie – państwo Samona* [The

first Slavonic state – the state of Samo], Poznań, 1949.

32 K. Tymieniecki, 'Z dziejów tworzenia się Europy w X w.' [The history of the formation of Europe in the tenth century], *Przegląd Zachodni*, XI, 1955, p. 139; F. Graus, 'L'Empire de Grande-Moravie, sa situation dans l'Europe de l'époque et sa structure interieure', in *Das Grossmährische Reich*, Prague, 1966, pp. 205–19; H. Łowmiański, *Początki Polski* [The beginnings of Poland], Warsaw, 1970, vol. IV, p. 230ff, p. 299ff.

33 R. Wallach, op. cit., p. 13; J. Fischer, in *Oriens, Occidens, Europa: Begriff und Gedanke Europa in der späten Antike und im frühen Mittelalter*, Wiesbaden, 1957, gives an excellent review of how the ideas that defined the Western community in the early Middle Ages functioned.

34 We must mention in particular two collections of studies out of the vast literature on the subject by two leading experts: F. Dolger, *Byzanz und die europäische Stattenwelt*, Darmstadt, 1972, and W. Ohnsorge, *Abendland und Byzanz*, Darmstadt, 1958 (esp. pp. 1–49: a study about the imperial idea and state ideology in the ninth and tenth centuries). Also, A. Michel, *Die Kaisermacht in der Ostkirche*, Darmstadt, 1959.

35 *MGH Epistolae*, V. p. 607; M. H. Serejski, op. cit., p. 97.

36 Cf. F. Dolger, 'Europas Gestaltung im Spiegel der frankisch-byzantinischen Auseinandersetzung', in *Das Vertrag von Verdun 834*, ed. T. Meyer, Leipzig, 1943, pp. 207–73, and in the collection *Byzanz . . .*, op. cit., pp. 282–369.

37 'Liudprandi relatio de legatione constantinopolitana', in *Liudprandi episcopi cremonensis opera omnia*, Hanover, 1877 ('Scriptores Rerum Germanicarum'), pp. 136–66. A list of works about Liudprand is given in W. Ohnsorge, *Konstantinopel und der Okzident*, Darmstadt, 1966, p. 177.

38 For differences in the customs of the 'Greeks' and the 'Latins', see R. Wallach, op. cit., p. 31ff; F. Chabod, op. cit., pp. 38–42.

39 Above all P. E. Schramm, *Kaiser, Rom und Renovatio*, Darmstadt, 1962.

40 For a review of the subject of German unity, see H. von Srbik, *Deutsche Einheit: Idee und Wirklichkeit von Heiligen Reich bis Königgrätz*, Munich 1935, vol. I, p. 15ff; G. Tellenbach, *Die Entstehung des deutschen Reiches*, Munich, 1940; *Die deutsche Einheit als Problem der europäischen Geschichte*, ed. C. Hinrichs and W. Berges, Stuttgart, 1960; G. Labuda, 'Tendences d'intégration et désintégrations dans la Royaume Teutonique du X au XIIIe siècle', in *L'Europe aux IX-XIe siècles: aux origines des Etats nationaux*, Warsaw, 1968, pp. 77–91.

41 Cf. L. Santifaller, 'Otto I, das Imperium und Europa', in *Festschrift zur Jahrtausendfeier der Kaiserkrönung Ottos des Grossen*, Vienna, 1962; a review of the state of research into Otto's empire is given in

Otto der Grosse, ed. H. Zimmermann, Darmstadt, 1976 ('Wege der Forschung', vol. 450), including bibliography.

42 *Liudprandi relatio* ..., op. cit., 12, p. 142: '... id est Romanorum nomine, quicquid ignobilitatis quicquid timiditatis, quicquid avaritiae, quicquid luxuriae, quicquid mendacii, immo quicquid vitiorum est, comprehendentes.'

43 F. Chabod, op. cit., p. 38.

44 On this subject, see in particular C. Erdmann, 'Das ottonische Reich als Imperium Romanum', in *Ottonische Studien*, ed. H. Beumann, Darmstadt, 1968, pp. 174–203, and W. Ohnsorge, 'Konstantinopel im politischen Denken der Ottonenzeit', in *Festschrift*, F. Dolger, pp. 388–412.

45 J. Baszkiewicz, *Państwo suwerenne w feudalnej doktrynie politycznej do początków XIV w.* [The sovereign state in feudal political doctrine up to the beginning of the fourteenth century], Warsaw, 1964.

46 M. Uhlirz, 'Das Werden des Gedankes der Renovatio Imperii Romanorum bei Otto III', in *Settimane di Studio del Centro Italiano di studi sull'Alto Medioevo*, Spoleto, 1955, vol. II: *I problemi comuni dell'Europa post-carolingia*, pp. 201–19.

47 Cf. W. Dzięcioł, *Imperium i państwa narodowe* [The empire and national states], London, 1962.

48 P. Skubiszewski analyses a miniature depicting these four symbolic figures in 'W służbie cesarza, w służbie króla: temat władzy w sztuce ottońskiej' [In the service of the emperor, in the service of the king: the subject of power in Ottonian art], in *Funkcja dzieła sztuki* [The function of the work of art], Warsaw, 1972, pp. 17–72 (esp. p. 38ff), including bibliography on the subject to date.

49 *Vita quinque fratrum eremitarum*, *Monumenta Poloniae Historica* [MPH], new series, IV/3, p. 44: 'ineuteratae Rome mortuum decorem renouare superuacuo labore insistit.'

50 J. Baszkiewicz, op. cit., p. 115.

51 R. Folz, *Le souvenir et la légende de Charlemagne dans l'Europe germanique médiévale*, Paris, 1950.

52 G. Barraclough, *The Mediaeval Empire: idea and reality*, London, 1950.

53 J. Baszkiewicz, op. cit. (chap. 2), in an excellent exposition on the subject, links the doctrine of *dominium mundi* rather one-sidedly with Germany's aims for political expansion.

54 W. Ullmann, *The Growth of Papal Government in the Middle Ages*, London, 1949; M. Pacaut, *La Théocratie: l'église et le pouvoir au Moyen Age*, Paris, 1957; E. Potkowski, 'Papiestwo a państwa europejskie' (XIII–XVw.) [The papacy and the European states (XIII–XV centuries)], in *Katolicyzm średniowieczny* [Medieval Catholicism], Warsaw, 1977, pp. 9–106.

55 J. H. Powell presents the basic controversy surrounding this pope in a rather simplified form in *Innocent III: view of Christ or lord of*

the world?, Boston, 1963 ('Problems in European Civilization').

56 W. Fritzemeyer, *Christenheit und Europa*, Munich and Berlin, 1931, p. 5.

57 S *Thomae Aquinatis Summa Theologiae*, 'Suppl. questio XXVI', art. 1: 'Ecclesia assimilatur congregationi politicae . . .'

58 A. Hauck, *Der Gedanke der päpstlichen Weltherrschaft bis auf Bonifaz VIII*, Leipzig, 1904, p. 44ff.

59 Cf. W. Sawicki, 'Prawo międzynarodowej średniowiecznej christianitas' [The law in international medieval *christianitas*], *Roczniki Teologiczno-Kanoniczne KUL*, XIV/5, 1967, pp. 21–40; the author overestimates the unifying role of institutions and the law in relation to *christianitas*.

60 P. E. Schramm's works are fundamental on this subject, a synthetic outline of which the author himself gave in his papers 'Die Staatssymbolik des Mittelalters', in X *Congresso Internazionale di Scienze Storiche*, Rome, 1955, vol. VII, pp. 200–1, and 'Il simbolismo dello stato nella storia del medioevo' in *La storia del diritto nel quadro delle scienze storiche: atti del primo congresso internazionale della Società italiana di Storia del diritto*, Florence, 1966, pp. 247–67.

61 P. Rousset, 'La notion de chrétienté aux XIe et XIIe siècles', *Moyen Age*, LXIX, 1963, pp. 191–203.

62 G. Ladner, 'The Concepts of "Ecclesia" and "Christianitas" ', *Miscellanea Historiae Pontificiae*, XVIII, 1954, pp. 49–77.

63 A. Dupront, 'La croisade après les croisades', in P. Alphandéry, *La Chrétienté et l'idee de croisade*, Paris, 1959, II, ('L'Evolution de l'humanité', XXXVIII), p. 275.

64 G. Barraclough rightly draws attention to this in *History in a Changing World*, Oxford, 1955, p. 38ff.

65 Cf. J. Schmidlin, 'Frühmittelalterliche Missionsmethode', in *Katholische Missiongeschichte*, Steyl, 1924.

66 'Ebonis Vita Sancti Ottonis episcopi babenbergensis', II, 12, in *Monumenta Poloniae Historica*, new series, Warsaw, 1969, VII/1, pp. 74–5.

67 S. Piekarczyk deals with these processes with reference to the Germanic peoples in *Barbarzyńcy i chrześcijaństwo: konfrontacje społecznych postaw i wzorców u Germanów* [Barbarians and Christianity: confrontations of social attitudes and examples among Germanic peoples], Warsaw, 1968, esp. p. 327ff.

68 Cf. F. Flaskamp, *Die Missionsmethode des hl. Bonifatius*, Hildesheim, 1929 ('Geschichtliche Darstellungen und Quellen', 8); G. Schmurer, *Die Anfänge des abendländischen Völkergemeinschaft*, Freiburg im Breisgau, 1932, vol. I, p. 202.

69 C. Deptula, 'Krąg kościelny płocki w połowie wieku XII' [The sphere of the Church in Płock in the second half of the twelfth century], *Roczniki Humanistyczne*, VIII/2, 1959, pp. 5–122; 'Niektóre aspekty stosunków Polski z cesarstwem w wieku XII' [Some aspects

of Poland's relations with the empire in the twelfth century], in *Polska w Europie* [Poland in Europe], Lublin, 1968, pp. 35–92; and 'Płock kościelny u progu reform XIII wieku: Biskup Lupus i jego czasy' [The Płock Church on the threshold of reform in the thirteenth century: Bishop Lupus and his times], *Roczniki Humanistyczne*, XXI/2, 1973, pp. 43–90.

70 A letter written in the 1160s by a certain abbot from Gembloux, who was warning his friend against the dangers of settling in Poland, provides interesting evidence of how widespread such migrations were: O. Górka, 'List Gwiberta z Gembloux do scholastyka Arnulfa [Guibert of Gembloux's letter to the scholar Arnulf], *Kwartalnik Historyczny*, XL, 1926, pp. 27–38. (Guibert writes: 'nolite incognitum laboriosum et siluosum iter . . . nolite nos incaute extere et barbare genti immergere', ibid., p. 33.) Herbord also writes in the life of Saint Otto about the dearth of *litterati* in Poland: *Herbordi Dialogus de Vita S. Ottonis*, III, 32: 'Itaque in Poloniam peregre vadens ubi sciebat litteratorum esse penuriam', in *Monumenta Poloniae Historica*, new series, VII/3, 1974, p. 197.

71 Cf. B. Geremek, 'Chiesa', in *Enciclopedia Einaudi*, Turin, 1978, vol. II, p. 1087ff.

72 T. Rosłanowski sketched a review of research and problems in 'Przegląd nowszych badań nad historią wypraw krzyżowych' [A review of the latest research into the history of the Crusades], *Kwartalnik Historyczny*, LXV, 1958, pp. 1311–35; bibliographies are in H. E. Meyer, *Bibliographie zur Geschichte der Kreuzzüge*, Hanover, 1960, J. B. Brundage, *The Crusades: a documentary survey*, Milwaukee, 1962, F. Cardini, *Le crociate tra il mito e la storia*, Rome, 1971, and D. Bigalli, 'Oriente e occidente di fronte alle crociate', *Studi Storici*, XIV, 1973, pp. 931–9.

73 L. Koczy, 'Narody w pierwszej wyprawie krzyżowej' [The nations in the first Crusade], *Teki Historyczne*, XI, 1960, pp. 41–96; the author aptly points out the significance of the linguistic and ethnic variety of the *Christi membra* that made up the first Crusade (*linguis, tribubus et nationibus differentia*).

74 On the idea of the crusade in particular, see. C. Erdmann, *Die Entstehung des Kreuzzugsgedankens*, Stuttgart, 1935; M. Villey, *La croisade: essai sur la formation d'une théorie juridique*, Paris, 1942; E. Delaruelle, 'Essai sur la formation de l'idée de croisade', *Bulletin de littérature ecclésiastique*, 1941, pp. 24–45, 86–103; 1944, pp. 13–46, 73–90; 1953, pp. 226–39; 1954, pp. 50–63; 1960, pp. 241–57; P. Alphandéry, *La Chrétienté et l'idée de croisade*, Paris, 1954–9, vols I–II, ('L'Evolution de l'humanité', XXXVIII).

75 P. Alphandéry, op. cit., vol. I, p. 215.

76 This is the sense of Urban II's famous speech at the Council of Clermont in 1095, in which he directed his appeal above all to the French knights: *Receuil des historiens des croisades, historiens occidentaux*, Paris, 1866, III, p. 728. Similarly in the bull *Cor nostrum*

in 1181 Alexander III addressed those who were accustomed to the business of war: P. Jaffe, *Regesta pontificum Romanorum*, Leipzig, 1888, II, no. 14360.

77 Cf. L. Winowski, 'Stosunek średniowiecznej Europy do obcych innowierców' [Medieval Europe's relationship towards foreign heretics], *Prawo Kanoniczne*, IV, 1961, pp. 593–680.

78 S. Runciman, *The Eastern Schism: a study of the papacy and the Eastern Churches during the eleventh and twelfth centuries*, Oxford, 1955.

79 Participation in the Crusades was of course much more widespread; it covered Greek Christendom and the eastern limits of medieval Europe. On Ruthenia's participation in the Crusades, see V. T. Pashuto, 'Mesto drevnei Rusi v istorii Evropy' [Ancient Ruthenia's place in the history of Europe], in *Feodal'naia Rossiia vo vsemirno-istoricheskom protsesse* [Feudal Russia in the world-history process], Moscow, 1972, p. 198ff.

80 L. Brehier, *L'Eglise et l'Orient au Moyen Age: les croisades*, Paris, 1907; J. Ebersolt, *Orient et Occident: recherches sur les influences byzantines et orientales en France avant les croisades*, Paris and Brussels, 1928; W. M. Daily, 'Christian Fraternity, the Crusaders and the Security of Constantinople, 1097–1204, *Medieval Studies*, XXII, 1960, p. 78ff.

81 G. Duby, 'Au XIIe siècle: les "jeunes" dans la société aristocratique', *Annales ESC*, 19, 1962, pp. 835–46.

82 P. Toubert, 'Croisades d'enfants et mouvement de pauvreté au XIIIe siècle', Recherches sur les pauvres et la pauvreté, IV, 1965–6.

83 We can point to the example of the crusader movement, that is the so-called *capuciati*, recruited from among the peasants of southern and central Poland, who in reply to Alexander III's appeal at the Third Lateran Council of 1179 set off to fight armed bands in their own country, and in exchange they received the promise of such indulgences as were granted to the crusaders; the lords and bishops were later compelled to return them to order by force. A. Luchaire, *La Société française au temps de Philippe Auguste*, Paris, 1909, p. 10ff.

84 This interpretation of German colonization, against a background of other settlers' migrations at the time, is set out in *Die deutsche Ostsiedlung im Mittelalter als Problem der europäische Geschichte: Reichenau Vortrage 1970–1972*, ed. W. Schlesinger, Sigmaringen, 1975, esp. p. 802 (result of the discussion written by K. Zernacka).

85 R. Wallach, op. cit., p. 24ff.

86 A. Brackemann, *Zur politischen Bedeutung der kluniazensischen Bewegung*, Darmstadt, 1955.

87 D. Sinor, 'Les relations entre les Mongols et l'Europe jusqu'à la mort d'Arghoun et de Bela IV', *Cahiers d'Histoire Mondiale*, III/1, 1956; A. F. Grabski, *Polska w opiniach obcych X–XIII w.* [Poland in the eyes of foreigners in the tenth to the thirteenth centuries],

Warsaw, 1964, chap. VIII; V. T. Pashuto, 'Mongolskii pokhod vglub' Evropy' [The Mongol invasion into the heart of Europe], in *Tataro-Mongoly v Asii i Evrope: sbornik statei* [Tartar-Mongols in Asia and Europe: a collection of articles], Moscow, 1977, pp. 210–27.

88 *Monumenta Germaniae Historica, legum sectio IV, Constitutiones et acta publica*, III, no. 401; O. Halecki, 'Diplomatie pontificale et activité missionnaire en Asie aux XIIIe et XIVe siècles', in *XIIe Congrès International des Sciences Historiques*, Vienna, 1965, Rapports, II, p. 10, emphasizes the role that Innocent IV ascribed to Poland, Lithuania and the Halicz region of Ruthenia in the struggle against the Mongols.

89 On the influence of this panic on thirteenth-century eschatology, see D. Bigalli, *I Tartari e l'Apocalisse: richerche sull'escatologia in Adam Marsh e Ruggero Bacone*, Florence, 1971 (esp. p. 50, about the organization of the defence of *universitas christianorum*).

90 J. Karwasińska, 'Państwo polskie w przekazach hagiograficznych XI i XII wieku [The Polish state in eleventh- and twelfth-century hagiographic accounts], in *Początki państwa polskiego* [The beginnings of the Polish state], Poznań, 1962, vol. I, pp. 233–44.

91 K. Bosl, *Mensch und Gesellschaft in der Geschichte Europas*, Munich, 1972, p. 230: 'war das Zentrum seiner geistigen Existenz nicht mehr Prag, sondern Rom und hier vor allem das griechisch-lateinisch-slavische Emigrantenkloster San Alessio . . .'

92 *Monumenta Poloniae Historica*, VI, p. 587ff.

93 *Li livres dou tresor de Brunetto Latini*, ed. J. Carmody, Berkeley and Los Angeles, 1948, p. 206.

94 G. Le Bras, *Institutions ecclésiastiques de la Chrétienté médiévale: préliminaires*, Paris, 1959 (Histoire de l'Eglise', XII/1), p. 45ff.

95 J. Kłoczowski, 'O historię porównawczą społeczeństw europejskich: struktury społeczne, polityczne i kulturalne Europy XIII w.' [About the comparative history of European societies: social, political and cultural structures in thirteenth-century Europe], *Przegląd Historyczny*, XLVII, 1976, pp. 527–35.

96 K. Bosl, in *Europa im Mittelalter: Weltgeschichte eines Jahrtausends*, Bayreuth, 1975, p. 229, aptly points out that, inasmuch as the First Crusade demonstrated the growing prestige and power of the papacy, the later history of the expeditions led to growing dissatisfaction with the riches of the Church and with the secularization of the papacy: 'Man begann an der Stellvertretung Christi durch einen verweltlichten Papst zu zweifeln.'

97 This was mentioned by A. Gieysztor, *La Pologne et l'Europe au Moyen Age*, Warsaw, 1962, p. 3, and G. Arnaldi, 'Regnum Langobardorum – Regnum Italiae', in *L'Europe aux IXe–XIe s.*, pp. 105–22, warning against an excessively unifying 'European' perspective.

98 (Pseudo-)Brocardus, *Directorium ad passagium faciendum: receuil*

des croisades, ed. C. Koehler, Paris, 1906, vol. II, p. 382.

99 M. J. Wilks, *The Problem of Sovereignty in the Later Middle Ages*, Cambridge, 1962.

100 J. Baszkiewicz sets this out, op. cit., pp. 372–95.

101 We have already referred above to most works on this subject. D. Hay's *Europe – The Emergence of an Idea*, Edinburgh, 1957, 2/1969, remains the best study.

102 D. Hay, 'Sur un problème de terminologie historique: "Europe" et "chrétienté" ', *Diogène*, 17, 1957, pp. 50–62.

103 C. E. du Boulay, *Historia Universitatis Parisiensis*, Paris, 1665–73, vol. IV, p. 409: 'Supponendum est quod prope istam Europam habitant his temporibus Christiani. Unde nulli vel pauci principes christiani dominantur extra Europam.'

104 L. R. Loomis, 'Nationality at the Council of Constance', *American Historical Review*, XLIV, 1939, pp. 508–27.

105 G. D. Mansi, *Sacrorum conciliorum nova et amplissima collectio*, vol. XXVII, col. 1058–70. Analysis of this text is in L. R. Loomis, op. cit., and in D. Hay, *Europe . . .*, op. cit., p. 77ff.

106 G. D. Mansi, op. cit., col. 1066: 'Orientalis vero plaga sive Ecclesia Christianitatis obedientiae papalis in Europa . . .'

107 D. Hay, *Sur un problème . . .*, op. cit., p. 57.

108 W. Fritzemeyer, op. cit., pp. 18–29.

109 M. Małowist, *Wschód i Zachód Europy w XIII–XVI w.* [The East and West of Europe in the thirteenth to the sixteenth century], Warsaw, 1973; J. Kłoczowski, 'Rozwój środkowowschodniej Europy w XIV wieku' [The development of Central-Eastern Europe in the fourteenth century], in *Sztuka i ideologia XIV w.* [Fourteenth-century art and ideology], ed. P. Skubiszewski, Warsaw, 1975, pp. 13–52; G. Labuda, 'Europa "gotycka" XIV w.' ['Gothic' Europe of the fourteenth century], in *Gotyckie malarstwo ścienne w Europie środkowowschodniej* [Gothic mural painting in Central-Eastern Europe], ed. A. Karłowska-Kamzowa, Poznań, 1977, pp. 7–23; H. Samsonowicz, 'Changes in the Baltic Zone in the twelfth to sixteenth centuries', *Journal of European Economic History*, IV, 1975, pp. 655, 672; and 'Europa Jagiellońska czy jednością gospodarczą?' [Jagiellonian Europe or economic unity?], *Kwartalnik Historyczny*, LXXXIV, 1977, pp. 93–100.

110 W. Abel in particular undertook this in his works *Agrarkrisen und Agrarkoniunktur in Mitteleuropa vom 13. bis zum 19. Jahrhundert*, Berlin, 1935; id., *Die Wüstungen des ausgehenden Mittelalters*, Stuttgart, 1955. Cf. also F. Braudel, *La Méditerranée et le monde méditerranéen à l'époque de Philippe II*, Paris, 1949, Eng. trans., London, 1972, 1973, vol. I; and *Civilisation matérielle et capitalisme*, Paris, 1967, p. 100ff (Eng. trans., London, 1973).

111 K. Bosl, *Mensch und Gesellschaft in der Geschichte Europas*, op. cit., p. 53ff (chap. 3, *Der Aristokratische Charakter der mittelalter-*

lichen Gesellschaft in Europa: Versuch über Mentalität). F. Heer, *Europäische Geistesgeschichte*, Stuttgart, 1965, p. 56, even says: '1000 Jahre Europa bedeuten 1000 Jahre Vorherrschaft des europäischen Adels', with the proviso that he calculates the 'European millennium' from the ninth century.

112 O. Brunner, *Adeliges Landleben und europäischer Geist*, Salzburg, 1949. Critical comments about Brunner's conception (in the margins of his famous book *Neue Wege der Sozialgeschichte*, (Göttingen, 1956) were made by F. Braudel, *Historia i trwanie* [History and endurance], Warsaw, 1971, pp. 316–33.

113 M. Weber, *Economy and Society: an outline of interpretive sociology*, trans. E. Fischoff, New York, 1968.

114 G. Sjoberg, *The Preindustrial City*, Glencoe, IL, 1960; L. Mumford, *The City in History*, New York, 1961; F. Braudel, *Civilisation matérielle et capitalisme*, chap. 8 (esp. p. 391ff).

115 J. Ortega y Gasset, in *La rebelión de las masas*, Madrid, 1931 (Fr. trans., Paris, 1961, p. 12ff), pointed out that the West is precisely a civilizing unit in the Middle Ages. Europe is only the physical expanse in which that unit is realized.

116 N. Schachner has put together earlier literature about universities in *The Medieval Universities*, London, 1938, p. 377ff; a more recent bibliography is given in the work of S. Steling-Michaud, 'L'histoire des universités en Moyen Age et à la Renaissance', in *XI Congrès International des Sciences Historiques*, Stockholm, 1969, vol. I: *Rapports*, pp. 97–143.

117 For apt remarks about this process: J. Le Goff, *Les intellectuels au moyen âge* ('Le temps qui court', 3), Paris, 1957.

118 A. Borst, *Der Turmbau von Babel*, Stuttgart, 1957; B. Kürbisówna, 'Kształtowanie sie pojęć geograficznych o Słowiańszczyźnie w polskich kronikach przeddługoszowych' [The formation of geographic concepts about the Slav world in Polish pre-Długosz chronicles], *Slavia Antiqua*, IV, 1953, pp. 252–82; A. F. Grabski, *Polska w opiniach obcych X–XIII w.* [Poland in the eyes of foreigners in the tenth to the thirteenth century], Warsaw, 1964, chap. 4, and *Polska w opiniach obcych XIV–XV w.* [Poland in the eyes of foreigners in the fourteenth to the fifteenth century], Warsaw, 1968, p. 120ff; F. Šmahel, *Idea národa v husitských Cechách*, Prague, 1971, p. 152; J. Banaszkiewicz, *Kronika Dzierzwy: XIV-wieczne kompendium historii ojczystej* [Chronicle of Dzierzwa: a fourteenth-century compendium of the history of the fatherland], Wrocław, 1979. An important item in this field is F. Graus's work *Lebendige Vergangenheit: Überlieferung im Mittelalter und in den Vorstellungen von Mittelalter*, Cologne and Vienna, 1975.

119 Cf. D. Hay, *Europe . . .*, op. cit., chap. 1; D. de Rougemont, op. cit., p. 9ff.

120 B. Stachón reviews the subject in *Polityka Polski wobec Turcji i*

akcji antytureckiej w wieku XV do utraty Kilii i Białogardu (1484)
[Polish policies on Turkey and anti-Turkish action in the fifteenth
century to the loss of Kilia and Bialgorod (1484)], Lvov, 1930
('Archiwum Tow. Naukowego we Lwowie', dz. [inv.] II, vol. VII).

121 The text of the proposed treaty is in the Archiwum Główne Akt
Dawnych, *Metryka Koronna* [Crown register], vol. XI, fo.
578–87. A publication of the Czech Academy of Sciences – *The
Universal Peace Organization of King George of Bohemia: a
fifteenth-century plan for world peace, 1462/1464*, Prague, 1964 –
contains an edition of the text and a political-legal study by
V. Vaněček. From the literature on the subject special mention
must be made of R. Heck, 'Czeski plan związku władców europejskich z lat 1462–1464 a Polska' [The Czech plan for a union of
European rulers in 1462–1464 and Poland], in *Studia z dziejów
polskich i czechosłowackich* [Studies of Polish and Czechoslovak
history], Wrocław, 1950, and G. Polišensky, 'Bohemia, the Turk
and the Christian Commonwealth (1462 to 1620)', *Byzantino-
slavica*, XIV, 1953.

122 Here we can mention in particular the fourteenth-century plan of a
French jurist and publicist who mused on *omnium credentium una
respublica*, which would have been organized under the adminis-
tration of the councils set up to regain the Holy Land: see
P. Dubois, *De recuperatione Terre Sancte*, ed. C. V. Langlois,
Paris, 1891 ('Collection de textes pour servir a l'enseignement').

123 *The Universal Peace Organization . . .*, op. cit., p. 71: 'Spurcissimi
denique Teucri, qui a diebus paucissimis primo inclitum Grecorum
imperium deinde quam plures christianitatis provincias et regna in
suam potestatem redigere . . .'

124 Cf. F. Bujak, *Studia geograficzno-historyczne*, Cracow, 1925,
pp. 114–37.

125 *Tractatus quidam de Turcis*, Nürnberg, c. 1477; I use the following edition: *Nürnberg ex tip. Conrad Zeniger, 1481*. 'Nam in
XXVI annis Turcus perfidus dua imperia, IV regna, XX provincias
et CC urbes suo imperio subiugavit . . .'

126 Georgius de Hungaria, *De ritu et moribus Turcorum*, G. Teutoni-
cus et Sixt. Riessinger, Rome, c. 1481–3; I use the example in the
Vatican Library. This treaty is preserved in a copy entitled
Tractatus de moribus, conditionibus et nequitia Turcorum
(Lat. 9522, pp. 41–67) with the annotation *scriptus 1499*; this
undoubtedly refers to the date when the copy was ordered (if it
indicated the date when the work was written it would mean that
the author was nearly eighty years old at the time). F. Bujak, op.
cit., p. 130, mistakenly identifies this manuscript with the Latin
edition of *Pamiętniki Janczara* [The memoirs of a janissary]. See
note 128.

127 Georgius de Hungaria, op. cit., chap. 3: 'Quam terribilis, quam
timenda est secta Turcorum.'

128 *Pamiętniki Janczara, czyli Kronika Turecka Konstantego z Ostrowicy napisana między r. 1469 a 1501* [The memoirs of a janissary, or the Turkish chronicle of Konstanty of Ostrowica written between 1469 and 1501], ed. J. Łoś, Cracow, 1912 ('Biblioteka Pisarzów Polskich', vol. 63).

129 On the state of the subject, see P. Chaunu, *L'expansion européenne du XIIIe au XVe siècle*, Paris, 1969 ('Nouvelle Clio', no. 26). J. P. Roux gives an interesting account of contacts between Central Europe and Asia in *Średniowiecze szuka drogi w świat* [The Middle Ages seek a path in the world], trans. T. Rosłanowski, Warsaw, 1969.

130 Cf. B. Olszewicz, *Legendy geograficzne średniowiecza* [Geographical legends of the Middle Ages], Cracow, 1927 (e.g. about where paradise is situated, p. 55ff).

131 Y. Renouard, 'L'Occident mediéval à la découverte du monde', *L'Information historique*, March–April 1955, pp. 49–57, and in a collection of studies by the same author, *Etudes d'histoire mediévale*, Paris, 1968, vol. II, pp. 661–75.

132 D. Hay, *Europe ...*, op. cit., p. 90ff; the information in L. Kretschmer's fundamental work *Die italienischen Portolane des Mittelsalters*, Berlin, 1909, still retains its value.

133 Cf. A. Gieysztor, 'Polska w El Libro del Conoscimiento z pol. XIV wieku' [Poland in El Libro des Conoscimiento from the second half of the fourteenth century], *Przegląd Historyczny*, LVI, 1965, pp. 397–412; distinctions are also made between individual countries by means of heraldic illuminations, but the difference between Christian countries and others is of particular concern.

134 W. Fritzemeyer, op. cit., pp. 18–29; cf. also A. Berg, *Enea Silvio de Piccolomini (Papst Pius II) in seiner Bedeutung als Geograph*, Halle, 1901.

135 *Pio II Lettera a Maometto II*, ed. G. Toffanin, Naples, 1953.

136 *Cosmographiae vel de mundo universo historiarum liber I*, in *Aeneae Sylvii Piccolominei ... opera quae extant omnia, Basileae 1551*, in *Opera omnia*, op. cit., fo. 281–386.

137 *Europa in qua sui temporis varias historias complectitur liber I*, in *Opera omnia*, op. cit., fo. 387–471.

138 Enea Silvio Piccolomini writes of it thus in the foreword: 'Quae sub Frederico tertio eius nominis imperatore apud Europeos, aut qui nomine Christiano censentur, insulae, homines, gesta feruntur memoratu digna ...' (ibid., fo. 387).

139 Ibid., fo. 394, chap. 4: 'De Turcarum origine et propagatione, victu, vestitu, et moribus eorum.' It is significant that the description in the case of the Turks is of a land, not of a people; in this way Turkey is not linked with Europe.

140 *Opera omnia*, op. cit., pp. 290, 291, 305, 308; Enea Silvio Piccolomini is, perhaps, the first Latin writer to use this form (D. Hay, in *Europe ...*, op. cit., p. 86, reminds us of the form

Europico in Boccaccio's *Comento alla Divina Comedia*); cf. W. Fritzemeyer, op. cit., p. 28.

141 Cf. note 138.

142 *Opera omnia*, op. cit., p. 445.

143 J. Tazbir, 'Poland and the Concept of Europe in the Sixteenth–Eighteenth Centuries', *European Studies Review*, 7, 1977, p. 32.

144 *Laurentii Vallae, De falso credita et ementita Constantini donatione declamatio*, ed. W. Schwahn, Leipzig, 1928, p. 54: 'Qui sunt fines occidentis? ubi incipiunt? ubi desinunt? Num ita certi constitutique sunt termini occidentis et orientis meridieique et septentrionis, ut sunt Asiae, Africae, Europae?'

145 *Opera Omnia*, op. cit., p. 284: 'Europa per Hispaniam, Italiam et Peloponnesum australior est, parallelum qui per Rhodum ducitur attingens in septentrionem per Germaniam et Norvegiam maxime protensa.'

146 *Opera Omnia*, op. cit., p. 285: 'Europae et Asiae coniunctio fit per dorsum quod inter paludem Meotim et Sarmaticum oceanum excurrit supra Tanais fluvii fontes.' This sentence was taken from Ptolemy with slight alterations. E. Wislotzki gives the best exposition on the geographic views of Europe's eastern border in: *Zeitströmungen in der Geographie*, Leipzig, 1897, pp. 399–440.

147 *De Constantinopolitana clade ac bello contra Turcos congregando*, in *Opera Omnia*, op. cit., epistola CXXXI, pp. 678–89.

148 Ibid., p. 679: 'ex duobus Christianitatis oculis alterum erutum, ex duabus manibus alteram aputatam dicere possumus.'

149 Ibid., p. 678: 'Nunc vero in Europa, id est in patria, in domo propria, in sede nostra, percussi caesique sumus.' There is also a copy of this discourse in the codex of Sędziwój of Czechło. Cf. J. Wiesiołowski, *Kolekcje historyczne w Polsce średniowiecznej, XIV–XV w.* [Historical collections in medieval Poland in the fourteenth and fifteenth centuries], Wrocław, 1967, p. 100.

150 K. Buczek, 'Maciej Miechowita jako geograf Europy Wschodniej' [Maciej Miechowita as a geographer of Eastern Europe], in *Maciej z Miechowa, 1457–1523*, Wrocław, 1960, p. 80ff, gives an exemplary account of the knowledge in this field ('Monografia z dziejów nauki i techniki', vol. XV).

151 Herodotus (IV, 20 and 100) recognizes the Tanaïs, that is the Don, as the border between the Scythians and the Sauromats. He later ascribes to it the role of border between Europe and Asia, while Ptolemy (III, 5) recognizes the Tanaïs as the border between European and Asian Sarmatia. Cf. S. Czarnowski about ancient geographical knowledge in 'Argonauci na Bałtyku: konwencje a rzeczywistość w kształtowaniu się greckich pojęć geograficznych' [The Argonauts in the Baltic: conventions and reality in the formation of Greek geographical concepts], in *Dzieła* [Works], Warsaw,

1956, vol. III, pp. 242–60.

152 R. Buczek, op. cit., p. 132, n. 174: the Camaldolite Fra Mauro, in the 1458 map of the world, takes the Volga to be the frontier of Europe.

153 The treatise which the Polish diplomat Mikołaj Rozemberski (Nicolaus de Rozemberg Polonus) wrote in 1503 on the order of Emperor Maximilian I, entitled *Exploratio compediosa de situ, moribus, diversitate Scithicarum gentium* (Biblioteka Czartoryskich, MS 26, pp. 593–619), marked the border of Scythia on the Volga: H. Barycz, 'Rozwój nauki w Polsce w dobie Odrodzenia' [The development of science in Poland in the Renaissance], in *Odrodzenie w Polsce* [The Renaissance in Poland], Warsaw, 1956, vol. I, pt 1, p. 125.

154 A. F. Grabski aptly points this out in *Polska w opiniach Europy Zachodniej XIV–XV w.* [Poland in the eyes of Western Europe in the fourteenth and fifteenth centuries], op. cit., p. 451.

155 B. Strzelecka, 'Odrodzenie "Geografii" Ptolomeusza w XV w: tradycja kartograficzna' [The renaissance of Ptolemy's 'Geography' in the fifteenth century: cartographic tradition], *Czasopismo Geograficzne*, XXXI, 1960, pp. 343–55.

156 Cf. A. F. Grabski, *Polska w opiniach obcych X–XIII w.* [Poland in the eyes of foreigners in the tenth to thirteenth centuries], op. cit., chap. 2, about the collapse of ancient schemes and the development of geographical knowledge.

157 T. Ulewicz, *Sarmacja: studium z problematyki słowiańskiej XV i XVI w.* [Sarmatia: a study of the Slavonic question of the fifteenth and sixteenth centuries], Cracow, 1950 (Bibl. Studium Słowiańskiego UJ, series A, no. 7).

158 Cf. in particular F. Bujak about Długosz's geographic reasoning: op. cit., pp. 91–105; J. Kornhaus, *Jan Długosz, geograf polski XV w.* [Jan Długosz, Polish geographer of the fifteenth century], Lvov, 1925 (*Prace Geograficzne*, no. 5).

159 *Ioannis Dlugossii, Annales seu Cronicae incliti regni Poloniae*, Warsaw, 1964, vol. I, p. 67: '... aliquando Sarmaticum nominatur Mare, quod in littoribus suis Sarmate sive Poloni regiones et urbes possideant ...'

160 Ibid., pp. 74–6.

161 Ibid., p. 89; 'A veteribus autem scriptoribus et historiographis Sarmacia Europica appellatur, et tam Rutheni, quam Poloni Sarmate nominantur.'

162 Ibid., p. 66.

163 Cf. K. Pieradzka, 'Genealogia biblijna i rodowód Słowian w pierwszej księdze "Annales" Jana Długosza' [Biblical genealogy and the origin of the Slavs in the first book of Jan Długosz's 'Annales'], *Nasza Przeszłość*, VIII, 1958.

164 *Ioannis Dlugossii Annales ...*, op. cit., p. 67: 'Bisancium insuper, sive Constantinopolitana urbs in Europa sita est.'

165 Cf. A. L. Khoroshkevich, 'Terminy "Russiia" i "Moskoviia" v 9–13 knigakh "Annalov Pol'shi" IAna Dlugosha [The terms 'Russia' and 'Muscovia' in Books 9–13 of Jan Długosz's 'Annales'], in *Cultus et cognito: studia z dziejów średniowiecznej kultury* [Studies from the history of medieval culture], Warsaw, 1976, pp. 203–8.

166 In particular, *Ioannis Dlugossii Annales* . . ., op. cit., p. 169.

167 Ibid., p. 90.

168 W. Senko, *Wstęp do studiów nad Janem z Głogowa* [Introduction to studies of Jan of Głogów], *Materiały i studia Zakładu Historii Filozofii Starożytnej i Średniowiecznej* [Materials and studies of the Institute of the History of Ancient and Medieval Philosophy], Wrocław, 1964, series A, vol. III, pt 2, p. 36; M. Zwiercan, *Jan z Głogowa, Polski Słownik Biograficzny 1962–1964* [Polish dictionary of biography, 1962–1964], vol. X, p. 452.

169 L. A. Birkenmajer, *Stromata copernicana*, Cracow, 1924, p. 105ff.

170 F. Bujak, op. cit., p. 42ff.

171 *Biblioteka Jagiellońska*, MS no. 2729, fo. 113–49; we are using Bujak's precis (op. cit., pp. 33–41), which describes this little work as an anonymous treatise by a Cracow professor at the very beginning of the fifteenth century. W. Senko, op. cit., p. 36, believes that Jan of Głogów's manuscript notes (BJ MS no. 2703, bk. 127–32) and the notes on the incunabula made up the initial editions of the treatise.

172 T. Ulewicz, op. cit., p. 43ff.

173 F. Bujak, op. cit., p. 75 (the note reads: 'haec tabula habet Sarmatiam asiaticam, nunc dictam Moszkowiam').

174 Cf. E. Wislotzki, op. cit., p. 403ff.

175 *Descriptio Sarmatiarum Asianae et Europianae et eorum quae in eis continentur*, Cracow, 1521 (this third edition was considered, while the author was still alive, to be fundamental); there is a Polish translation of the work by Tadeusz Bieńkowski, Warsaw, 1976.

176 B. Olszewicz, 'Geografia polska w okresie Odrodzenia' [Polish geography in the Renaissance], in *Odrodzenie w Polsce* [The Renaissance in Poland], Warsaw, 1956, vol. II, pt 2, p. 342.

177 This subject demands further research. T. Ulewicz, op. cit., p. 56, poses the question whether Maciej of Miechów omitted Poland in his description of European Sarmatia 'in order to avoid uttering platitudes'; H. Barycz, 'Maciej z Miechowa: studium z dziejów kultury naukowej Polski doby Odrodzenia' [Study of the history of scientific culture in Poland during the Renaissance], *Nauka Polska*, VI/3, 1958, p. 97, thinks that the *Opisanie* [Description] might have been a supplement or a fully developed section of a planned work about the Slav world. We must mention here that Maciej of Miechów did not refer to Poland in the introductory, general definitions of European Sarmatia either; perhaps he wanted to treat the

Polish lands, between the Odra and the Vistula, separately – as he did with the Czech lands – like a traditional part of the Latin sphere, and the ancient division of Germania-Sarmatia restricted him in this arrangement.

178 *Descriptio Sarmatiarum* . . ., ibid., bk II, §I, chap. 3 (Polish trans., p. 72).

179 K. Buczek, op. cit., p. 141, suggests that here it is a question of the method of pacifying the freshly captured lands by the Moscow rulers, which Maciej of Miechów recognized as evidence of their way of life.

180 *Descriptio Sarmatiarum* . . ., ibid., bk II, §II, chap. 1 (Polish trans., p. 76).

181 E. Wislotzki, op. cit., *passim*.

182 Cf. T. G. Masaryk, *Russland und Europa*, Berlin, 1913.

183 G. Vernadsky, *Kievan Russia*, New Haven, 1948, p. 1ff, presents the problem of Ruthenia (and Russia) belonging to Europe; G. Stökl, 'Die politische Religiosität des Mittelalters und die Entstehung des Moskauer Staates', *Saeculum*, II, 1951, pp. 393–415, declares himself for the Europeanness of the state of Moscow in the first period of its existence.

184 O. Halecki, *Borderlands of Western Civilization: a history of East-Central Europe*, New York, 1952, p. 145; cf. C. Toumanoff, 'Moscow, the Third Rome: Genesis and Significance of a Politico-religious idea', *Catholic Historical Review*, 40, 1955; W. Lettenbauer, *Moskau, das dritte Rom: zur Geschichte einer politischen Theorie*, Munich, 1961; A. L. Goldberg, 'K predistorii idei "Moskva – tretii Rim" ', in *Kulturnoie naslediie drevnei Rusi*, Moscow, 1976, pp. 111–16.

185 This was a subject for discussion at a congress of historical sciences in Warsaw in 1933; cf. J. Bidlo, 'Ce qu'est l'histoire de l'Orient européen', *Bulletin d'information des sciences historiques en Europe orientale*, VI, 1934, pp. 11–73; M. Handelsman, 'Quelques remarques sur la définition de l'histoire de l'Europe orientale', ibid., pp. 74–81; O. Halecki, 'Qu'est ce que l'Europe orientale?', ibid., pp. 82–93.

4

Poland and the Cultural Geography of Medieval Europe

'The land of the Poles is far from the routes of pilgrimage and is little known to any save those seeking trade who travel through it to Russia.' These words were written at the beginning of the twelfth century by Gallus Anonymous, a foreigner living in Poland and entrusted with the task of chronicling the deeds of its ducal house and the history of the country over which it ruled. In this way, that author defined the very limits of a civilization of which Polish culture was a distant representative, situated on the periphery of the Christian West but also lying astride trade routes radiating from Byzantium.

Before considering the medieval beginnings of Polish national culture or the establishment of a Polish state which was so crucial for its emergence, we must briefly examine the extent to which elements of Polish medieval culture represented a continuation of an earlier Slavic tradition. We may then consider how that tradition was affected by Poland's entry into the orbit of Western-European Christendom by outlining the major areas of cultural contact.

For centuries, the Mediterranean basin had been a developed and creative centre of civilization. Continental ethnic communities were stimulated by it and turned towards it to exchange people, goods and information. These people, whom classical tradition described as barbarians, expressed their desire to approach this advanced civilization and partake of its material culture by their continual raiding expeditions and even tribal migrations. Natural conditions, however, impeded contacts between the Slavic peoples and the Mediterranean: mountains barred the way into Greece and Italy while further obstacles were offered by the central and lower Danube, the Sudetan and Carpathian mountains and the impassable forests throughout the region. All these ensured that the Slavs would at best remain on the periphery of the classical world.

Archaeology has contributed a rich store of material evidence of the contacts between the Roman empire and the lands stretching between the Baltic and the Carpathians. The graves of tribal notables dating from the first to the third centuries contain many luxury items which originated in the Roman provinces, or even in Italy itself. Of these burial sites, perhaps the best known are the 'princely' graves at Lubieszów near Gryfice in western Pomerania and at Łęgo Piekarskie near Turek in Wielkopolska. Such remains suggest that Roman influence was not restricted to articles of luxury, prestige or entertainment, but extended to the most fundamental concerns of everyday life: imports from the Roman provinces included various utensils, especially tools. Treasure hoards have also been discovered: one at Grodna near Sierpc contained some six thousand coins which testify to active trade with Roman merchants who were most probably attracted by Baltic amber. The demand for high-quality ceramics from the Roman provinces, especially Gaul, fostered an extensive commercial network which necessitated the establishment of intermediate centres from which the Slavic lands could be reached for regular trade. Finally, Roman influences can also be detected in the techniques which the Slavs applied to metallurgy, pottery and agriculture.

Undoubtedly the tribal elites among the Slavs were affected by such contact with the Roman world, and at least some of these influences were to exert a permanent impact on their material and spiritual culture. One must not, however, exaggerate the extent and weight of this influence since it did not affect basic Slavic psychological attitudes – their way of experiencing or sensing the world and their perception of the relationship between man and nature. Indeed, for the first millennium of the Christian era, the Slavs partook only marginally of the classical tradition, while the migratory movements which occurred around the middle of this period destroyed existing commercial and cultural contacts, though they did at least bring some Slavic tribes into closer proximity to the Roman empire.

The true cultural shape of these early Slavic communities was defined largely by experiences, habits and knowledge developed indigenously. Aleksander Gieysztor, for example, has drawn attention to the diverse materials, varied forms and technical mastery which their local art displayed, even when serving the most mundane needs. This accumulated expertise was enriched over time, though it was material culture which was primarily affected thereby; there was less continuity of development in spiritual culture as long as there was no basic instrument of transmission and preservation such as writing. Transmission through tradition is more resistant to innovation as it preserves the customs, rituals, signs and gestures of a culture. On the other hand, it must be admitted that language is continually being enriched; while being passed from generation to generation and thereby in its own way transmitting a particular world view, it also accumulates social experiences and therefore change. Even before the Slavic migrations irrevocably fragmented the tribes of Slavdom and thrust at least some of them into radically different circumstances, the structure and vocabulary of the spoken Slavic languages had already manifested considerable complexity and maturity, permitting the expression of diverse economic activities, social phenomena and psychological states.

When considering which elements of Polish culture at the beginning of the eleventh century represented a continuation of the earlier Slavic tradition, one should really treat the entire Slavic world as a unit. The evidence recorded by travellers and chroniclers usually treats the Slavs *en bloc*, offering general sketches of their customs and rituals. For example, when beginning his history of the Polish state, Gallus Anonymous felt it necessary first to locate Poland within the Slavic world by describing it as 'the northernmost part of the Slavic regions'. Similarly, he intended his rhetorically exaggerated paean to its natural wealth to apply equally to all the Slavic lands, 'where the air is healthy, the soil fertile, the forest flowing with honey, the waters teeming with fish, the knights warlike, the peasants industrious, the horses sturdy, the oxen apt for the plough, the cattle rich in milk and the sheep heavy with wool.' Linguistic data testify to the

irrecovably
loose

continuing community of the Slavic nations in the common-root language discernible in the speech of its offshoots, while archeology demonstrates the similarities in their material culture and social organization.

Recent research has been sceptical of a common Slavic culture continuing much beyond the great migrations between the fifth and seventh centuries which divided and separated the Slavs. The Jewish traveller Ibrahim ibn Yaqub observed that, 'if it were not for disputes caused by the proliferation of divisions in their branches and fragmentation into tribes, no people would be able to match their strength.' By the beginning of the Christian era, the western Slavs had emerged as a linguistic unit distinct from their eastern brethren, and the process of differentiation among tribal groups continued in subsequent centuries. The first among them to create a state were the Moravians in the south, and the high level of material culture and prosperity which they achieved eventually influenced the Czech and Slovak tribes and even penetrated into the southernmost Polish lands. At the other extreme, the northernmost of the western Slavs were strongly affected by the proximity of the sea. The Polabian and Pomeranian Slavs carried on a commerce which involved even the Arabs, as is demonstrated by archeological finds of Arab money, eastern silks, and silver or glass-work decorated with oriental motifs. Diverse natural and geopolitical circumstances compounded by the influence of different cultures deepened and perpetuated divergent trends in the evolution of particular Slavic tribes, eventually fragmenting irrecoverably the cultural unity of the Slavic world. By the beginning of the second millennium of the Christian era, these tendencies took on a greater significance because of an acceleration in the social and institutional development of distinctive ethnocultural communities both in the Slavic lands and in other regions of Europe.

By the decision of its Piast rulers in the latter part of the tenth century, Poland found a place in Europe within the orbit of Western Latin Christendom. It is unclear whether or not this was the result of a conscious choice; indeed it is not known whether the elites of the Piast state even saw the issue in terms of a distinct choice. In contrast, the chroniclers of Kievan Rus recorded that grand duke Vladimir heard representatives of various religions – the Bulgars speaking for Islam, the Germans for Latin

Christianity, the Khazars for Judaism, and the Byzantines for Orthodoxy – before opting for the last, a decision which placed Rus firmly within the Byzantine cultural orbit. This traditional account probably reflected the historical reality of a Kievan Rus assailed by a multitude of cultural influences.

The West emphasized its links to the classical heritage by proclaiming the twin theories of *translatio imperii* and *translatio studii* to account for shifts in the centre of power and civilization away from the Mediterranean. A more direct continuation of that heritage, however, existed in the Byzantine empire, which regarded Western Europeans as barbarians, as Bishop Liudprand of Cremona discovered during his embassy to Constantinople. Under the Macedonian dynasty, Byzantine culture flourished, the university in Constantinople developed its philosophical and legal faculties, Greek literature preserved the ancient traditions while adding new elements of popular narration, and architecture and the decorative arts evolved forms which were to characterize Byzantine culture to its end.

Centres of Byzantine culture were established among the southern Slavs, developing unique characteristics and a particular intensity which was felt throughout the Slavic world, and the winning of Kievan Rus for Greek culture brought the latter yet nearer to the borders of the western Slavs. Following the conversion of Bulgaria, Greek missionaries penetrated into the central Danube and Moravia and even reached the southern regions of Poland itself, but one cannot see in this any significant link to Byzantine civilization or its economic and political structures. The artistic and intellectual impact of Byzantine culture on medieval Poland has received only limited treatment and awaits systematic research. There is fragmentary archeological evidence of commercial contacts, a few artistic imports, some minimal influence on local art, and perhaps a predilection for jewellery, as was mentioned by Gallus Anonymous. That is what we know at present of Byzantine influence in Poland, and it is weak and circumstantial at best. Perhaps more significant is the fact that Mieszko II (1025–34) is said to have known not only Latin but Greek. This could at least potentially have given him access to the world of Greek thought and writing, though obviously it was in the first place proof of an unusually good education. In any case, the fragmentary evidence we have of the earliest book collections in Poland mentions no Greek titles whatsoever. It would seem, therefore, that as early as the tenth century there was a stronger tendency in Poland towards the West than towards the East, and the decision of its Piast rulers now unambiguously confirmed this. History had clearly linked the rising Polish state to the Europe which was emerging from the Carolingian rather than from the Byzantine tradition.

For the Carolingian world, the lands of barbarian peoples stretched beyond its borders on the *limes Sorabicus* and *limes Saxonicus*. The empire's expansion was directed towards them, and its fortified advanced positions on the left bank of the Elbe and on the upper Danube pointed at the western Slavic tribes. At the same time, some manufactures reached Poland from the Frankish lands, among them silver inlaid weapons recently discovered near Szczecin. This Carolingian interest in the Slavic world continued and became political with the emergence of Ottonian imperial policy in the tenth century. Indeed, historians are still investigating the precise nature of the legal and political ties which developed between the east Frankish state and its Slavic neighbours.

Within the context of the Ottonian court's Eastern policy, the Slavic lands were a. vital element of the imperial structure. Otto I even went so far as to despatch Bishop Wojciech to Kievan Rus in 961, an event which historians see reflected in the above-mentioned chronicles (p. 135) describing Vladimir's reception of Germans representing Latin Christianity. Such a policy was more obviously realized in the case of the Czechs and the Poles, and Otto III even considered 'Sclavinia' to be one of the four components of the empire. A well-known miniature dating from the Ottonian period shows four regions doing homage to the emperor: Roma (Italia), Gallia, Germania and Sclavinia. Thus Poland not only entered into the *res publica christiana*, but was considered to be a partner of the three political successors to the Carolingian empire. The meeting at Gniezno in the year 1000 between Otto III and the Polish duke Bolesław Chrobry was recorded in the *gestae* with a Byzantine symbolism intended to introduce the Polish ruler into the Ottonian family of kings.

Regardless of subsequent relations, such political gestures conditioned the way in which Poland accommodated Western models. The emerging Polish state decisively influenced the consolidation of distinctive Polish cultural and ethnic characteristics, but, at the same time, the ruling dynasty and the elites made great efforts to adapt Poland to the culture of post-Carolingian Europe by accepting the models already established in the West; the results of these efforts can be found in the country's legal system, its administrative organization and its social practices. This process of acculturation was hardly unique or peculiar to early Piast Poland or to its Slavic contemporaries; the same had happened at different times to every part of the barbarian world from which Europe was slowly beginning to emerge.

Tenth-century Europe was characterized by volatile political structures, impermanent borders and unstable authorities. The Ottonian initiatives seemed to promise that Europe might first be born in Germany, but they failed to have permanent results. Western Europe had been divided into two great linguistic regions, the Germanic and the Romance, and it was the latter which assumed the lead in disseminating medieval culture. The great movements which were to affect the whole of Christendom were all born here – the Crusades with their critical influence on social mobility and the collective imagination, the Cluniac reforms of monastic life, the birth of the Cistercian order which reconciled agrarian society with the missionary expansion of Christianity, and the rebirth of education and scholastic life. These movements subsequently spread in vast circles, though their influence weakened as they moved further from their intellectual source.

Centres of learning sprang up along the axis between the Loire and the Main rivers, that is, between central France and the southern German lands. They usually developed around the cathedrals and larger monasteries, and among them we find Fleury, Reims, Chartres, Orléans, Tours, Angers, Laon and Tournai. There were, however, similar centres in other areas. In England, Canterbury, York and Winchester played a comparable role, while in Spain, Vich, Ripoll, Cuxa and Montserrat emerged to exert a continental influence. At the same time the German monasteries at Echternach, Cologne and St Gall developed into important cultural, ecclesiastical and educational centres. As a result, the original cultural skeleton of the Carolingian world was fleshed out by these additional centres. One must also emphasize that an important role in this process was played by the patronage of various princes. Of particular significance was the emerging concept of monarchy, which sought sacral confirmation of its authority and prestige by supporting the cultural work of the monasteries. Thus, for example, the emperor Henry II wanted Bamberg to be the leading centre of imperial influence, and indeed it did become a fundamental model for ecclesiastical organization in the Slavic lands converted to Western Christianity.

In the year 1000, European culture was effectively composed of many isolated islands. Certain centres might exert a wider influence and enter into close contact with other centres, but natural barriers such as mountains, rivers and forests continued to limit communication. Cultural activity was the product of great effort directed at overcoming these natural obstacles rather than being the result of the kind of osmotic process which might occur in conditions of dense human settlement and accelerated circulation of ideas, customs and products. As we have already seen, the fact that the Greek world had reached the borders of Poland did not mean that it could exert any real influence there or offer an alternative to Western culture. Because of Poland's geographical and historical situation, efforts by the Piasts to adopt more advanced cultural models inevitably had to turn towards the Latin West, and it was from that direction that influences entered Poland, with great consequences for the development of its culture.

Above all, there was foreign immigration into Poland. Efforts to convert the country to Christianity and organize an ecclesiastical structure created an immediate demand for educated personnel capable of conducting missionary work and filling church offices. Such people, initially at least, were supplied by Western monastic and episcopal centres located either in nearby Moravia and Bohemia, or in the empire and even in Italy. At the beginning of the eleventh century, the Hermits of St Romuald settled in the western regions of Poland, first in Międzyrzecz and then in Kazimierz Biskupi near Gniezno, but they maintained close ties with their original abbey in Italy. Lively contacts also existed between Polish ecclesiastical institutions and those in Lorraine, one important consequence of the fact that the wife of Mieszko II, Rycheza, came from that area. The archiepiscopal see of Cracow was occupied by Aaron, a Benedictine from Brunvillare who had previously resided at Stavelot in the diocese of Liège. He was accompanied to Poland by another Benedictine from the abbey of St James in Liège. Equally lively contacts were maintained with south German centres such as Regensburg and Bamberg. It was from the latter that a mission set out to convert the pagan Pomeranians during the reign of Bolesław Krzywousty (1102–38).

Such ecclesiastical immigration was not confined to the earliest phase of conversion, and Polish churches and monasteries continued to benefit from an influx of Westerners. An initiative by the congregation at Arrouaise led to a foundation at Sobótka in 1110, which was later transferred to Wrocław. Premonstratensians settling in Silesia and Małopolska in the middle of the twelfth century continued to maintain an exchange of personnel with their parent centres for some time after coming to Poland. The first bishops of Piast Poland were foreigners, among whom Jordan, Unger, Poppo and Reinbern were all from Germany. During the reign of Bolesław Krzywousty, Swidger, the Bishop of Kujawy, came from Bamberg, while the brothers Walter and Alexander of Malonne administered the dioceses of Wrocław and Płock. Indeed, the activities of artistic and intellectual circles in Płock during the administration of Alexander and of his successor, the Franconian or Bavarian Werner, constitute an excellent example of the profound significance such immigration of church officials had for Polish culture.

Cultural transmission was also facilitated by migration in the opposite direction, as Polish clerics journeyed to Western centres. It was even said that there was a Polish prince from Bolesław Chrobry's family among St Romuald's students in Ravenna, though little else is known of him. Poles occasionally entered foreign monasteries, but more frequently they merely visited them and other educational centres for the sake of learning. Sent abroad to study, they returned with the holy books, treatises, and encyclopedic works, the intellectual tools which enabled them to perform their spiritual functions and introduce their acquired knowledge of Western practices, artistic forms and ideas into their own dioceses. Such learning sometimes served as a stimulus to literary activity in the case of individuals such as Master Vincent, but it was more often applied to the Church's spiritual and political work, which was more highly esteemed than writing. Matthew, Bishop of Cracow, is probably one of the interlocutors in a dialogue appearing in one of Master Vincent's chronicles. It is clear from this that he was a learned personality, well versed in Latin; yet we have no examples of his writing save for a letter to Bernard of Clairvaux, urging that Christian luminary to visit Poland and lead a mission into Rus. Iwo Odrowąż was a splendid representative of medieval Latin culture, serving as Leszek Biały's chancellor between 1206 and 1218 and then as Bishop of Cracow, but he too left no writings despite his high intellectual reputation, his contacts with leading Western intellectuals and the wealth of books in his library. Catholicism's international character stimulated travel, especially to Italy, and the chronicles report that Gedko, Bishop of Cracow, together with Giles of Mutina, brought the relics of St Florian from Modena to Cracow.

Clerical migration enriched ecclesiastical culture and stimulated creative activity, which remained a monopoly of the Church for some time, but it also overwhelmingly influenced the political practices and administrative structures of the ducal court and government. Gallus Anonymous, a Western European at Bolesław Krzywousty's court, undertook to write the first Polish chronicle, 'so as not to eat Polish bread for nothing'. Clerics, who in many cases were of foreign birth, also directed the diplomacy of the Polish state. For example, Bishop Reinbern was sent by Bolesław Chrobry (992–1025) as ambassador to the Kievan court, where, however, he was imprisoned.

Migration touched the secular realm as well as the spiritual one. There were already Western knights in the armies of Bolesław Chrobry and we know that his expedition to Kiev in 1018 included a contingent of German warriors. Other Western knights accompanied Kazimierz I Odnowiciel ('the Restorer', 1034–58) on his return to Poland in 1040, and chronicles speak of hundreds of foreign warriors, though this may be something of an exaggeration. The German chronicler Thietmar relates the story of a Saxon knight, Erik, who, pursued in his own country for murder, found sanctuary in Bolesław Chrobry's army. Indeed, Bolesław's favour towards foreign soldiers was noted by Gallus Anonymous, who reported that 'any brave newcomer gaining a good reputation in his service was no longer considered a knight but a royal son; whenever the king heard that any one of them was having difficulties ... he bestowed a profusion of gifts upon him ...'. Memories of these foreign knights were occasionally incorporated into the family traditions of their descendants, especially in the preservation of their names, as in the case of the family name Bałdrzych, which comes from Balderic (Baudry). It should be added that Poland's armies were also augmented by immigrants from its nearer neighbours, such as Bohemia and Rus, where similar chivalric practices had also been established.

Poles might come into contact with Western chivalric society through occasional embassies or through the Crusades. There were only a few Polish Crusaders, the best known of whom was Henryk Sandomierski, the youngest son of Bolesław Krzywousty. Nevertheless, this great movement did influence the thinking and culture of the Polish nobility in a much broader way than simply by impinging on the experiences of a few individuals. Even though Poles appeared only infrequently on the great routes of pilgrimage which formed the medium of commercial and cultural exchange in Latin Christendom, individual encounters still contributed to a definite geographical and intellectual image of Polish culture. Annalists took pains to record that Iaxa of Miechów set out for the Holy Land in 1162: for the collective imagination, recording the fact of a journey to the Near East was no less significant than an actual encounter between a magnate from Małopolska and the people and products of both East and West.

Among Poland's foreign contacts, those enjoyed by the ruling dynasty were especially significant since they affected court life, which in turn influenced the manners of the entire ruling elite. Above all, princely marriages enriched court practices and stimulated artistic creativity, certainly to a greater extent than any other diplomatic initiatives by the Piasts. The dynasty was especially familiar with the imperial court. Bolesław Chrobry resided there as a hostage for some time, and Mieszko II was a prisoner there. Kazimierz I Odnowiciel was familiar not only with the imperial court but also with that of Hungary and with smaller temporal and spiritual centres along the Rhine. The imperial court, moreover, frequently played host to Polish knights and barons. Wars, too, stimulated the dissemination of ideas, particularly since they involved a confrontation between rival military tactics and techniques as well as a confirmation of the fact that a common cult of chivalry existed on both sides.

We have less information about economically motivated migrations. The earliest travellers' accounts emphasize that Poland lay at the crossroads of the great continental trade routes. Though a sizeable Jewish colony settled in Przemyśl, it was able to remain in contact with its co-religionists scattered throughout Europe. Foreign merchants visited Poland to satisfy the demands of the elite for luxury items, but their influence seeped out far beyond their fortified settlements. The Book of Henryków mentions a wealthy Walloon active in Wrocław whose descendants entered the nobility. Among such early contributors to Polish culture were foreign architects and artisans whose names have not been recorded by the chronicles. On the other hand, we can speak with even less confidence about the independent foreign activities of Polish merchants. Merchants from Cracow and Wrocław probably operated along the routes leading east and south through Rus, and they were also probably active in a small colony at Pereyeslav. There may have been Polish activity along the commercial routes leading west, but this was at best only sporadic.

By the thirteenth century, these individual contacts had swelled into a mass migration and colonization which affected groups of people living in small villages as well as in larger towns. By this time, foreign immigration was affecting the language and customs not only of the elite, but of the common people as well.

The transfer of goods and ideas sometimes accompanied human migration, but sometimes it operated quite independently. It would be useful to attempt some overall assessment of the balance of artistic imports, or the circulation of manuscripts and of stylistic influences. Initially such imports served the demands of the church and the ducal court, though individual items might occasionally be found among the furnishings in private dwellings. For example, an imported bronze bowl has been discovered in the grave of a twelfth-century knight at Czersk. Research into the history of art, music, literature, law, material culture and technology has assembled an impressive body of information dealing with foreign borrowings, but for the present the geographical origin of foreign influences in these areas will be presented in only the most general form.

Inventories of Polish imports single out Saxony as a particular source, as the artistic and manufacturing centre at Hildesheim supplied the Polish Church with basic ecclesiastical utensils. Saxon workshops also supplied minor liturgical objects such as small pitchers and dishes for washing hands. The Bavarian role is exemplified by the richly illuminated manuscript from the monastery of St Emmeran at Regensburg, known as the Emmeran Codex. Other artistic items in Polish church treasuries testify to the influence of manufacturing centres in France and lower Lorraine, with croziers, reliquaries, enamels and metal work originating in centres such as Limoges. The previously mentioned connections between Poland and Arrouaise are manifested by magnificent princely diadems from lower Lorraine dating from the middle of the thirteenth century. Goblets found at Trzemeszno may also have originated there, though recent research has suggested that they may have been produced locally. Dinant specialized in cast-metal goods, some of which found their way to Poland. Other luxury items came from northern Italian or even Sicilian workshops: twelfth-century textiles discovered in the gardens of the abbey at Tyniec probably came from Palermo, though the possibility of Anglo-Saxon provenance cannot be ruled out.

Few of the artistic items preserved in Polish collections originated in Byzantium or in the Orient. Commercial connections and minimal Polish participation in the Crusades left no trace in the inventories of surviving art works. Among the few examples of such links are a silver casket of Arabic origin, a silver reliquary found at Łęczyca, which was a richly decorated example of twelfth-century Byzantine craftsmanship, and some glasses with engraved decorations.

Library inventories of the eleventh and twelfth centuries suggest a similar pattern of origin for imported manuscripts, especially the liturgical texts connected with missionary work, though there were also a few literary and private texts as well. Few of these initial imports have survived, and many of the medieval manuscripts preserved in Polish collections entered the country much later. In any case, the manuscripts and miniatures illustrating them which circulated in Poland were the products of scriptoria and artists from all over Europe. Contributions came from nearby neighbours such as the Czechs and Germans as well as from more distant French and Italian sources. Of particular importance were links with the miniaturists and scribes of the Moselle region, who supplied the demands of abbeys, missions, ecclesiastical officials and the ducal court itself. Private commissions also became more frequent. By the middle of the twelfth century the canons of Płock were importing legal treatises directly from Bologna, and it may be assumed that by that time this was a fairly common practice.

The handful of examples presented above suggest the geographical distribution of Polish artistic contacts in this early period. The importance of the art of the Moselle region should especially be stressed since a synthesis of diverse European artistic influences was developed there which supplied Poland with a large number of models, products and people, all of which influenced the subsequent evolution of Polish art. Michał Walicki has seen echoes of this influence in the Romanesque carvings in Wrocław, Strzelno and Czerwińsk, in illuminated manuscripts from Czerwińsk and Płock, in various examples of gold work and even in certain sections of the great doors of Gniezno Cathedral.

From the eleventh century there was a considerable effort made to adapt Western legal norms and systematically combine them with local customary law. Even before Roman law suffused Polish jurisprudence, collections of canon law were used by the Church. The pre-Gratianic *Collectio triparta* was already known in Gniezno and Cracow from the middle of the twelfth century, while Master Vincent's chronicle testifies to the author's familiarity with jurisprudence and his facility in the use of legal concepts. The princes and barons also needed people familiar with the law for day-to-day administration and they themselves frequently referred to available law codes. Thietmar recorded of Bolesław Chrobry, 'whenever he himself felt or was persuaded by some Christian reminder that he had greatly sinned, he ordered the canons to be brought to him that he might determine the way the sin might be atoned for, after which, in the spirit of the laws set down there, he attempted to do penance . . .'.

A mere listing of specific examples will offer no general idea of the numerical significance of the artistic work circulating in Poland during these centuries. Certainly it was not great and was considerably less than in the greatest centres of Latin Europe. Poland received works of only modest calibre and Polish culture was nourished only by the reflected brilliance of Western artistic and intellectual centres through the mediation of secondary centres of production and distribution. Polish culture in these centuries was obviously peripheral and remained so at least until the end of the twelfth century. Such a comparative judgement, however, applies only to the culture of Poland's elite, which fused foreign learning with foreign artistic expression. On this cultural level, Piast Poland could not equal the models which it imitated. The same cannot be said for popular culture, which evolved in ways similar to the developments affecting all European culture in this period.

Medieval culture was syncretic, that is, it joined structures inherited from the barbarian world with elements of the classical heritage. It also operated within the framework of an agrarian society and therefore it also depended on its structures. The classical world view and its notion of man's place in that world did not correspond exactly to the experiences or rhythm of medieval social reality. The traditional religious beliefs and customs of German and Slavic barbarians were intimately linked to their everyday practices and to their own ideas about the relationship between man and nature or man and man. Expanding Christianity accepted and adopted fragments of these beliefs and practices in order to combat paganism as a system and better to perform its social functions. Whenever it set itself the goal of interiorizing the faith of the masses, it achieved this by adopting some of their traditional customs and practices. At the same time, the Church consolidated a monopoly over all higher forms of culture, particularly those associated with the written word. The intellectual culture of the Church emerged from the simplified didactic system of encyclopedic knowledge prevalent in late antiquity, and it therefore developed in opposition to and largely in isolation from the popular culture of lay society.

The syncretism of cultural models is even more obvious if one turns one's gaze from the Church to medieval laymen. Aristocratic life styles grew out of blood ties and were intended to strengthen feelings of common family bonds. This concentration on relation by blood really originated in barbarian concepts, upon which Christianity superimposed its own doctrine of the family with which it became intermingled. The same occurred with the chivalric ideals that arose out of the value structures of a

chivalric

warriors' world, but which were sanctioned by a Church that even associated them with its own monastic obligations.

Poland's entry into the Latin world exposed it not only to a wealthy and functioning intellectual culture, but also to social models and practices which were produced by a fusion of barbarian and Christian values. This syncretic culture was then exported to Poland and other countries where it went through another process of fusion. During this second process of acculturation a significant layer of local traditions, customs and even rituals was preserved within the new Christian framework. What Western Christian culture adopted from the barbarians in Western Europe, and what it subsequently incorporated of local Polish tribal traditions, constitute two different cultural layers which, in the end, are difficult to distinguish in the historical evidence which we possess from the first centuries of Piast Poland.

Because Poland's participation in the Latin culture of the Western elites was still relatively circumscribed, the cultural distance between Polish social elites and the masses was not yet as great as in the West. Consequently cultural barriers were weaker, interaction between elite and popular culture was stronger, and the penetration of folklore into the highest cultural circles was thereby facilitated.

Medieval Poland's ties to the Latin West were complicated by the need to accept foreign cultural models while at the same time continuing the development of the indigenous culture. By way of comparison, one might refer to what the sociologist and cultural historian Stefan Czarnowski wrote in reference to the Romanization of Gaul: 'the acceptance of a foreign culture does not inevitably result in the disappearance of everything which hitherto constituted the indigenous culture ... A great deal of what Celtic Gaul possessed survived not only the loss of tribal independence, but even the Roman empire, the Merovingian and Carolingian eras, and the long centuries of French history – it continues until the present day.' These words, *mutatis mutandis*, can also be applied to the Latinization of Piast Poland.

The international nature of medieval culture was connected with the role and character of the Catholic Church and with the function of Latin as its universal language. This offered both the possibility and the necessity of contacting the main centres in the West. The news of St Wojciech's (Adalbert's) martyrdom reached

Rome at the same time as the first information about Poland and its inhabitants. The course of Polish history was even affected by the decisions taken on the banks of the Tiber, but the reverse was also true in the sense that Poland was vital for the realization of both papal and imperial policies. It was important that the strongest influences either in terms of ecclesiastical personnel or artistic models originated in imperial territories, either in the Romance areas around Liège, or in the Germanic lands of Bavaria and Franconia. This had a significant influence on the nature of the ideal of court and state evolving in Poland, while at the same time creating an awareness of the independent role of a Polish monarchy within the constant structure of imperial ideology. Indeed, we can see one curious example of this fusion in the twelfth-century attempt to introduce the veneration of the emperor Henry II in the diocese of Płock.

Ultimately, perhaps the most interesting aspect of all of these changes pertains to the realm of perception, particularly the perception of space: the local horizon which had been limited to immediate surroundings was now suddenly confused with global concepts that were introduced into the common view of the world by news of pilgrimages to the Holy Land or by the arrival of products and merchants from distant regions of the world. Despite this kind of foreign influence which upset the traditional assumptions, it must be admitted that, because of the limited nature of warfare, the restrictions on human migration and the impediments to the circulation of ideas, medieval man's awareness of space continued to be defined largely by narrow local limits.

Bibliography

A. Gieysztor, 'Christiana respublica et la politique orientale de l'Empire', *Renovatio imperii* (Faenza, 1963).
——, 'Les paliers de la pénétration du christianisme en Pologne au Xe et XIe s.', *Studia in onore di A. Fanfani*, I (Milan, 1962).
——, *La Pologne et l'Europe au moyen âge* (Warsaw, 1962).
W. Hensel, 'La contribution du monde slave', *Sources archéologiques de la civilisation européenne: actes du colloque international organisé par le secrétariat général de l'AIESEE sous le haut patronage et avec le concours de l'UNESCO, Mamaie 1–8 Sept. 1968* (Bucharest, 1970).

——, 'Die materielle Kultur der Slawen im 6–10 Jahrhundert', *Acta II Congressi Internationalis Historiae Slavicae Salisburgo–Ratisbonensis, Anno 1967 Celebrati* (Wiesbaden).

T. Manteuffel, 'Problèmes d'intégration et désintégration des états européens aux IXe et Xe siècles', *L'Europe aux IXe–XIe siècles* (Warsaw, 1968).

5

Geography and Apocalypse: The Concept of Europe According to Jakub of Paradyż

The question of 'European consciousness' touches on fundamental elements of historical culture which concern both the past and the present. Historical reflection on the concept of Europe has been intensive throughout the twentieth century, and particularly since 1945, following the experience of a total war which began in Europe and of totalitarian ideologies and political movements whose origins were also European. A shadow of uncertainty has fallen over the sense of identity of a common civilization. As a result of this attitude the common fates of European culture, and the consciousness of belonging to a common culture such as has been ascribed to the nations and peoples of Europe in the distant past, have been overestimated. There are still too few objective studies on this subject. One area for investigation of the real history of the European idea is the history of words, the manner in which they were used, their scope and given content.

In the medieval vocabulary the term 'Europe' occurs with varying intensity and meaning.[1] It is not until the close of the Middle Ages that it is used rather more generally in Latin writings, no longer restricted to the technical terminology of geographical descriptions; it becomes a concept with a historical and cultural content, increasingly widely used in historical or philosophical works. At the same time the concept of *christianitas* is employed less frequently, the result of an early humanistic concern for reconstructing the classical Latin canon, a growing awareness of the existence of Christianity beyond the confines of obedience to Rome, and the development of national monarchies, which were preparing the ground for the rise of particularism in church structures within specific states or even the development of 'national' churches. This concept of Europe, developing out of the traditional concept of medieval universalism, was more appropriate to the new situation than its predecessors. Without exaggerating the importance of the changes occurring in the terminology used in Poland's Latin writings of the fourteenth and fifteenth centuries, and especially the extent to which these changes reveal the evolution of social consciousness, it is possible to treat the question of employing a concept of Europe as crucial if the processes of modernizing culture and mentality that occurred at the close of the Middle Ages are to be understood. This applies above all to the way of thinking among the church elite of that period; it was precisely within those circles that the ideas, programmes and concepts that shaped the consciousness of those times were formed.

The extent to which a concept of Europe was used in Polish medieval writing still needs to be researched in detail, taking in, besides historical works – it is enough to mention Długosz's discourse on geography – minor texts of an encyclopedic, geographical, theological or even literary nature. I should like to draw attention to a discourse on Europe written by one of the leading representatives of Polish theology in the fifteenth century, first a Cistercian, then a Carthusian, Jakub of Paradyż.

Several copies of the work *De malis huius saeculi per omnes aetates*, written in the 1440s, have been preserved in libraries in Wrocław, Pelplin and Cracow, and in several dozen German libraries, demonstrating the considerable sphere of the author's influence.[2]

The circulation of the treatise was no more than that of a manuscript book; it has not been printed in modern times, but has been included among the published writings of Jakub of Paradyż on the subject of church reforms. The author writes about these reforms in an unusual way, since he discusses the question of moral renewal among Christians and the reform of morality. The treatise is an ambitious attempt to present a history of evil. After a short description of the theory of evil, Jakub of Paradyż expounds the 'story of sin' in the Old and New Testaments –

which occupies half the treatise – in order then to reveal the evil
that exists in his own time and to define the tactics and weapons
for the battle against sin and evil customs. This construction cor-
responds to the general view held by Jakub, who looks at the
world from an eschatological standpoint. It is foretold that sin
and depravity will increase when the earthly world nears its end,
and that is why the Holy Bible advised that *illa tempora pericu-
losa* be carefully observed. It is enough to compare the Christian
life of two or three hundred years ago with that of the present,
and there could be no doubt that, 'if people were silent, the
stones would cry out.' The nearer the end of the world, the more
depraved man's moral behaviour becomes. History is the ceaseless march of depravity. This applies to nature and to people:
when the world began the earth was more fertile, and men lived
longer. It is the same with men's morals, which become more
depraved with each day.[3]

In the middle of the treatise, between the commentary on the
Bible and the section that presents the history of evil in the contemporary world, there is an exposition of the geography of
Christianity. This is dictated by the logic of the work's overall
construction: geography is treated under the cloak of evil, as is
history. History, according to Jakub of Paradyż, is not a series of
events following the laws of chronology or absolute time according to man's calendar, which is measured in days, months and
years. Here time is organized qualitatively; there is a fundamental
turning-point, created by the division between sacred history as
written in the Old and New Testaments and contemporary history, whose subject is the history of the Christian faith and the
Church. In a history which is described somewhat misleadingly
as contemporary, a certain depth of time appears; evolution is
traced by authorities summoned to support the theories or to
illustrate them. Examples are drawn from hagiographical literature to demonstrate that Christian life was nearer to achieving
perfection in the past; reference is sometimes made to ecumenical
councils, popes or the schisms of the previous decades. The purpose is to emphasize the underlying turning-point and fundamental differences; not only is contemporary history tarred with the
brush of evil but it also causes the spread and increase of the evil
that is leading to the end of the world. Its purpose and character
are defined by the fact that the geographical exposition is

constructed around this turning-point and at the heart of the treatise; evil extends into space as well as time.

As the apostles dispersed they set in motion the dissemination of Christianity beyond the frontiers of Judea. Sent to foreign nations, they carried the word of God to Greece, Asia, Africa and the farthest corners of the earth. Finally the apostle 'princes', Peter and Paul, directed their teachings towards Europe, that is, towards the city of Rome, France and the maritime nations to the north and west.[4] Others followed in their footsteps and carried the word of God further afield. Jakub of Paradyż goes on to enumerate the countries of this later Christianizing process, 'as far as us', and they are Denmark, Sweden, Germany, Ruthenia, Prussia, Poland, Hungary, Livonia, England and 'the countries lying near the arctic pole'.[5] The words *ad nos* are significant, for they define the author's true geographical horizon.

In the East, in Asia, India and Africa, the work of the apostles and their pupils had a different fate. Pseudo-apostles, false prophets and heretics appeared; the unity of the Church was torn by schism and heresy. Where there had once been numerous faithful, few remained. Pagans and Saracens had taken over the sites of Christ's Passion and other holy places. The lands once occupied by the Ephesians, Thessalonians, Galatians, Philippians, Macedonians and Corinthians, to whom St Paul had written letters from his Roman prison, were now in the hands of pagan and Saracen rulers. It was a similar story in Africa, where St Cyprian had been Bishop of Carthage, and, later, St Augustine Bishop of Hippo. Vast tracts of land and masses of people had come under the power of the prince of darkness.

I detect a personal note between the lines of Jakub's description of the dissemination of Christianity. It is the view of someone who knows well the Bible and the scholarly works of the church fathers. Apart from regret at the loss of the holy places there is a nostalgic statement that beyond the reach of the Christian faith there were places known to him from reading learned books. 'I do not know', he writes 'if there are many Christians there today.'[6] There is none of the pedantry of the scholar in these words, but rather the nostalgia of someone who knows the world of the past, and the pessimism of an observer of contemporary times. In the summary of the development of Christianity which concludes Chapter XIV of *De apostolis*, a picture emerges of catastrophes rather than of successes, of losses not gains. Only one region avoids this: Europe.[7]

The true exposition of the geography of faith begins at this point. Jakub of Paradyż devotes a whole chapter to it, announcing a description of the lands of the faithful and unfaithful (XV: *Descriptio partialis terrae fidelium et infidelium*). The astronomers, he says, calculate that there are seven *mundi climata*, but on the basis of my limited knowledge it cannot be said that any of them is wholly devoted 'to the true Christian faith'.[8]

For – the author knows this from reliable sources and from his own experience – it is enough to distance oneself somewhat from Cracow, the royal city and capital of the Polish kingdom, in order to meet a mixture of nationalities. In certain towns there are even two places of worship, 'that is, belonging to the unfaithful Ruthenians and the faithful Christians'.[9] Both faithful and unfaithful are to be found under the rule of one and the same monarch, living side by side for ever in the vast territories of Ruthenia and Lithuania. Jakub of Paradyż takes this opportunity to praise his ruler. He presents 'an eye-witness account' of the fact that he is a very Christian and Catholic king who uses his power as befits a Christian monarch. His parents were Christian; it was his father, Władysław, who converted huge numbers of Ruthenians and Lithuanians to Christianity, appointed their bishops and built many churches. Finally he emphasizes the Polish king's policy of tolerance, which forced no one to become a Christian and allowed everyone to continue to worship as their forefathers had.[10]

Looking to the East from Cracow Jakub notes that in Lvov ('sixty miles from Cracow') Catholic churches also coexist with Orthodox, and the further we go the fewer and more scattered are the 'real Christians'.[11] He sees a similar situation in Lithuania, where 'there are not many Christians but there are many forest areas full of wild beasts.'[12] Other peoples live alongside the Lithuanians: Tartars and 'other nations, I don't know what they are called.' The people live there *ritu bestiarum*, worshipping various gods they themselves invented. Referring to a reliable informer[13] Jakub of Paradyż notes that it is possible to reach the Holy Land that way by land. It is here that the countries we read about in the Bible and in historical works are situated. The following list of those countries would seem to outline the geographical horizon which the learned books spread beyond the window of the monastery cell: Ethiopia, Constantinople, Arabia, the Kingdoms of Sheba and Tarsus, India, Antioch, the paradise on Ararat, Babylon, Nineva, Assyria, Syria, the lands of the Medes and Persians, Egypt, Libya and 'many other kingdoms besides'.

Following the example of St Augustine, Jakub divides the lands according to the four corners of the earth and places Asia so that it extends from the southern boundaries, via the East to the West; Africa from the southern regions to another part of the West; and Europe so that it occupies the western territories.[14] The East, identified as Asia, and the West, identified as Europe, form the basic division of the populated world. It is Asia which is named the largest and most noble part of the world; it is here that the centre of the earth is to be found and here lie the bones of many holy apostles, but now it is ruled by idolatry and unbelievers. This demonstrates the extent of the rule of evil over the world.[15]

The place from which Jakub of Paradyż observed Asia was Cracow. He continues his description by returning once more to the Polish capital. To the right of Cracow lie Hungary, Dalmatia and Croatia. These countries remain Catholic, but the Kingdom of Hungary is already under threat. Buda, which is apparently sixty miles from Cracow, is on the route to Transylvania, and that borders Turkey, a country of infidels which touches Asia. This is the end of the Christian world.[16] Unbelief is spreading: the Turks have occupied a large part of the Kingdom of Hungary. And at this point Jakub reminisces about recent events connected with Władysław Jagiellończyk (killed by the Turks, *ut famatur*) taking the Hungarian throne.

'To the left' of Cracow lies Prussia, 'whose territory is not vast but is eminently noble and peaceful'. It possesses sea coasts and, via Gdansk, the roads lead to England, Flanders, Scotland, Denmark and Norway; these are Christian countries. And that is all; not a word about the fact that Teutonic Knights have settled there, that those Prussian lands are a crusader state! Apparently there are still some unbelievers in the far north, but there are Christians in Sweden, Denmark and Norway. If we move further on we come to Ireland, where we find St Patrick's purgatory, and to Britain, whence St Ursula came. Thus we reach Rome[17] and

Spain, where the name of Christ is known everywhere. But Jakub is not certain how far the Catholic faith extends 'beyond Rome'.

The conclusion is pessimistic: the Christian faith occupies only a small, sorry part of the inhabited lands in relation to the huge areas in the power of the prince of darkness. 'Real Christians' are confined and under siege from unbelievers; if they were not in the powerful embrace of Christ's care, the pagans would already have swept them off the face of the earth. The prophesy of the Bible has been fulfilled and the Scriptures have already been taught throughout the whole world. There is no nation, even on the most distant island, which the word of God and the name of Christians have not reached, and yet there are few believers on earth. It is time for the second coming of Christ. If we study history we find no part of the world where the Christian faith has not been taught.[18] The time of the apocalypse is coming. It falls to our generation to experience the last days of life on earth and the end of the world.[19] Let the faithful cleanse themselves; let the unfaithful begin a punishment that will last for eternity.

A description of the history and geography of the world ought above all to lead – says Jakub of Paradyż – to reflection on the journey of faith from place to place, from nation to nation. That is what happened in Old Testament times when, in Abraham's day, the faith passed from the lands of the Chaldeans to the land of Canaan, where Jerusalem lay. The faith was born 'in the centre of the earth'; there lived Adam and Eve and their descendants, and there Christ appeared. In the centre of the world, 'where Jerusalem lies', the salvation, as related in the New Testament, took place and from there the news spread throughout the whole world. The apostles carried it to the East and the South, reaching the very frontiers of the world. In accordance with God's plan the Christian faith reached as far as 'that Europe', and its far corners where no apostle had yet travelled.[20]

The Catholic faith remained (*repausat*) in Europe in the care of the Roman Church, from which part of Greece had broken away half a century earlier – and here follows a reminiscence of the great debates between the Latins and the Greeks. Jakub adds with a certain scepticism that many hope for union at the present time, although memories of the Council of Florence were still alive. He sees the unity of the Roman Church in the hierarchy of church offices, obedience to papal orders, retention of the holy canons and uniformity of sacraments and rites.

Jakub of Paradyż concludes his description of the fate of Christianity and journeys of the faith with an astonishing reflection about the future of Europe: he is not in a position to say – for he has been unable to discover anything definite on the subject in the 'real Scriptures' – what the fate of Christianity in Europe will be. The description in the Bible of the fall of Christianity, which is to take place at the end of the world, poses the question of whether Europe will return to practising pagan rites.[21] We might also consider the question of whether those nations that have abandoned the faith will return to it. And Jakub does not answer that question; he admits his ignorance and leaves the solution to the problem to men who write more fluently or who are better at foretelling the future. He points out only that the Bible prophesies that before the end of the world the Jews will come to believe in the incarnation of Christ and that in fact many Jews are now converting. This demonstrates once again that Jakub of Paradyż's thesis on the history and geography of Christianity is guided by thoughts of the future; the apocalyptic horizon is always present.

The area of knowledge which can be called geographical is rather modest in Jakub's case, considering he represents an intellectual elite. It can be assumed that when he was formulating his description of the world he referred to one of the existing maps of the globe, in his imagination perhaps and not from sight of the material. The geographical information that he uses comes principally from the religious works he has read, sometimes from other people's information or from personal observation, or from current knowledge. I do not think that this devalues the testimony; for the requirements of a history of culture it even presents a certain additional value because it brings us somewhat closer to the level of current awareness.

It is significant that Jakub passes so directly from Cracow, which he knows best, to its surrounding area, then to neighbouring lands, in order to enter – seemingly effortlessly, without breaking the continuity – a world of countries and places known to him from reading the Bible. His passage from local and worldly geography to a geography of the world occurs in a natural way. The division of space is less abrupt and less obvious than the division of time, that is, the hiatus between secular time and holy time. When mentioning names he knows from both Testaments, Jakub seems to have no desire to demonstrate his erudition to the reader. The tone of modesty and a certain scepticism towards his own knowledge or acquired information on geographical subjects is not a writer's device or technique: it has an authentic ring. In his list of biblical names, where the names of countries, nations, towns and mountains are mixed up, I detect the dream of a Christian and reader of books; I find elements of the 'oneiric horizon' of the people of the Middle Ages. And in just this sense those unclear contours of current awareness appear between the lines of this treatise written by a theologian and moralist: the associations that occurred to someone who read the Bible were also those of *illiterati* – those who listened to sermons, public readings or stories and who looked at the iconographical decoration of the churches.

The association of space with historical events also appears as a significant feature of the geographical imagination. Space is recounted in tales: Africa is made up of those countries where St Cyprian and St Augustine were bishops; Ireland is the country where apparently the purgatory of St Patrick is to be found; England is associated with the places of St Ursula's hagiography; Pope Martin came from Panonia. It is not just a question of recording the spaces or a specific mnemotechnical procedure, but it is also a way of achieving ideological supremacy over space and its qualitative organization.

In the manner in which Jakub of Paradyż makes use of the concept of Europe the association between geographical and religious content is clear. As a result of the journey of faith it was precisely Europe that became the privileged place of 'real Christians'. The area of obedience to the Roman Church indicates its frontiers, according to the Polish monk. There is absolutely no recognition of the pluralism of Christianity within Europe. The Orthodox Church is treated as if it lies beyond the pale of faith and is considered *infidelitas*, as is paganism. So Europe is Catholic, and obedience to Rome determines its unity, as does the hierarchical organization of the Church, rising above national divisions, and the community of the liturgy, church law and religious teaching. I do not think it is possible to treat such an understanding of European community as a simple continuation of the traditional concept of universalism, except that there is no emperor. What remains of the centralist idea is recognition of the principle that the naming of prelates was to rest in the hands of the pope. Jakub of Paradyż is a firm conciliarist and he understandably places emphasis on recognition of the holy canons, unity of the church sacraments and community of rites. And so, above all, *cultus*: the community of culture is foremost.

It would be difficult to admit that the concept of Europe, expressed in this way, is used only as an element of the laicizing *instrumentarium* of thought. It replaces the concept of *christianitas*, but to a considerable extent it also perpetuates its fundamental substance.

Jakub of Paradyż's view of Europe is clearly local in nature; with a certain amount of exaggeration we might say that this is a Pole looking at Europe. The structure of the treatise, in which Cracow appears as the point of observation, demonstrates this, and the sequence of the description is indicated by the way in which individual countries are positioned in relation to Poland. Jakub presents the Turkish threat, which was one of the elements in the formation of an awareness of European community at that time, from the point of view of Jagiellonian Poland, reminding us of the role of Władysław Jagiellończyk and the battle of Warna. He notes Jagiełło's role in the Christianization of Ruthenia and Lithuania. He emphasizes the Christian character of the Jagiellonian monarchy, and does not treat it as a frontier margraviate of Christianity. This view of Europe and the world from Poland shows none of the characteristics of provincialism, for the whole of Europe is on the periphery.

It is surprising that the conversion of Lithuania to Christianity was treated so marginally. It was in fact a highly significant event for the identification of Europe with Christianity: after all, the last pagan country in Europe disappeared when Lithuania was converted. It could have been treated as evidence of the triumph of Christianity, but – according to Jakub – it was not.

This, however, is a result of the eschatological horizon of the work, which seems to place both time and space at the end of time. The fact that Europe is Christian is announced not as a success but as a disaster. The central point of the world is the Holy Land. Asia is the place of Christian dreams; Europe is Christian, but that means that it is the last refuge of a withering Christianity, and proof of the approaching end of time on earth.

Notes

1 I deal with this matter in more detail in Chapter 3 and in 'La notion d'Europe et la prise de conscience européenne au bas Moyen Age', in *La Pologne au XVe Congrès International des Sciences Historiques à Bucarest*, ed. S. Bylina, Wrocław, 1980, pp. 69–94. Bibliographical references can be found there. The conditions under which I wrote the present outline, in Jaworze, forced me to limit my scholarly apparatus to the indispensible minimum.

2 *Jakub z Paradyza: a collection of texts concerning church reforms*, ed. S. Porębski, Warsaw, 1978 (*Textus et studia historiam theologiae in Polonia excultae spectantia*, vol. VI), pp. 103–273; the edition was produced on the basis of the Pelplin manuscript.

3 This treatise is included in the introduction to the work, or *Proemium* (ibid., pp. 106–7), while the following statement occurs in the conclusion of the tract: 'quoniam vere dies mali sunt et mundus totus in maligno positus est' (ibid., p. 273).

4 Ibid., p. 187.

5 Ibid., p. 187: 'qui etiam ad nos usque ad Daciam, Sueciam, Germaniam, Russiam, Prussiam, Poloniam, Hungariam, Livoniam, Angliam et alia terrae climata sub polo arctica iacentia verbum Dei seminaverunt.'

6 Ibid., p. 188.

7 Ibid., p. 188: 'Tandem inoviolata fides ab illis praenominatis terris et mundi partibus, ubi coepit repulsa hodie in sola Europa est arctata.'

8 Ibid., p. 189.

9 Ibid., p. 189: 'scilicet Ruthenorum infidelium et christianorum fidelium'.

10 It is significant that Jakub of Paradyż considers Catholicism alone to be the 'true faith', counting the orthodox as 'unbelievers'; he also emphasizes tolerance of oligarchy *in sua perfidia remanentibus* (ibid., p. 189) and rejects the imposition of the faith by force. Cf. U. Borkowska's work *Treści ideowe w dziełach Jana Długosza: Kościół i świat poza Kościołem* [The substance of the ideas in the works of Jan Długosz: the Church and the world outside the Church], Lublin, 1983, on this question.

11 *Jakub z Paradyża*, op. cit., p. 189.

12 Ibid., p. 189.

13 Ibid., p. 190: 'a fide dignis accipi . . .'

14 Ibid., p. 190: 'Europa [continet] partem occidentalem, in qua nostra fovetur habitatio.'

15 Ibid., p. 190: 'Ecce mala mundi istis temporibus et in illis partibus.'

16 Ibid., p. 190: 'Ibique iterum fidelium terra finem habet.'

17 Ibid., p. 191: 'usque ad Romanam urbem quae inter occidentales computatur partes.'

18 Ibid., p. 192: 'Recensentes enim omnes historias, non reperimus terrae partem aliquam, in qua fides christiana no sit annuntiata.'

19 Ibid., p. 192: 'Nos sumus, in quos fines saeculorum devenerunt ... finis mundi est in foribus.'

20 Ibid., p. 193: 'in hac Europa, ad quem saltem quo ad eius fines nullus legitur Apostolus aut eorum convicim advenisse.'

21 Ibid., p. 194: 'Utrum vero Europa, relictura sit fidem conceptam et ad ritus gentilium reversura sicut ceterae nationes, puto, nil certum me in scripturis anthenticis aliquid legisse?'

6

The Nation-State in Twentieth-Century Europe

The growing pressures and demands of supranational integration have given rise to a degree of uncertainty as to the fate of the nation-state. This uncertainty is reflected both in the political realities and in the social consciousness of the West. The idea of 'Europe' seems hardly to have emerged from its teething period, yet the concepts of 'nation' and 'fatherland' are already faded; there seems to be no place for them in the idea of Europe and the concrete manifestations of it which we see today.

In countries further removed from Europe's political and cultural centres, however, the concepts of 'Europe' and 'nationhood' have evoked a much more immediate and heartfelt response. These are the countries of East-Central Europe: countries whose European identity is well grounded culturally and geographically, but not at all politically. It is here, on the Vistula, the Moldau or the Danube, that the idea of Europe has genuine roots in the aspirations of the people. Here, the nation – or the nation-state – is not something self-evident and well entrenched in history; it is a question, a hope, an aspiration. Moreover, it is precisely through this distant and much-desired European prospect that a nation can affirm its cultural identity and realize its existence as a political entity. In this part of the European continent there is no contradiction between 'Europe' and 'nations'; on the contrary, the two are mutually dependent. For while we naturally associate Europe with cultural diversity, it also represents, in the world of the late twentieth century, the antithesis of an imperial order: the universalism of European civilization is buttressed by its very rejection of a universal political order. For such a Europe, nations are the national basis of political organization – at least, this is how things should be from the perspective of East-Central Europe.

But is it not anachronistic, this cry of the weak demanding the right to their own state? It is, after all, global strategies that decide the effective world order; on the economic scene it is the multinational companies that play the leading role; the sovereignty of states is necessarily diminished and restricted, while mass culture, as it reduces artistic tastes and the consumption of goods to a bland uniformity, undermines the deepest foundations of national diversity. The nation-state seems to be a matter of genuine concern only in those places which the political programme of the French Revolution has not reached – or, to put it more precisely, where it was not implemented on a sufficiently long-term basis.

In the middle of the last century, during the Spring of Nations, the revolutionary force contained in the idea of nationhood became the common property of all Europe. Lewis Namier argues that intellectual circles around 1848 produced the richest and broadest range of programmes and ideas, which continued to be propagated and elaborated well into the last quarter of the following century; and it was indeed around 1848 that the fullest affirmation of national aspirations took place. The near-ubiquity of these aspirations was such that basing the organization of a state on ethnic bonds was considered an inalienable right; while the lack of one's 'own' state – that is, a nation-state – led to feelings of profound wrong and collective frustration. On the other hand one may assume that those nations which had never been forced to struggle for political independence, and, albeit obliged from time to time to defend it, enjoyed it as a natural right, lacked this deep national sensitivity, and consequently now have no qualms about availing themselves of supranational political organizations as instruments to meet the challenges of the future.

Thus the legacy of the revolutionary idea of the nation-state is a controversial one in Europe today. In East-Central Europe it defines a genuine, indeed fundamental, focus of social aspirations. The mini-nationalist movements which sometimes emerge within certain Western states, when the distinction between a desire for autonomy and aspirations to independent statehood seems fluid, are an extension of this front. One hardly supposes that the Bretons aspire to an independent state; but what about the Basques? Most European countries today, however, are intertwined within European, that is, supranational, organizations. The economic community, the European Parliament, European commissions and committees, regular inter-governmental consultations, the common projects of the political community, one united army and one government – all this has become a significant area of public life. In spite of all these factors, however, this tendency is not a strong one: voter turnout at elections to the European Parliament remains low, and the countries of the European continent seem afflicted with a permanent inability to articulate their common interests and goals. One thing, at least, is clear: in Europe today, the desire to affirm identity and independence as a nation-state coexists side by side with the aspiration to membership of supranational organizations and political institutions.

In order to come to understand the contemporary relevance of the revolutionary legacy, or indeed to reject it as anachronistic, we must first provide a more precise definition of the very concept of a nation-state. In seeking such a definition, we must identify the historical content inherent in the concept of a nation-state and describe the functional advantages of applying it in a social and political analysis of our time.[1]

The term 'nation-state' is a fusion of two separate concepts, those of 'nation' and 'state'. Both are history-laden. Whatever the meaning associated with each of them by various schools of thought, there has never been any doubt that they play the leading role on the historical scene, for they are the most obvious and natural tools for describing and understanding collectivities. Clearly, they are also a subject of study in themselves, in that they are the products of history, complete with birth certificate.

The state may be seen, in the wake of Max Weber, as an organization exercising a monopoly of power and constraint or, according to Hugh Seton-Watson, as an organization demanding loyalty and obedience from its citizens. Both contemporary events in Africa and our memory of Europe's past show that the state is an institution with a definite beginning.[2]

The birth of the state in the history of Europe is a distant event. We continue to imagine a time before the existence of states, rationalizing the historical nature of state structures. In the twentieth century, the gradual creation of states on other continents has strengthened the image of the state as a historical entity, although these states have been of a specific and modern kind, their basic reference being the ethnic group; this has been true even in cases where such a group has emerged only as a result of the creation of a post-colonial state. Even if it is true to say that groups of people have always and everywhere created a certain kind of political organization, it is nevertheless equally true that the 'monopolization of power' is a historical phenomenon. It has assumed diverse forms and derived its legitimacy in various ways. Indo-European ideology continued until the eighteenth century to provide the basic conceptual structures necessary to justify the power of a few over many. Later attempts to justify such power have involved appeals to the will of large collectivities, such as society or the nation.

In eighteenth-century thought the opposition between state and society[3] was so sharp and clear that one is sometimes justified in attributing to that time the birth of that particular distinction. Indeed, Otto Brunner believes that such a distinction was unthinkable within the framework of a state system.[4] But in fact the concept of the *societas civilis* was already emerging in the Middle Ages, from the great intellectual debates of the thirteenth century concerning the reception of Aristotle and the spread of Roman law. The distinction between state and society, absent from oriental models of historical evolution, plays an important role in the evolution of the West from the Middle Ages onwards.[5] The separation of the concepts of state and society which evolved in modern times brought out not only the restructuring of the social fabric which was taking place but also, and most importantly, a new conception of the state. The basic point of reference, both in the creation of states and in establishing their legitimacy, became the nation.

No less controversial is the time at which the idea of the nation can be said first to have emerged. In one view, nations are the product of the Middle Ages, created from a variety of ethnic communities, in particular multi-ethnic political organizations. In another, medieval ethnic communities do not deserve the name of nations, for they were either cultural and linguistic groups or Estate corporations which participated in decisions concerning the state. Nations, on the other hand, emerged only in modern times, as ethnic collectivities became political communities. At the root of these different ideas of nationhood lay the question of national consciousness and the degree of its spread; romantic glorifiers of the naturalness of national bonds, such as Ernest Renan, when he argued that the nation is a new phenomenon, sought their arguments in the realm of mass psychology. Later exponents of the modern theory of the birth of nations shifted the centre of gravity of their arguments to more objective criteria. In 1913, during debates on the social-democratic programme and the national question, Stalin is recorded as having remarked that the process of the liquidation of feudalism and the development of capitalism was also a process of the formation of people into nations. Not many years later, in 1929 – by which time his pronouncements had the force of an edict – he wrote categorically that 'nations did not and could not exist in the pre-capitalist era.' This gave rise to a certain terminological canon in Marxist historiography, whereby the concept of a nation was reserved for the modern era, or the era of capitalism, and terms such as 'nationality' were preferred when referring to earlier periods.[6] The basis for this distinction was the degree of cohesion and durability: before the capitalist era, ethnic communities lacked economic cohesion, and this made them unstable and short-lived. Behind the layers of doctrinal obstinacy and imprecise definitions, however, this historiographical debate also reveals a glimpse of the genuine fabric of the past: the diversity of forms which national bonds assumed at various periods of European history and the changing significance of those bonds in the social consciousness and ideology. But in spite of these changes the bonds were always of the same kind; it is therefore safe to assume that the nation is a long-lasting phenomenon.[7] The modern era brought with it a clear strengthening of national bonds, and in particular the spread of national consciousness to the masses and the peculiar fusion of society, state and nation. The concept of the nation-state expresses a new symmetry in the long history of the nation as a phenomenon.

'The Third Estate, which is nothing, becomes everything.' In these words, published on the threshold of the French Revolution, the abbé Sieyès combined a diagnosis of social reality with a programme. His pamphlet *Qu'est-ce que le Tiers Etat?* can be seen as being addressed to all those who had not enjoyed the privileges of blood or entry into the old structures of power. They had been used as instruments of power, had even, some- times, been its mainstay, but had been denied the entirety of their rights, as subjects, to participate in the exercise of power. Most striking in Sieyès' argument is its negative aspect: it is a rejection of the monopoly of class and the exclusive role of the aristocracy, and an attempt to demonstrate that such a monopoly contradicts the demands of public order. His positive programme, although less clear and ideologically controversial, concerns the creation of a new kind of public life – a new *polis*, a civil society in which the subject of the *ancien régime* becomes a citizen, or a nation- state which embodies the sovereignty of the people. François Furet describes Sieyès' programme as aiming to 'fonder la nation contre la noblesse.'[8] This applies to both the subjective and the objective elements of the project: the feeling of belonging to a community created by the will of the citizens, and the fact that a new nation is created by a community of people who have excluded the aristocracy and assumed responsibility for the state to which they have pledged their loyalty.

Thus the nation-state is neither a national state, that is, a polit- ical organization whose borders are identical to or concurrent with the borders which define the settlement of an ethnic group, nor a 'Staatsnation', that is, an ethnic community which has proved capable of assuming possession of its own state. It is a peculiar amalgam of the concepts of nation, state, society and a people. Its essence is the idea, born on the wave of the French Revolution, of combining power and the community, or, better still, basing power on the community. Such a conception of the birth of the modern nation casts a singular light on our under- standing of what the idea of a nation-state means in twentieth- century Europe; it affects our view of the strength and scope of ethnic bonds, the principles on which states exist and function, the relations between the governing and the governed, and the scope of community solidarity.

From the historical point of view the issue is a complex one. The modern idea of the nation was born in a dialectic of force and contract, particularism and centralization, conflict and community. The association of the nation-state with political democracy was the culmination of a long process, and the aberrations and paroxysms of nationalism in the twentieth century indicate that democracy is only one of many possible programmes for the nation-state. Territorial integration, the slow and gradual transformation of unstable dynastic states, which predominated in the political landscape of the eighteenth century, into large and populous dynastic states and finally into industrial nation-states, was a long process. The distribution of power among the various social strata underwent a similar process of evolution. Norbert Elias attributes the slow pace of the formation of nation-states to the fact that until the First World War the exercise of power was largely in the hands of the upper classes of the *ancien régime*.[9]

Certainly, in the case of France, which may be taken as the classical model, the extension of the sociological framework of the nation and the anti-aristocratic nature of the process by which the modern state came into being were clear and unwavering. In other countries this process was slower and less sharply marked, and its effects were slow in making themselves felt. The hiatus between the avowed will to change and the implementation of a programme of change was slow to disappear.

Marshall Ignacy Potocki, one of the authors of the Polish Constitution of 3 May 1791, made a remarkably significant confession in a letter written near the end of 1789 to one of his collaborators in the programme of reform. He wrote, 'I have tried not to offend foreigners by the use of aristocratic terminology. Our programme refers only to the nation and its citizens, but in fact the nation is the First Estate, and the citizens are the nobility. If other classes should one day have the desire and the will to be free, they will be able to say to the nobility, "we are the nation to a much greater extent than you"; and the nobility will find no reply to this.'[10] Thus this aristocrat and enlightened reformer was aware that, in the Poland of his day, the political nation was the nobility, and that other social forces were not yet ready to assume this role; at the same time he aimed to create the necessary legal and ideological framework for implementing the revolutionary programme. The argument of his programme was the reply to the question of who makes up the nation.

The nineteenth century retained the old framework, both in its social structures and in its main conflicts. The landed aristocracy and the court elites continued to repel the pressures of the industrial and financial middle classes; beyond these, the aspirations of the working classes towards some participation in political life were only beginning to emerge (indeed, they were used by the former as a weapon against the latter; both Disraeli and Bismarck appeal to the working classes in the struggle with industrial and liberal groups).[11] Where dynastic monarchies were built on relatively homogenous ethnic foundations, this process gained momentum through the creation of representative systems of government; elsewhere it led to the emergence of political movements whose programmes offered ethnic communities the possibility of creating their own state. None of this, however, entailed the spread of national consciousness. The masses were slow and reluctant to adopt the idea of a community with the upper classes, and the condition for convincing them of the intimate link between the individual and the public sphere was the development of culture and the growth of communication between those who make the decisions about the fate of the country and those who submit to them. But the principle had been formulated: the sovereignty of a state is grounded in its existence as a nation and as a civil society.

In modern history the nation-state has demonstrated its strength in a pragmatic way: it is the most effective. Karl Deutsch wrote, 'Where there is one nation, nation-states, whether communist or capitalist, have become the normal instruments of governing modern industrial societies.'[12] But this was far from being the case in most of modern Europe. At the turn of the eighteenth century, the idea of the nation-state could establish itself in this way within the already existing state borders of France, Great Britain, Spain or Holland, but certainly not in Germany or Italy or in Central or Eastern Europe. Both ancient and modern imperial structures stood in the path of its progress: the legacy of the Holy Roman empire and the Ottoman empire, and the new Habsburg empire. But the trend was unequivocal, and was realized with increasing momentum on a worldwide scale. From the fall of the Napoleonic empire to 1890, seven nation-states were added to the map of the world; another 25 appeared before the Second World War; and after 1945 a further hundred or so nations gained political sovereignty. In Europe itself, this trend has continued unabated for two centuries, leading to the general acceptance, in practice, of the political principle whereby each nation has the right to an independent state. Equally, there have been cases counteracting this trend, either because a country has lost its independence as a state or because of the emergence of a model of a dependent state.

The political beginnings of Europe were defined by 'master nations' (Namier) in competition with one another. At the Congress of Vienna the balance of power was distributed in such a way as to neutralize the predominance of France; at the same time, however, nation-states were consolidated. But fundamental to the success of the Congress of Vienna was the determination to base the new order on certain principles, and in particular on the strength of the principle of legitimism. The effects of this new order, safeguarded by an alliance of four powers, were long-lasting; but the chief unsolved territorial problem of the nineteenth century remained the question of what nation-states should be created in Central and Eastern Europe.[13] After both world wars, regardless of the fact that they were *world* wars, the organization of a new political order in Europe was the main problem, and the principle of ethnically based states was an accepted one. The states brought into being after the First World War, although two of them, Yugoslavia and Czechoslovakia, were composite creations, expressed the will to political independence on the part of those small and medium-sized nations bound together by cultural ties and by the memory of their past independence. That their aspirations could be fulfilled was the result of international decisions taken at a particular time, when the European powers which had initiated the Great War had lost their significance. But perhaps more important even than a weakened Russia, Austria and Germany was the disintegration of the empires of the Habsburgs, the Romanovs and the Hohenzollerns. These, let us note, were European empires, and therefore state creations fulfilling their 'imperialist' ambitions in relation to other European nations.

The Second World War did not entail the disintegration of an empire. The defeat of the Third Reich was of a different order: it was a case of a nation-state (the first in German history to encompass a whole nation) aspiring to the conquest and subjugation of other nations. This war left Europe unequivocally weakened in its role, relegated to the shadow of two competing superpowers. European states might be justified in seeing in both these powers a potential threat to their political, economic or cultural independence. But for the Eastern part of the European continent this aftermath of the war meant becoming part of an imperial system which was in contradiction to the basic structures of a nation-state, both in violating the principle of the sovereignty of a nation-state and in rejecting the democratic organization of public life.

The Second World War revealed the weakness of the post-Versailles order, which both the French system and the League of Nations were powerless to defend. Even at the start of the war, there was a clear and prevalent feeling that Europe was in a state of crisis. It was in Europe, after all, that totalitarianism was born, and the programmed destruction of the fundamental values of the European heritage was proclaimed to be a continuation of those values. This time the barbarians, that classical threat to Europe's civilization throughout its history, did not come from outside. Europe's infinite ability to question herself, her ceaseless self-doubt and capacity for self-criticism – a capacity to which Leszek Kołakowski attributes fundamental significance, seeing it as Europe's essential defining feature[14] – seems this time to be pushing her to the brink of an abyss, towards her own annihilation. Everything must be subjected to doubt, even the idea of the nation-state. Indeed, the idea of the nation-state most of all, since the motivating power behind the development of national socialism was nationalism.

At the beginning of the war, in February 1940, Namier, in considering the weakness and inconsistency of the post-Versailles system, wrote: 'The first task is to save Europe from the Nazi onslaught – a difficult task; but even greater will be the work of resettling a morally and materially bankrupt world on a new basis.'[15] This was a view embraced not only by intellectuals – a bitter reflection on the part of the clerks on the powerlessness of values and sound programmes; it was shared by the European political elite, and by the politicians whose task it was to determine the shape of postwar Europe. It was clearly imperative to uphold the principle of the nation-state; it was, after all, the Organization of United Nations which was responsible for the political balance of the new order, with the great powers guaranteeing its permanence, as they had after the Congress of Vienna.

But in practice the new map of Europe took shape in the course of Churchill and Stalin's schoolboy game of passing notes under the table; added to this was Roosevelt's distrust of European 'anachronisms', among them nationalism, the pejorative associations of which were easily extended to encompass the aspirations of nations, especially smaller nations, to their own independent state.

The post-Yalta European order, as it came to be known, emerged in the course of a lengthy political interchange and successive conferences of the allied powers. Its aim was to subdue Germany, which was responsible for unleashing both world wars. At the same time, however, the division of Europe into spheres of influence was also a constituent part of this new order, and this is hard to reconcile with the philosophy of imposing exemplary punishment on an aggressor. Need one recall the fate of Poland, whose subjugation (and partition) was the first act of aggression? Once an active subject of the war against the Axis, through its movement of armed resistance and the participation of its army, it became an object, and no more than an object, of the political negotiations which defined the postwar order. At one of the conferences Stalin is alleged to have referred to the small European nations as 'little birds, which should sing what they are told to sing'. Such an utterance may, of course, be put down to that notorious 'brutality' of Stalin's with which Lenin reproached him in his famous 'testament'; but it was also characteristic of the way in which the political fate of Europe and the world was decided. Regardless of the fundamental differences between the sides involved and the dissimilarity of their goals, programmes and political systems, the division of Europe into spheres of influence was an imperial principle in action; it was part of an imperial order.

It is a matter for debate whether such imperial systems necessarily conflict with the idea of the nation-state. The fact remains, however, that the decisions taken at Yalta, while clearly grounded on the same principles concerning the right of nations to their own state as guided Woodrow Wilson a quarter of a century earlier, and based, just as clearly, on the principles of representative democracy through which a nation determines the shape of its state, nevertheless sanctioned the end or at least the restriction of the sovereignty of small nations. This situation was certainly not created by the Yalta conference; it was the result of the balance of power and the distribution of armies. But it was accepted, at Yalta, Teheran and Potsdam, in the name of neutralizing conflicts.

The contemporary relevance of the principles involved in the idea of the nation-state can be considered from several aspects. The first and most obvious, perhaps even trivial, concerns the international balance of power. The second may be broadly defined as concerning internal political systems or community structures. Finally, the third concerns the conflict between national characteristics and the trend towards the economic, political and cultural unity of Europe. Each of these aspects of the idea of the nation-state is a tangle of ambivalent and contradictory currents, and it is because of this that the line between programme and analysis is so thin, and that a vision can so easily be mistaken for reality. In each of these areas hopes and dangers coexist.

No one questions the principle of the right of nations to self-determination; it is the basis of the European political order. It does not, however, remove the threat of hegemony. The current European political order, dominated by the rivalry between the United States and the Soviet Union, may be treated as one whole, with the possible threat of hegemony from one side or the other. But one can also exclude both powers from Europe, which is probably no less arbitrary than including them. Then the problems of Europe become internal ones. But the European political order is divided in the same way as Europe is divided; east of the Elbe the problem is the maintenance of the imperial system and the dependence of nations within it, while west of the Elbe the problem is the threat of hegemony. A brief comment will suffice on the situation east of the Elbe: there is no place in Europe today for imperial systems; the countries of Central and Eastern Europe must recover their national independence and their right to a sovereign state. This is what should happen, but the logic of history is governed by its own rules, or at least proceeds at its own pace.

The degree to which this process of 'historical necessity' can be speeded up depends to a great extent on how the situation evolves in the rest of the continent, and thus on relations between the Western states. For it is not true to say that implementing the principle of nation-states neutralized conflicts and ensured international harmony. As George Kennan said in 1954, 'The German problem in its present form was born in 1871, with the realization of German unity. The terrible European wars of our century reflect the fact that it has not been, and probably could not have been possible, to find an appropriate place within the European community of sovereign states for a Germany that was both united and sovereign.' The political history of the European continent is marked by the fear that one of the national states would attain hegemony in Europe, and this fear has been a permanent source of conflict and apprehension. Raymond Aron, a shrewd observer of the twentieth-century political scene, alluded to it in 1968: 'European national states, like Greek city-states much earlier, feared the hegemony of one state. The strongest among them represented the greatest threat, and came to assume in the eyes of the others the form of a common enemy liable to destroy the existing order.'[16] This feeling of threat affects in a negative way the degree to which we can see the nation-state as an effective instrument for safeguarding national interests. Its effects are also felt in the East, for in justifying the need for a 'protector' it also rationalizes the view that a condition of dependency is a natural and inevitable one for small states.

The German problem reveals the internal contradictions of national self-determination as a basis for international harmony. Throughout the European continent, the formation of nation-states was preceded by a relentless process of centralization, in the course of which conflicts between regions and provinces were played down, while regional and national ties were emphasized. In the case of Germany, the *Zollverein* of the nineteenth century was the foundation on which the nation-state was built; but a large degree of autonomy was retained, and Bavaria and Prussia, for example, remained profoundly divergent in their regional structures. But there is another aspect of the problem to be considered, quite apart from the political issues involved in a united Germany, that is Germany's entanglement in the relations between the two superpowers, and the fears of Germany's neighbours after the experience of two world wars; and it is an aspect which touches the heart of the German national problem. For the idea of the nation-state is underpinned by the assumption that a nation is a conscious or voluntary community, a *communauté volontaire*; but what is the basis of the German nation-state? How should its borders be determined and its limits defined? Ethnic or linguistic criteria will not suffice in this case, for while Germans inhabit the states on both sides of the Elbe, there are other territories beyond the boundaries of those states which are inhabited by German-speaking people. And the symmetry of Germany's 'two states' is a dubious one, because the difference between them does not reside merely in the divergence of their political systems. Władysław Gomułka is alleged to have remarked at one point that the German Democratic Republic was not a state, but a punishment for the war. The national consciousness of both German states has evolved in different directions, not always reducible to a common denominator; but the feeling of national unity is unquestionably there. Indeed, unofficial results at the Olympic Games are sometimes calculated jointly for the FRG and the GDR, although it is doubtful whether the supporters of both countries display a similar degree of unity.

In the case of Germany, the disintegration of the concept of the nation is linked not only to the constraints encountered in the nineteenth century in the realization of the idea of the nation-state, or to the problem of a divided Germany as it is today, but also to the German feeling of responsibility for Nazism. The 'historians' dispute' (*Historikerstreit*), the great debate over German responsibility for Nazism which has been going on in the FRG in recent years, has highlighted the difficulties of German identity today.[17] Nevertheless, a feeling of historical continuity is part of what makes up a nation; it is a constituent element of a nation's identity. No one who has read Fernand Braudel's last work, *Identité de la France*, can be in any doubt about this. But in the case of Germany the problem of apportioning responsibility for Nazism appears to remain an insurmountable obstacle. The appeal to a common history and the national spirit, to what Jürgen Habermas terms the conventional feeling of identity,[18] evokes the spectre of recent history and opens the way to a return of German nationalism, or at least, in the common view, creates the danger of such a return.

Thus the least painful solution to the 'German problem' may be sought in a supranational or an international context. One way would be to obtain Moscow's approval for uniting or confederating the two German states, which would have to involve the neutralizing or 'Finlandization' of both states or the creation of an entirely new entity. In 1952, Stalin, and later Khrushchev, alluded to such a possibility. The idea continues to have its adherents in Germany today. It seems unlikely, however, that the prospect of another Rapallo would enjoy either the support of the main political forces within the FRG or the necessary political conditions beyond its borders.[19] In any event, such a decision would take place within the context of the Soviet-American game, and would thereby be part of what we may, simplifying slightly, call an imperial order.

Another way to achieve the same end would be through the political integration of Europe, within which a place could be found for the German state. But the threat of hegemony would remain in such a case, for while the Federal Republic is techni-cally and economically the most powerful country of the Western community, the other German state is also economically the strongest of the Eastern block; uniting the two would therefore create a threat. The proponents of this solution argue that if the Federal Republic has not achieved hegemony within the Western community of states, it would be even less likely to do so within a united Europe, where both German states would account for a proportionately smaller part of the population.[20] A European community thus conceived would therefore have to overcome the post-Yalta division of Europe and achieve an independent role on the world political scene. Looked at realistically, such an argu-ment requires either great optimism or great patience. On the other hand, contemporary history is marked by violations of the principles of simple extrapolation.

Thus the case of Germany today reveals genuine difficulties in seeing the idea of the nation-state as a realistic working principle for Europe in the late twentieth century. But the solutions men-tioned above are situated outside the national context. Realistically speaking, and putting aside the temptation to indulge in hopes and desires, we must admit that there is a con-flict, on the one hand, between the Germans' due right to the unity of their state and nation and, on the other, both the current political order and the current state of German national con-sciousness.

This is a genuine problem. It nevertheless remains true that Europe's political geography confirms the significance of a harmonious relationship between nation and state, in which the state is the expression and the instrument of collective identity, the guarantor of the physical basis of the nation and the guardian of the national memory.

Turning to the question of the internal political system of the nation-state, we should note the striking divergence between the initial revolutionary principle and the political practice over the past two centuries. For a nation-state can be democratic or anti-democratic, parliamentary or authoritarian, and there is no connection between the ethnic homogeneity of its inhabitants and its system of rule. In the course of the twentieth century, political movements which aimed – sometimes successfully – to subvert the democratic order did so precisely in the name of state and nation. The idea of the nation implemented in the modern state, however, was based on an appeal to feelings of community, thereby favouring pro-democratic tendencies of a certain kind. Its vehicle was the trio of people, nation and state; yet history records numerous instances of conflicting relations between these three elements.

The 'people' saw the state as an alienated instrument of coercion, and opposed the idea of a nation because they rejected all ties and forms of solidarity with the upper classes. But the argument used in contesting the idea of the nation appealed precisely to national aspirations. In the Communist Manifesto, the famous words about workers without a fatherland were followed by a sentence about the national character of the proletariat; the proletariat, having obtained political power, was to transform itself into a national class, which in turn was to become a nation. This is not only an instance of polemical rhetoric, but a genuine demand.

But the very possibility of formulating such a demand was provided by the democratic content of the idea of the nation-state. Demands of this kind, whether made by the right or by the left, sometimes led to the wholesale destruction of the programme of the nation-state, and thus of the right to liberty as well as of the right of nations to self-determination. This can be put down to the ruthless and unjust dialectic of history, where power and interest have more weight than values and principles. But there are some genuine contradictions inherent in the political organization of a nation: its legitimacy derived from the community, but its implementation was regional. Tocqueville wrote of France at the time of Louis Philippe that it was governed on the principles of an industrial association, where thoughts of profit are uppermost in everyone's minds;[21] but the same surely holds true of every modern state, not only of the July monarchy. (F. C. Lane also refers to the state-as-enterprise.) The dream of independence and fulfilment of the 'general will' was constantly blocked by a wall composed of the practical necessities of politics and the social reality of nations internally rent apart. By its very nature the state (in Tönnies' categories more of a *Gesellschaft* than a *Gemeinschaft*) is not a community, but rather an aggregate of institutions and structures of power which together guarantee the existence of the individual and the group. But its ultimate justification is grounded in the common good of its citizens and on a constantly renewed social mandate. Thus the divergence of particular interests does not undermine the structure of the nation-state; it merely demands a pluralist political organization.

The history of political parties in modern European states indicates that the political expression of divergent interests was an instrument in the building of the national consciousness. The formation and functioning of mass political parties as normal institutions of the nation-state reflected a significant change in participation in political life, or in the 'distribution of power'. Because parties must rely on a wide social base, all their activities must be aimed at spurring as many people as possible into political activity. Both those parties which appeal to national feeling and those which oppose it extend the boundaries of the *polis*, thereby enlarging also the social scope of the process through which a nation shapes its state. At the same time, however, the combination of party political struggles, escalating conflicts among the social classes and economic and political groups, and the increasing conventionality of the parliamentary political game leads to profound internal divisions. There are many examples of political conflicts which engendered sharp and long-lasting divisions within national societies, such as the Dreyfus affair in France or the assassination of Gabriel Narutowicz, the first president of independent Poland. But this feeling of dichotomy, the conviction that each nation contains within it two different nations, has always been present in the modern social consciousness, and does not require dramatic conflicts to be made apparent. In every nation-state there is a part of the nation which feels deprived of its rights to such an extent that it perceives no solidarity binding it to the rest, just as a part of every nation feels, because of the difference of its living standards, education, customs, manners and behaviour, not only set apart from other classes but also inferior to them. Thus Disraeli's remark about 'two nations' appears to express a universal truth.

The idea of the nation-state was beset by difficulties from the very beginning. It was Marat who said that the poor have no fatherland; and Augustin Thierry produced a political and historiographical theory about two nations sharing one territory. The problem with which they were concerned involved more than just the differences between the social classes; they saw a deep dividing line running through the body of society, creating in the social consciousness a sharp dichotomy between 'us' and 'them'. The criteria on which this division was based were property (both Tocqueville and Marx agree on this) and perhaps exploitation (according, this time, only to Marx). Both led to that simplest of directly observable divisions in society, its division into 'rich' and 'poor'; but the sharpness of the dichotomy depended on the introduction of the political element: the contrast between the appropriation of power by some and the expropriation of others.

Participation in public life is a significant element in this division. The French Revolution divided citizens into 'active' and 'passive'; conservative thought at the time of the Restoration differentiated between 'the nation' and 'the people'; the July monarchy's conception of the *pays légal*, while it did not establish different rights for different sections of the population, nevertheless sanctioned differences in the exercise of those rights; and, finally, the modern distinction between the political establishment, with its system of 'party oligarchy', and the masses is based on claims about the increasingly technical and professional nature of politics. But the feeling of there being 'two nations' is above all a genuine part of the social consciousness; it is a feeling that a certain order has been violated or disrupted. It expresses the need for a political community.

It hardly needs pointing out that the extension of the social scope of public life in the course of modern history was not synonymous with mass politicization. From the middle of the nineteenth century the principle of universal suffrage brought politics into the centre of social life. The opposition movements of 1968 questioned this central role of politics and the extent to which it had become the norm in the institutions of Western states (while in Poland and Czechoslovakia, at the same period, the object of opposition was the system of political monopoly and the exclusion of society from any participation in or influence on political decisions). The collapse of the radical utopias of 1968 and the shock at the violence of the conflict between the younger generation and the established order did nothing to mitigate the growing distrust of the institutions of political life. This distrust was also directed towards political parties; it was expressed not only through a rejection of the traditional division into right and left but also in a deep suspicion of the way in which the games and rivalries between political parties were conducted in a representative system. Behind the current lack of trust and interest in politics it is possible to discern the need for a system in which consensus and solidarity play a greater role.

There is an ambiguity inherent in the very idea of the nation-state, in the sense that it is a continuation of the Jacobin tradition whereby the sovereignty of a people is linked to the omnipotence and omnipresence of the state. But this surely does not entail the expansion of the state's oppressive role in the life of the individual; on the contrary, it should involve the expansion of the state's role as guarantor, organizer and guardian. Recent experience suggests, however, that hypertrophy of the state is a very real danger. With the twenty-first century looming closer, the old liberal claim that the less there is of the state the better, and democratic socialism's equally old distrust of the state (which may be summed up in the principle that there should be just as much state as is needed), begin to assume a new significance.

But there is another aspect of the idea of the nation-state, in which many natural, organic and community elements in the relationship between state and nation are embedded in contractual, conventional and arbitrary structures (as Tönnies remarked, real societies are a mixture of *Gesellschaft* and *Gemeinschaft*). It is in those aspects of the idea of the nation-state which emphasize the community that its contemporary relevance may be seen. Totalitarianism is the implementation of a programme of state omnipotence, and depends on the depoliticization of the masses;

representative democracy feels itself undermined by a general lack of interest and refusal to participate in political life. The idea of the nation-state can make sense for the future only if it can prevent the former while supporting the latter.

Turning, finally, to the question of Europe and nations, we return to our initial problem, namely the possible conflict between nations and the nation-state on the one hand and Europe's tendency towards integration on the other. This tendency seems to have emerged not only from ideas and political programmes but also from certain objective phenomena – the very phenomena which were once the basis for the creation of nation-states, and which now favour the gradual obliteration of state borders and the unity of the European continent.

This is certainly true of the economic sphere. The development of the market played an important role in the formation of nation-states. It was above all a means of integrating the territory of the state and extending and strengthening internal ties, linguistic and cultural as well as economic. The realities of the market also favoured the expansion of freedoms, since territorial integration was accompanied by demands for the free movement of goods and the creation of a complementary system of regional specialization (or regional division of labour). A similar process is now taking place throughout Western Europe. Economic integration has in recent years been felt more and more to be a requirement of the times; the current rate of progress of technology, sometimes dubbed the third industrial revolution, may even have made it a condition of Europe's continued survival.[22] As James Reston wrote in 1987, 'There is a risk that in the next century Europe will become economically what it is geographically – namely, a small peninsula of the Eurasian continent, dependent, comfortable and complacent.'[23] Although integration within the European Economic Community is surely proceeding at a good pace, the gap between Europe and the economic world powers is widening, and the relentless rise of unemployment figures (eight million in 1975, more than 19 million, most of them young people, in 1986) reflects a certain inefficiency. In such circumstances extending the process of integration eastwards might be not only an act of compassion but also a means of hastening and revitalizing the development of Europe as a whole. This is unlikely to happen on the economic front, but less so within the context of

Europe's political integration.

The dream of political unity for Europe began to grow after the last war, with the diminishing of the role of the great European powers and the growth of frustration at the extent to which world politics had become dominated by the superpowers. The time had come to implement at least parts of this dream. These have not yet reached the 'critical mass' stage, but the general climate of opinion, both among political elites and in society as a whole, is favourable. The prospect of political unity is brought closer by the similarity of the political systems of the countries of Western Europe, where the democratic organization of public life and the community of fundamental values seem to be firmly rooted. The Scandinavian countries pose a problem in the North and Turkey and Greece in the South, but the main problem is posed by the countries of Eastern and Central Europe. Their European aspirations are based on the same fundamental values, but also include their emergence from the condition of political dependence. The traumatic experiences which the nations of these countries have suffered have given rise to fears for the survival of their own national communities.[24] For this reason they might hamper rather than assist the process of integration, and their attachment to the idea of the nation-state, either as an unfulfilled dream or as a disrupted reality, might be as great an obstacle to European integration as the post-Yalta division of Europe. For the moment we cannot know how much truth there is in such a supposition. What is certain, however, is the importance of defining the relationship between the nation-state and the vision of a united Europe.

Predictions concerning the disappearance of national barriers in Europe[25] were accompanied by the conviction that nation-states would be supplanted by a community which would create a state political organization encompassing Western Europe or even the whole continent – or, to be more precise, the subcontinent. This would be possible only if Europeans could come to be bound by feelings of closeness and unity analogous to those which bind Frenchmen, or Poles, or Dutchmen, among themselves. The transition from nation-states to the state of Europe would require that Europe usurp the place of one's country as a fatherland. Many of the necessary conditions for such a transition, both psychological and objective, have already been

fulfilled. There are elites which spark feelings of European identity; there is a community of traditions and values; there is also a
common repertoire of symbols and myths. And yet the European
community has not achieved a status analogous to that of the
national communities which go to make it up – not even on the
humble scale of Western Europe. Both culturally and politically,
it seems, Europe is fated to be *ex pluribus unum*.

The framework in which the European nation-states have been
situated up to now is certainly changing, owing to integration.
Experience suggests the possibility of international federations,
and of Europe as a unity of states. The federal alternative seems
to me to be the most promising, for it would allow the process of
evolution to continue, and would enjoy the support of the existing structures of nation-states because it would express their
interests. The federal alternative could take many forms: a
Scandinavian and a Western federation, a Balkan and Central-
European one, or a European union consisting of several federations. But even if the future does belong to the state of Europe,
the idea of the nation-state is not dead as long as national feelings remain alive. The Polish historian Benedykt Zientara ends
his book on the nations of medieval Europe with the following
words: 'While nations exist, while there is a variety of languages
in which each word multiplies the richness of meanings, while
national literatures retain their individual character, which
derives from a different way of experiencing the human predica-
ment, allegedly always and everywhere the same – while all these
things exist, the richness of European culture will not be extinguished, and the understanding of man's variety of experiences in
other, distant lands and civilizations will not perish.'[26] I agree
with him.

I have considered the idea of the nation-state as a foundation
of public life, and above all as a political problem. In considering
the relevance of this concept today I have emphasized its first
part – the nation – even though the legacy of the revolution
places the emphasis on the second – the state. It is in linking the
principles of political organization to the concept of nationhood
that I have sought the possibility of promoting community ties
among people. In this way I have tried to demonstrate the vital
strength and the rationality of the idea of nationhood in the
modern world, and its intimate connection with the rights of

individuals and groups, with general participation in the *polis*, and with democracy.

Yet the experiences of the twentieth century clearly reveal nationalism to be a dark and threatening force. Its destructive and aggressive potential has certainly diminished in the realities of postwar Europe, but its spectre continues to haunt Europe. East and West alike. I believe, however, that it is by denigrating the idea of nationhood that we open the way to a return of nationalism on the social and political scene; for in rejecting the idea of nationhood we surrender it to nationalism. Nationalism manipulates the idea of nationhood while concentrating on the development of the state. But in the model of the nation-state which has become the common property of Europe, the state is tempered and restricted by the 'sovereignty of the people', and in the interplay between aspirations and realities one can discern not only conflicts of interest but also feelings of brotherhood and solidarity – those elements of human relationships which, because of their emotional content, sit uncomfortably in the conceptual apparatus of the sociologist or the historian.

Notes

1 K. Deutsch, *Nationalism and Social Communication*, Cambridge, MA, 1953; F. Chabod, *L'idea di nazione*, Bari, 1961; E. Lemberg, *Nationalismus*, I–II, Reinbek, 1964; J. Szűcs, *Nation und Geschichte*, Budapest, 1981.
2 H. Seton-Watson, *Nation and State*, Boulder, CO, 1977.
3 *Staat und Gesellschaft*, ed. E.-W. Böckenförde, Darmstadt, 1976 (Wege der Forschung, B.171).
4 O. Brunner, *Neue Wege der Sozialgeschichte, Vorträge und Aufsätze*, Göttingen, 1956.
5 J. Szűcs, *Les Trois Europes*, Paris, 1985, p. 24; cf. W. Ullman, *Medieval Foundations of Renaissance Humanism*, London, 1977; W. Conze, *Nation und Gesellschaft: zwei Grundbegriffe der revolutionären Epoche*, Historische Zeitschrift, B.198, 1964, pp. 1–16.
6 B. Zientara, 'Nationale Strukturen des Mittelalters: ein Versuch zur Kritik der Terminologie des Nationalbewusstseins unter besonderer Berücksichtigung osteuropäischer Literatur', *Saeculum*, 32, 1981, pp. 301–16.
7 B. Vilar, 'La nation', in *La nouvelle histoire*, ed. Jacques le Goff, p. 442; here the nation is referred to as long-term, the nation-state as medium-term and national movements as short-term.

8 F. Furet, *Penser la Revolution française*, Paris, 1978, p. 66.
9 N. Elias, 'The process of state formation and nation building', in *Transactions of the Seventh World Congress of Sociology*, Sophia 1972, vol. III, p. 277.
10 E. Rostworowski, *Legends and Facts of the Eighteenth Century*, Warsaw, 1963, p. 294.
11 N. Elias, op. cit., p. 282.
12 K. Deutsch, *Politics and Government*, Boston, 1970, p. 87.
13 L. B. Namier, *Conflicts: studies in contemporary history*, London, 1942, p. 7.
14 Leszek Kołakowski, 'Looking for the barbarians', in *Can the Devil be Saved?*, Warsaw, 1985; French version in *Commentaire*, 1980.
15 L. B. Namier, op. cit., p. 18.
16 Both quotations are taken from: H. Wagner, 'The German problem', *Aneks*, 46–47, 1987, p. 81.
17 *Aneks*, 46–47, 1987; and *Esprit*, 10, 1987.
18 *Die Zeit*, 11 July 1986.
19 F. Stern, 'Germany in a semigaullist Europe', *Foreign Affairs*, 1980, pp. 867–86.
20 H. Wagner, op. cit., pp. 70–92.
21 Alexis de Tocqueville, *Souvenirs*, vol. I, in *Oeuvres Complètes*, vol. 12, Paris, 1964.
22 M. Richonnier, *Les metamorphoses de l'Europe*, Paris, 1985, p. 252.
23 *International Herald Tribune*, 1 June 1987.
24 I. Bibo, *Misère des petits etats d'Europe de l'Est*, Paris, 1986, p. 161.
25 E. H. Carr, *Nationalism and After*, London, 1945.
26 B. Zientara, *The Dawn of European Nations*, Warsaw, 1985, p. 360.

Index